EATING FOR
diabetes

Also Available in Marlowe & Company's Healthy "Eating" Series

Eating for Pregnancy:
An Essential Guide to Nutrition with Recipes for the Whole Family,
by Catherine Jones with Rose Ann Hudson

Eating for IBS:
175 Delicious, Nutritious, Low-Fat, Low-Residue Recipes to Stablize the Touchiest Tummy,
by Heather Van Vorous

Eating for Acid Reflux:
A Handbook and Cookbook for Those with Heartburn,
by Jill Sklar and Annabel Cohen

Eating Well After Weight Loss Surgery:
Over 140 Delicious, Low-Fat, High-Protein Recipes to Enjoy in the
Weeks, Months and Years after Surgery,
by Patt Levine and Michele Bontempo-Saray

Eating Gluten Free:
Delicious Recipes and Essential Advice for Living Well
without Wheat and Other Problematic Grains,
by Shreve Stockton

What to Eat When You Can't Eat Anything:
The Complete Allergy Cookbook,
by Chupi and Luke Sweetman

If the label says caution, warning or danger

Take old cleaners, fertilizers, pesticides and similar items to the Household Hazardous Waste Facility for safe disposal. Located at the Tacoma Recovery & Transfer Center, 3510 S. Mullen St. No charge for Tacoma and Pierce County residents. **cityoftacoma.org/hazwaste**

Make your own all-purpose cleaner

Mix the following ingredients in a bowl or bucket:

- ¼ cup baking soda
- ½ cup borax (found in the laundry section of grocery stores)
- ½ cup white vinegar + 1 gallon water

Stir briskly to dissolve the baking soda and borax. To make this cleaner in a spray bottle, reduce the recipe to fit and fully dissolve the ingredients to avoid clogging the nozzle. This recipe works well on countertops, floors and walls. Use with a reusable mop, sponge or rag.

cityoftacoma.org/greenercleaners

cityoftacoma.org/environmentalservices
City of Tacoma • Recycled and Recyclable • Sept/Oct 2015

SURFACE WATER • SOLID WASTE • WASTEWATER
ENVIRONMENTAL SERVICES DEPARTMENT

A little TAGRO
can work a lot of magic on your lawn

Give your yard a little love this fall, and you'll be ready to enjoy a beautiful lawn next spring.

1. Thatch or plug dense or well-rooted lawns.
2. Mow the lawn short.
3. Spread a thin layer (about 1/4-inch deep) of TAGRO Mix.
4. Water well, and get ready to enjoy a lush and lovely lawn.

Consider overseeding your entire lawn. Spread grass seed over the TAGRO Mix on your existing lawn at about half the rate needed for a new lawn.

TAGRO products – Mix, Topsoil, Potting Soil and Aged Black Bark – are available year-round for pickup or delivery.

TAGRO
2201 E. Portland Ave., Gate 6
(253) 502-2150 tagro.com

TAGRO
City of Tacoma

EATING FOR

diabetes

A Handbook and Cookbook—
with More than 125 Delicious, Nutritious
Recipes to Keep You Feeling Great and
Your Blood Glucose in Check

Jane Frank

MARLOWE & COMPANY
NEW YORK

EATING FOR DIABETES
*A Handbook and Cookbook—with More than 125 Delicious, Nutritious Recipes
to Keep You Feeling Great and Your Blood Glucose in Check*

Copyright © 2004, 2005 by Jane Frank

Published by
Marlow and Company
An Imprint of Avalon Publishing Group Inc.
245 West 17th St. • 11th Floor
New York, NY 10011

AVALON
publishing group incorporated

Previously published in the United Kingdom in 2004 in somewhat different form as
The Basic Basics Diabetes Handbook. This edition published by arrangement with Grub Street.

Library of Congress Cataloging-in-Publication Data is available.

ISBN 1-56924-365-4

9 8 7 6 5 4 3 2

Book design by India Amos and Pauline Neuwirth, Neuwirth & Associates, Inc.

Printed in the United States

contents

acknowledgments

Without all the help I was given by three groups of people this book would never have been written. First the people with diabetes who kindly agreed to be interviewed: David, Dorothea, Gay, Henrietta, Jean, Laura, Mike, and Rona. Together they helped me to be aware of the role that diabetes plays in people's lives, and they gave me a better understanding of the disease. Henrietta, in particular, has not only given me insights into the physical implications of diabetes but has also demonstrated that, while the illness can sometimes be a trial, it can also be spiritually enriching.

The second and indispensable group of people consists of all those, either diabetics or nutritionists, and sometimes both, who tested and commented on the recipes. Special thanks go to Alexandra Aitken, Lynn Alford-Burow, Marion Billingham, Kay Clarke, Josie Cowgill, Fiona McDonald Joyce, Rona MacInnes, Linda Marais, Nicola Phipps and Jake, Sara Shakespeare, Coreen Tucker, David Wallace and Kasumi Hatazawa, Penny Williams and Craig Brown, and Liz Wright. Not only did they correct me where I went wrong, and gave me honest opinions about the taste and appearance of my creations, but they also ensured that all the recipes went through a robust testing process, and are therefore, if not foolproof, at least as unambiguous as I could make them.

For going through my facts with a fine-toothed comb and correcting my tendency to obscurity, my heartfelt thanks go to my husband John and to my old colleague Mike Frazer. And finally, I owe a huge debt of gratitude to Gay Patton, a diabetes nurse and educator and a diabetic herself, who read through the introduction very carefully and made many constructive comments. Thank you all.

introduction

It is neither alarmist nor an exaggeration to say that we are in the midst of an epidemic of diabetes in the Western world, but simply a statement of fact. In 2002 it was estimated that there were nearly 20 million in the United States with diabetes.[1] It is appearing increasingly in the developing world too, especially in Asian countries such as Korea and Taiwan and in urban populations in India and Pakistan.[2] The number of people with diabetes globally is currently estimated at 194 million, and that number is predicted to rise to 366 million in 2030, according to the International Diabetes Federation and World Health Organization statistics.

Why is diabetes on the increase? Epidemiologists say that it is due to our more and more sedentary lifestyle, the overabundance of processed foods and, more specifically in Europe and America, an aging population.[3] Diabetes is associated with obesity, but recent findings indicate that the diabetes epidemic will continue even if levels of obesity remain constant. But because obesity continues to rise, it is likely that the predictions for diabetes are actually an underestimate.[4]

Diabetes research has made enormous progress over the last few years, and a much greater understanding of the disease, its causes and risk factors, has developed. However, some of the advice given to people with diabetes has not always kept pace with the research. This book aims to fill that gap. The information and the recipes it contains are based on the latest research and on informed medical opinion. However, I hope the recipes are simple enough for anyone to cook. This book is intended both for people with diabetes, whether they have been newly diagnosed or whether they are old hands, and also for those people who are aware of the risks of diabetes and who wish to minimize those risks by modifying their diet.

what is diabetes?

PUT SIMPLY, DIABETES is a condition in which there is too much glucose (sugar) in the blood. This glucose comes from the carbohydrate foods in our diet, and is the principal source of energy for the muscles and the brain. The level of blood glucose is normally strictly regulated by two hormones called insulin and glucagon, secreted by the pancreas, at between 70–100mg/dl (milligrams per deciliter of blood) when the stomach is empty, and up to 140mg/dl just after a meal. Working in tandem, the function of insulin is to lower blood glucose while that of glucagon is to raise it. In diabetes, this mechanism fails to work, and the blood-glucose level is abnormally high. This could be either because the pancreas makes too little or no insulin, or because the cells become resistant to insulin and fail to respond to its message.

signs and symptoms

THE FIRST EFFECT of high blood-glucose levels, above 160–180mg/dl, is that glucose passes into the urine because it can't get into the cells where it is needed. This glucose makes the urine of a person with undiagnosed diabetes sweet, hence the name "diabetes mellitus"—"mellitus" deriving from the Greek word for honey. In response to these high levels of glucose, the kidneys excrete more fluid in an attempt to dilute the urine. This results in the need to pass urine more frequently (polyuria), which, in turn, causes extreme thirst (polydipsia). The excessive fluid loss often causes the patient to lose weight, which may make them feel very hungry (polyphagia). Polyuria, polydipsia, and polyphagia are the three classic symptoms of diabetes. Other symptoms include extreme fatigue, blurred vision, nausea, and tingling or numbness in the hands and feet. Frequent or recurring infections and slow wound healing are also signs of undiagnosed diabetes.

A simple fasting plasma-glucose test can confirm whether or not you have diabetes. The test is given in a lab or at the doctor's office, usually in the morning, after fasting since the previous evening. If the fasting plasma-glucose level is 126 mg/dl or higher on two occasions, even after not eating for eight hours, it usually means that the person has diabetes.

Fasting serum insulin levels are often tested as well. They should be under 20 mcU/ml (micro unit per millileter) and ideally under 5 mcU/ml. High insulin levels after an 8-hour fast mean that the cells are resistant to insulin. Any fasting insulin level over 20 mcU/ml is a major problem and is a risk factor for diabetes.

types of diabetes

THERE ARE TWO main types of diabetes mellitus: Type 1 and Type 2. About 5 percent of people with diabetes have Type 1, while the remainder are Type 2. The two types are very different from each other, although management of both conditions is broadly similar.

Type 1 or Insulin-Dependent Diabetes Mellitus (IDDM)

In this type, which used to be called juvenile diabetes to distinguish it from the later-onset Type 2, the symptoms listed above begin suddenly and must receive immediate medical attention. If it is not recognized immediately, a condition called diabetic ketoacidosis (DKA) may result. Although there is a lot of glucose in the blood, the cells can't use it because there is no insulin. The body interprets this as starvation, and so it uses fat as a source of energy instead. The breakdown of fat cells results in the formation of ketones, strong acid compounds that make the blood more acid (ketoacidosis). The acid/alkaline balance of the blood (the pH), like the blood-sugar level, is normally kept within strict limits (a pH of 7.35–7.45) by various mechanisms, one of which is the exhalation of carbon dioxide. Breathing out reduces the level of acid in the blood, so a person going through diabetic ketoacidosis will breathe deeply and rapidly in an attempt to make the blood less acid. The exhaled acid on such a person's breath smells like pear drops. Without treatment, diabetic ketoacidosis can result in coma and eventually death. People with established Type 1 diabetes can develop ketoacidosis if they miss an insulin injection or become stressed by an infection, an accident, or a serious medical condition.

Type 1 diabetes is sometimes further classified into three subtypes:

Immune-mediated diabetes (Type 1A). This form results from auto-immune destruction of the beta cells of the pancreas. Interestingly, about 5 percent of people with autoimmune diabetes also have celiac disease (an autoimmune disorder of the digestive tract that is triggered by gluten in wheat and other grains, and which leads to a malabsorption of all nutrients, primarily of fat).

Idiopathic diabetes (Type 1B). Some forms of Type 1 diabetes have no known cause. Some diabetics have permanent insulin deficiency and are prone to ketoacidosis but have no evidence of auto-immunity. This form of diabetes is strongly inherited and is more common in people of African or Asian heritage.

Latent Autoimmune Diabetes in Adults (or Slow Onset Type 1, LADA or Type 1.5). This is Type 1 diabetes appearing in adulthood (over the age of 30). These patients do not immediately require insulin for treatment, are often not overweight, and have little or no resistance to insulin. They are often diagnosed as Type 2 because they are older and will initially respond to diabetes medications because they have adequate insulin production.[5] One major benefit to this type is that when their blood sugars are controlled, people with Type 1.5 usually do not have the high risk for heart problems more often found with the high cholesterol and blood pressure seen in true Type 2 diabetes.

david:

DAVID IS A VERY unusual Type 1 diabetic, in that he was not diagnosed until the age of 36, so he could more properly be said to have Latent Autoimmune Diabetes in Adults (LADA, also known as Type 1.5). He was put onto Metformin initially, but after a while this appeared not to be working. This is not surprising as the primary action of this drug is to overcome insulin resistance, whereas David's problem was not insulin resistance so much as poor insulin production. Eventually he was put on insulin therapy, and he now takes two types—Humalog at meal times, and a new long-lasting insulin called Lantus at night. The latter is supposed to last for 24 hours, but in practice David finds that it is not as beneficial as he had hoped, and often doesn't last long enough.

David describes himself as a "foodie" in that he enjoys his food and is not prepared to deprive himself of the pleasures of the table. Typically for a person with LADA, he is not overweight. When first diagnosed with diabetes, he consulted a dietitian, but found that the advice he was given was basic, old-fashioned, and unsympathetic to his lifestyle. The emphasis was on processed foods such as baked beans, but David would never consider eating this sort of food. He did, however, broadly follow the recommended diet for the first two or three years, and then, unwilling to let his diabetes take over his life, he started "flouting the rules." For ten years his blood-glucose levels were reasonably well-controlled, but they are now higher than they should be—typically 8–15 mg/dl, though he is not sure why. He has quite a stressful job, and it could be that this is a contributory factor. He exercises twice a week, and although he is well aware that exercising more frequently would help to moderate his blood-sugar levels, David is a pragmatist and knows that he would not be able to find the time. At his 6-monthly checkups with the diabetes specialist, he has seen his HbA1C scores (see page 17) creeping up, and he is obviously concerned about this. The only real difference diabetes has made to his life is that he feels tired a lot of the time, but thankfully has none of the other complications of diabetes.

Breakfast for David, as for nearly all of my interviewees, often consists of porridge, as it is very good for moderating blood-glucose levels. He also finds rice-based dishes help, though he is wary of relying too much on rice as it is a high-carbohydrate food. He gave up sugar in his tea and coffee long before he was diagnosed with diabetes, and he is lucky in that he doesn't have a particularly sweet tooth in any case. David feels that there isn't a lot of nutritional help for diabetics who really enjoy their food, so I hope he will find something of interest in this book.

■ ■ ■

Type 2 or Non-Insulin Dependent Diabetes Mellitus (NIDDM)

In Type 2, the same symptoms as those associated with Type 1 occur, but they progress gradually. They may not all be present, and sometimes people with Type 2 have no obvious symptoms at all, and are not even aware that they have diabetes. Such people may go undiagnosed for several years. As insulin deficiency progresses, symptoms may develop. Increased urination and thirst are mild at first and may gradually worsen over weeks or months. Ketoacidosis is rare. If the blood-glucose level becomes very high—usually as a result of added stress such as an infection or drugs—the person may develop severe dehydration, which may lead to mental confusion, drowsiness, or seizures.

One of the reasons Type 2 diabetes may remain undiagnosed for a long time is that many of its symptoms, such as increased urination, lack of energy, weight loss, skin infections, wounds that are slow to heal, or erectile dysfunction in men, are also complaints commonly associated with aging. By the time a person is diagnosed, he or she may already be suffering from the complications of diabetes. Since untreated diabetes can cause blindness, kidney failure, heart disease, and strokes, it is important to get it diagnosed and treated as soon as possible, particularly if you are in a high-risk group.

■ ■ ■

mike

MIKE WAS DIAGNOSED as Type 2 less than a year before I interviewed him, but five years before that he had suspicions that he was already diabetic. At that time he went to the doctor with a lot of what he describes as "little things"—skin irritation when he shaved, spots, sensitive skin, general lethargy—but there was never anything specific on which to pin these symptoms. On one of these visits to the doctor's office he saw another physician instead of his usual GP. The physician did a urine test that showed that Mike's urine glucose was very high. In the physician's opinion he was definitely diabetic, but on subsequent occasions his blood glucose, although high, was within normal limits. He was told he was glucose intolerant. The only dietary change he made at that time was to switch from sugar to sweeteners.

Mike's work involved a long commute on the interstate or highway, and he was under a lot of pressure when he got into the office each day. By early 2003, he was feeling completely exhausted, and only kept himself going by eating chocolate and sweet snacks on the road. Then when he got home in the evenings he didn't feel like eating a proper meal. He was aware that his blood-sugar levels were soaring, but he had almost ceased to care. Things came to a head one evening and he finally collapsed under the strain. He was diagnosed as diabetic after a glucose-clearance test.

Mike keeps his diabetes under control by choosing low-GI foods when possible. This is all right if he is at home or when he and his family go on self-catering trips, but less easy when he has to stay in hotels on business. The only information he was given when he was first diagnosed was a pamphlet from a national diabetes organization that advised consumption of bread, potatoes, and pasta, and suggested swapping sugar for sweeteners, and didn't mention the GI at all. He discovered low-GI eating by talking to a friend. When he mentioned the GI to his diabetes nurse, her response was "Oh, it's 5 years since I looked at the glycemic index."

In Mike's opinion there is not enough quality help for people newly diagnosed with diabetes. He would like to see clear indications on food labels as to whether a food is good or bad for blood-glucose control. An example is yogurts, which are promoted as a healthy food, but which can be very high in sugar. He is still driving a lot, and comments that when you want a snack, the only options available while traveling are sweet snacks such as chocolate, or fatty and salty snacks. He makes sure he always has nuts and raisins in the glove compartment of his car to help him avoid either of those unhealthy options.

Complications from Type 2 diabetes in adults can often be reduced or prevented with medicines, weight loss, and exercise. However, it is uncertain what the prognosis is for those who start the disease in childhood rather than in adulthood, of whom there is an increasing number. Many doctors predict that complications will emerge in early adulthood.

Maturity-Onset Diabetes of the Young (MODY)

This is a hereditary form of diabetes usually occurring in people under the age of 25. MODY can often be controlled with diet or medication in the early stages. It differs from Type 2 diabetes in that patients have a defect in insulin secretion or glucose metabolism, and are not resistant to insulin. MODY accounts for about 2 percent of diabetes. Because MODY runs in families, it is useful for studying diabetes genes.

Gestational Diabetes

Gestational diabetes is a type of diabetes that occurs in pregnancy, and usually disappears after the baby is born. If not treated, it can cause serious problems for both the mother and the baby. Women belonging to high-risk ethnic groups, such as Afro-Caribbean, Hispanic, South or East Asian, are statistically more likely to get gestational diabetes. Other risk factors are overweight, age, family history of diabetes, having had gestational diabetes with a previous pregnancy, or having previously had a stillbirth or a very large baby.

Diabetes Insipidus

Despite the similar names, Diabetes Insipidus is not related to Diabetes Mellitus. It is a relatively rare condition that occurs when the kidneys are unable to conserve water, resulting in very diluted urine. Diabetes Insipidus can usually be managed by drinking adequate fluids and following a low-sodium diet.

the causes of diabetes

EXPERTS CONTINUE TO be at odds over the causes of diabetes, particularly of Type 1.

Type 1

There appears to be a genetic component in about 10 percent of people with Type 1. The most commonly accepted theory for its development in the other 90 percent is that viral infections, particularly those of the digestive system, cause the immune system to attack and destroy the islet cells of the pancreas where insulin is produced, rendering them unable to make insulin. Strongly implicated is the family of coxsackie viruses—polio-related viruses that cause upper respiratory infections. This is not a new theory—epidemiological studies in the 1960s, for example, showed that coxsackie outbreaks in various regions were followed by an increased incidence of diabetes.

Researchers in Finland have discovered that babies fed on cow's milk formula, particularly those with diabetic siblings, are five times more likely to develop Type 1 diabetes.[6] This may be because cow's milk contains insulin, and the babies may be making antibodies against the cow's insulin. These antibodies then go on to destroy the insulin-producing cells in the baby's pancreas. To support the theory that Type 1 is an autoimmune disease, 75 percent of people with diabetes have antibodies to their own pancreatic cells.[7]

Type 2

In general, the risk of developing Type 2 diabetes rises with age, particularly after the age of 40. There is some hereditary component, so anyone who has a close relative with the disease might be considered at risk. Women who had diabetes when pregnant (gestational diabetes—see page 6) are at greater risk too. High blood pressure and membership of a high-risk ethnic group (such as Afro-Caribbean or Hispanic groups) also contribute to the risk. But the greatest risk factor is obesity. It is arguable whether obesity is the cause of diabetes or a symptom, along with diabetes itself, of pancreatic failure, but there is no doubt that obesity accompanies diabetes. Not all diabetics are overweight, but 90 percent of people who go on to develop Type 2 are overweight.

Unfortunately, Type 2 is now appearing in younger and younger people, especially in the United States but now also in the UK. Childhood Type 2 diabetes is characterized by obesity, high blood-glucose levels and insulin resistance. Doctors blame the increasing diabetes trend on unhealthy diets and inactivity. Children with diabetes tend to be especially large for their age. Many also have a skin condition called acanthosis nigricans, dark patches around the neck and other skin folds, which is a sign of insulin resistance.

dorothea

AT A SPRIGHTLY 82, Dorothea is the oldest of my interviewees and has had diabetes for thirty years. When she was about 50, she began to experience a terrible thirst, accompanied by itching all over her body. She went to the doctor and was swiftly diagnosed as having diabetes. This was a terrible shock to Dorothea. There was no diabetes in the family and she couldn't think where it had come from. She was started on medication, and given help with managing her diet, but it quickly became apparent that she needed insulin. She was resistant to this at first, dreading having to cope with the injections, but eventually became used to it.

The recommended diet for diabetes thirty years ago appears to have made no distinction between refined and complex carbohydrates, and the Glycemic Index hadn't been invented. By current standards the diet recommended to Dorothea seems designed to maintain rather high blood glucose, relying heavily on tea and crackers between meals, toast for breakfast and a sandwich for lunch. Interestingly, before she had diabetes, Dorothea used to drink a lot of milk, but she was told to cut back on her milk consumption. She still largely follows the diet she was given back then, having her main meal in the evening consisting of a protein food, two potatoes and lots of vegetables, always with a small piece of fruit for dessert.

Two years ago Dorothea developed age-related macular degeneration, the effect of which she describes as like having a "big black thing" in the center of her vision. This makes it impossible to read, and she has to rely on a family member to read her mail for her. Drawing up her doses of insulin would be difficult too, without the help of a nurse, who visits three times a week to draw up the insulin for the following day.

Along with many other diabetics, Dorothea was recently switched to the human insulin, and finds as a result that her blood sugar is much harder to control. She has always suffered from hypoglycemia (see page 13), for which she carries glucose tablets around with her. When she was on the porcine insulin, she says, she always knew when a hypoglycemic episode was coming on, as she would start yawning. But now, on the human insulin, she has no warning. She has also found that her blood sugar gets very low at bedtime, so she has started having a cookie before going to bed to keep the blood sugar up during the night. This is typical of Dorothea's cheerful determination to cope with the vicissitudes of having diabetes.

risk factors for type 2 diabetes

Metabolic Syndrome

Also known as Syndrome X or insulin resistance, this is a collection of symptoms that, taken together, predispose a person to developing Type 2 diabetes. It can and usually does coexist with the other risk factors.

To qualify for metabolic syndrome, a person must have at least three of the following characteristics:

- ▶ A waist measurement of more than 40" in men or 35" in women. In addition, a waist to hip ratio of more than 0.75 is considered a risk factor for diabetes
- ▶ High levels of triglycerides and LDL (low-density lipoproteins)—the "bad" cholesterol
- ▶ Low levels of HDL (high-density lipoproteins)—the "good" cholesterol. Low is considered to be less than 50 mg/dl (milligrams per decileter) in women and less than 40 mg/dl in men
- ▶ Blood pressure greater than 12/80mm Hg
- ▶ High levels of blood glucose
- ▶ Insulin resistance, which means that although the person may be producing enough insulin, the body cells are not heeding its message and taking up glucose as they should. The result is very often the coexistence of high blood glucose with excess circulating insulin

Poor Dietary Choices

Most experts now agree that diets high in overall carbohydrates contribute to both diabetes and obesity by increasing the body's production of insulin. As long ago as 1935, Dr. H. D. C. Given pointed out the correlation between carbohydrate intake and diabetes.[8] More recently, Michel Montignac[9] has embraced a similar theory, now rapidly gaining credence, which states that obesity and Type 2 diabetes coexist as symptoms of a pancreas that is not working properly and is producing too much insulin (hyperinsulinemia). This surplus eventually causes insulin resistance. The reason the pancreas is producing too much insulin in the first place is a diet too high in refined carbohydrates and sugar.

To complicate the picture further, a diet low in fat, for example so-called heart-healthy diets, can contribute to diabetes. If you remove fat, you are going to be left with too many carbohydrates. That will increase insulin, and anything that increases insulin over a long period of time is going to give you a higher risk for diabetes. So the danger of a so-called low-fat diet is not the low fat, but the high carbohydrate content.

There are good fats and bad fats, however. A diet high in hydrogenated fats—those fats found in processed foods—seems to increase the risk of Type 2 diabetes. As far back as the 1920s Dr. S. Sweeney produced reversible diabetes in his medical-school students by feeding them a diet high in refined vegetable oils for 48 hours.

Three long-term studies have recently shown that the foods most associated with a higher risk of Type 2 diabetes are: deep-fried potatoes, white bread, white rice, crackers and soft drinks.[10]

Chromium Deficiency

A deficiency in the trace mineral chromium could be a contributory cause of Type 2 diabetes. Elevated insulin levels increase excretion of chromium, so people who receive insulin injections will tend to become deficient in chromium. Under normal circumstances, chromium works with insulin in allowing the cells to absorb and utilize glucose. A deficiency of chromium has been found to increase insulin requirements, so that a vicious cycle develops. Many Type 1 diabetics are also deficient in chromium.

Stress

Diabetes often develops after a stressful event such as a heart attack or car accident. Evidently emotional stress triggers hormonal responses. In particular insulin levels might fluctuate wildly—this is called posttraumatic dysinsulinism—with the result that blood glucose also fluctuates. This is in itself stressful and it is easy to see how poor insulin control can eventually result in mood swings, from depression to hypomania.[11]

henrietta:

Henrietta is the most unusual case of diabetes that I have come across, and is equally interesting to the many doctors who have cared for her over the years. Trauma accompanying the birth of her first child, now a strapping young man in his early twenties, triggered her diabetes. She lost 10 pints of blood during the Caesarian section, and the hospital was slow to get a transfusion in place. For three months after the birth, Henrietta was very weak—she had lost half her body weight, and was unable to feed her baby. Then the classic symptoms of diabetes began to appear—she became very thirsty and needed to urinate frequently, and her sight was affected. When she was diagnosed, she was found to need a very small dose of insulin indeed, and ever since has needed less than 10 units daily, sometimes in doses as small as half a unit. Henrietta is what is known as a brittle diabetic, in that her diabetes is particularly hard to manage. She used to have frequent hypoglycemic episodes on the porcine insulin, but manages better with the human insulin. Occasionally she uses Humalog, but only in an emergency when she is given a high-carbohydrate meal, perhaps at a dinner party.

Henrietta eats a very healthy diet. She doesn't avoid sugar completely, but is careful to balance high-GI carbohydrates with low-GI carbohydrates and protein. She long ago found that artificial sweeteners upset her digestive system, so she avoids these. She relies quite heavily on sugar-free muesli and porridge with which she will often have a banana. She cooks a lot of vegetarian dishes, but is aware that roast peppers and parsnips, for example, are high-sugar foods, so she would never eat them on their own, but always with a low-GI food or some protein. She does eat baked potatoes, but has discovered that the skins make her blood glucose leap up, so she usually removes the skin.

Henrietta suffers from some of the complications of diabetes. Her legs were damaged during the birth of her first child, the skin on her legs is very thin and she bruises easily. Any wound on her legs is slow to heal. She always wears support bandages on her legs and makes sure to keep the blood circulating as much as possible by never sitting down for too long. Now she is starting to experience some neuropathy in her arms as well. She looks after her health carefully, walks everywhere and swims frequently. The worst thing, she finds, is that she is always tired, and has to make a conscious effort to rest as much as possible—about 10 hours a night—even if she is not asleep all that time.

Industrial Air Pollution

Dioxin intake by inhalation and/or ingestion has been revealed in published journals to be associated with an increased incidence of diabetes. Recent Israeli research has shown chronic exposure of fat or muscle cells to even low levels of free radicals produces insulin resistance and Type 2 diabetes.[12] In Sheffield the hospital admissions for diabetes were recorded per 1,000 people as 4 in the center of the city but as high as 11 in the eastern part of the city that is affected by pollution from dioxins emitted by the city incinerator and a castings plant.[13]

the long-term implications of diabetes

DIABETES IS SUCH an important issue because of the long-term effects of the disease. The complications of diabetes are serious. They include heart disease (2–4 times more likely in diabetics than in nondiabetics, high blood pressure (twice as common in diabetics), strokes (mortality rates from this disorder are three to six times higher in diabetics) and peripheral vascular disease (that is, diseases of the blood vessels outside the heart and brain, often a narrowing of vessels that carry blood to the leg muscles). There are several complications of diabetes that develop over time. These include damage to the retina of the eye (retinopathy), which can lead to impaired vision and even blindness. Other complications are damage to the blood vessels (angiopathy), the nervous system (neuropathy), and the kidneys (nephropathy). Studies show that keeping blood-glucose levels as close to the normal, nondiabetic range as possible, may help prevent, slow, or delay harmful effects to the eyes, kidneys, and nerves.

High blood-glucose levels over an extended period result in glucose attaching to proteins until the proteins cease to function properly. This is called the glycosylation of proteins and, at the cellular level, is the ultimate cause of diabetic complications. Glycosylation reactions happen normally in the body, controlled by enzymes, but in diabetes the process is speeded up or uncontrolled. For example, cholesterol-carrying proteins that have been glycosylated are unable to bind to receptors that tell certain liver cells to stop manufacturing cholesterol. As a result, too much cholesterol is manufactured. For diabetics, the most significant glycosylation is that of hemoglobin, the molecule in our red blood cells that carries oxygen around the body. This glycosylation is measured by the HbA1C test (see page 17).

Glycosylated proteins eventually turn into Advanced Glycosylated End Products (AGEs) and their formation increases with the level and time that blood glucose is elevated. Glycosylation of the proteins in the lens of the eye can result in cataracts. AGEs also trigger the production of free radicals by the immune system. Free radicals are unstable molecules that can damage the DNA of cells. This increased level of free-radical damage translates into high risk of developing many of the degenerative diseases. It has been found that people with metabolic syndrome, many of whom go on to develop Type 2 diabetes, have low-antioxidant status.[14] It is therefore especially important that people at risk of diabetes protect themselves from free-radical damage by eating a diet high in antioxidants, such as vitamins C and E, and by taking antioxidant supplements. (This is covered in more detail in the section on nutritional management.)

Hypoglycemia

Hypoglycemia means low blood sugar and is one of the effects of diabetes. People with diabetes unfortunately often experience hypoglycemic episodes when their blood glucose is not under control. It may seem illogical that low blood sugar is the most dangerous effect of diabetes, which by its very nature is a disease of high blood sugar. However, hypoglycemia arises if the person with diabetes injects too much insulin, or takes too high a dose of diabetes drugs. It can also occur if the person skips a meal or delays eating, drinks too much alcohol or exercises without eating beforehand. Low blood sugar, caused either by excess insulin or by lack of glucose from the diet, will lower the blood sugar too much, which causes the body to release adrenaline. The role of adrenaline is to mobilize energy stores and convert them into glucose. It also causes symptoms of nervous-system stimulation and starves the brain of glucose, which can cause confusion and abnormal behavior. Severe hypoglycemia will result in coma and is eventually fatal. One diabetic I interviewed who has many years' experience of hypoglycemia, comments: "I never know when I have a hypoglycemic epoiside coming on, and only realize it when I become ludicrously depressed, clumsy, repetitive, and exhausted. When I do realize what's happening, I have a large drink of orange juice. As I start to get better, usually after half an hour, I will test my blood and then have a small bowl of sugar-free muesli . . . You need to rest after an episode—they are shattering to the system and need care and time to recover from."

medical management of diabetes

BEFORE 1921, WHEN insulin was first discovered, people with diabetes usually died, as there was no way to control their blood-glucose levels. Today, people with Type 1 diabetes can manage their condition with insulin, and people with Type 2 diabetes either use medication to control their blood glucose, or manage the disease with diet and exercise alone. Some people with Type 2 also take insulin.

When a person is first diagnosed with diabetes, he or she is given a full medical examination. Their diabetes team will then work with them to develop a program of care that suits them and includes diabetes-management goals—this may take the form of a record for them to keep. If they are lucky, they will also be seen by a certified diabetes educator—who is usually a nurse or dietitian. Insulin-dependent diabetics are shown how to inject, look after their insulin and syringes and dispose of needles. They are also shown how to test their blood glucose and test for ketones, know what the results mean and what to do about them, and informed about hypoglycemic episodes: when and why they may happen and how to deal with them. People on tablets are given instruction on blood or urine testing and have explained what the results mean and what to do about them.

For anyone with diabetes, Type 1 or Type 2, always check with your health-care provider or public-health agency to see if you are entitled to any free examination (such as eye or foot care), medications, or supplies. A certified diabetes educator will also be able to provide this information.

Type 1

Insulin

Type 1 has been managed conventionally with insulin and a carbohydrate-based, low-fat diet. The carbohydrates in such a diet inevitably put large amounts of glucose in the bloodstream, and frequent insulin injections have to be administered to bring these high levels of glucose in the blood down to normal. When the illness is first diagnosed, most Type 1 diabetics are still producing some insulin, but this tapers off over time. Some researchers believe that if the illness is caught soon enough, a very-high-fat-and-low-carbohydrate diet might obviate the need to inject insulin at all, or at least to need as much insulin. As it is, sufferers of Type 1 diabetes require insulin injections for the remainder of their lives. Unfortunately, insulin cannot be taken in tablet form because it would be broken down in the stomach before it could work. There are different types of insulin, and these can act very differently in different people. The insulin may be packaged in vials, cartridges, or prefilled pens. The cartridges are used with pen injectors and the vials are used with syringes. Prefilled pens are disposable pen injectors, prefilled with insulin.

There are three main types of insulin, which are also available in various combinations in premixed form. Rapid-acting insulin can be injected just before or just after eating and lasts for between two and five hours. Long-acting insulin is more slowly absorbed and lasts around 24 hours. It is taken only once a day, in the evening. Short-acting insulin is usually taken 15 to 30 minutes before a meal and has its peak action within two to six hours after injecting. It can last for up to eight hours. Medium and long-acting usually have their peak activity between four and 12 hours after injecting and can last from eight to 30 hours. They are often used in combination with short-acting insulin.

A few years ago "human" insulin replaced insulin derived from pigs. This new insulin was achieved using recombinant DNA technology, which means that it is genetically modified. It is not human at all, but a synthetic insulin chemically similar to human insulin. Many of the people I interviewed for this book complained of difficulty in controlling their blood sugar on the human insulin. It was first introduced, under pressure from the large drug companies, because many scientists and doctors believed that it would have many benefits over the older type of insulin precisely because it was "human," but thousands of people complained that it made blood-glucose levels harder to manage. Nevertheless, pig insulin is rarely used now, if at all.

laura:

LAURA, WHO IS in her early thirties, has had diabetes since she was two years old, so she has known nothing else. She remembers that when she was a child her parents had to weigh all of her food and work out the grams of carbohydrate it contained, and that she was not allowed to eat sugar. She sees a nutritionist regularly, and about three years ago gave up dairy and wheat. Her blood-glucose levels have come down considerably since she made these changes to her diet, and so she needs less insulin at each injection than she used to. Where she used to use 20 units a day, now she only uses 12 units. She now uses an insulin pen four times a day, five minutes before eating, along with the longer-acting insulin at bedtime to take her through the night. She was moved from porcine insulin to human insulin about eight years ago, but, in common with many other people I interviewed, finds the human insulin provides less control over blood glucose than the porcine insulin.

When I asked Laura how diabetes affected her life, she replied that diabetes is boring. She thinks about carbohydrates in general, without being particularly aware of the Glycemic Index. Carbohydrates for her are usually rice, noodles, potatoes, and rye bread. She does occasionally suffer from mood swings, and becomes irritated if her blood-glucose levels are low. She has occasionally had hypoglycemia for no reason that she could identify, and actually passed out a couple of times.

Type 2

Type 2 diabetes is managed either with drugs or with diet and exercise alone. Occasionally people with Type 2 need insulin, either on its own or with drugs. I was surprised to find that several of the older Type 2 people I spoke to were on insulin.

gay:

GAY, A DIABETES educator and nurse, has herself had Type 2 diabetes for 15 years. Three months ago she was put onto two different types of insulin: Lantus, which she takes at night, and Novo Rapid, a relatively new and extremely fast-acting insulin, immediately before a meal. She finds that the big advantage of Novo Rapid is that it is out of the system again within 3–5 hours, reducing the risk of hypoglycemia and the necessity to have meals exactly on time. Unlike David, she has found the Lantus very effective, in that it does not have a significant peak and does last 24 hours, although it has the slight disadvantage of having to be taken at exactly the same time each night. Gay comments that this regime has completely revolutionized her life, in that she can now eat when she pleases. With her extensive knowledge of diabetes and how to manage it, she has always kept her blood glucose well under control, and her HbA1C has been consistent at 6.5 percent since she started insulin. However, she was delighted to find that, after three months on the new regime, it actually went down to 6.3 percent. Gay comments that with the Lantus and Novo Rapid regime, snacking should not really be necessary on a regular basis, as this regime mimics the body's own mechanism much more closely, i.e., a constant background low-level supply of insulin with postprandial surges (that is, the Novo Rapid provides a surge of insulin to cope with the normal surge in blood glucose as a result of eating carbohydrates).

Drugs

Diabetes drugs work by lowering the blood glucose. They do this either by stimulating the pancreas to produce more insulin, or by helping the body to use the insulin that it does produce more effectively.

Sulphonylureas (e.g., Chlorpropamide) work by stimulating the cells in the pancreas to make more insulin. Unfortunately, they can cause your blood-glucose levels to fall too low, causing hypoglycemia, and can also cause weight gain. Prandial glucose regulators are shorter-acting. They are taken during a meal and work by stimulating your pancreas to produce more insulin. Biguanides (e.g., Metformin "Glucophage") work in two ways. They help to stop the liver from producing new glucose and also overcome insulin resistance by making insulin carry glucose into muscle and fat cells more effectively. Side effects include upset stomach, nausea and diarrhea, and in some cases a serious condition called lactic acidosis. Alpha glucosidase inhibitors (e.g., Acarbose) work by slowing down the absorption of starchy foods from the intestine, thereby slowing down the rise in blood glucose after meals. Side effects can include gas, a feeling of fullness or diarrhea. Thiazolidinediones (e.g., Actos) are a new family of tablets that overcome insulin resistance, enabling the body to use its own natural insulin more effectively. Side effects can include headaches, edema (fluid retention), weight gain and, less commonly, upper respiratory tract infections.

jean:

JEAN WAS DIAGNOSED with diabetes fourteen years ago when she had to go into the hospital for a hip replacement. Two years before that she had visited her doctor complaining of excessive thirst, but at that time the doctor told her this was healthy and normal. She was prescribed Metformin to begin with, but this caused unpleasant gastric side effects, so the dose was lowered and combined with insulin. Jean continued on this therapy until early 2003, but she is now on insulin alone as her pancreas is no longer able to make any insulin of its own. She takes 34 units of insulin a day, of two different types: one before breakfast that takes half an hour to kick in, and one at bedtime that works instantly. Jean has invested in a sophisticated battery-driven glucose meter that she uses on her arm rather than on her finger. She has found that different meters record different levels of blood glucose, which can be quite confusing.

When Jean feels she is about to have a hypoglycemic episode, she has learnt to take three glucose tablets all at once, and this brings her blood glucose up quickly enough to avert hypoglycemia. If she wakes up with a low blood-glucose reading of 5, she allows herself a spoonful of sugar in her tea, and this is enough to keep her blood sugar steady until breakfast. At breakfast she has half a grapefruit, one Weetabix with milk and an apple juice. This keeps her going through the morning and she finds she doesn't need a snack at all in the morning, though she may have a cookie with tea in the afternoon. She makes lots of homemade soups, and eats plenty of fresh green vegetables. She normally eats fresh fruit for dessert, especially strawberries, but if she is out at a restaurant she might just try a spoonful of something like pudding. Jean seems to be very in tune with her diabetes, and knows only too well that if she eats sugar, sugar products, potatoes, and bread her blood sugar will go sky-high, and this gives her the self-discipline to avoid or severely limit those foods. As she says, "once you know you have diabetes, you know you've got to take care of it. If you don't, you're in trouble."

■ ■ ■

Blood-Glucose Monitoring (Type 1 and Type 2)

Blood-glucose monitoring is an essential tool for controlling diabetes. It can help to maintain day-to-day control, detect hypoglycemia, assess control during any illness, and help to provide information that can be used in the prevention of long-term complications. Blood glucose is monitored with the help of a blood-glucose meter. There are many different sorts of glucose meter, some of which are downloadable to a computer so that you can keep track of your blood-glucose fluctuations easily. Glucose meters measure blood glucose in mg/dl. The range of values the meter registers can be as wide as 0–600 mg/dl, whereas normal blood glucose is generally 70–100 mg/dl. Any values outside the normal range are registered as low or high.

HbA1C

This is a vital long-term blood sugar reading. The HbA1C score represents the level of glycosylation of hemoglobin in the blood (see page 12). The amount of hemoglobin that forms HbA1C will depend on the concentration of glucose that the hemoglobin is exposed to and the length of time it is exposed to a given concentration of glucose. So consistently high blood sugar over an extended period of time will cause a greater percentage of hemoglobin to be damaged in this way. A patient's HbA1C level is used to predict the likelihood of complications from diabetes. It is important to achieve a score of less than 7 percent on the HbA1C test. The HbA1C level changes slowly, over 10 weeks, unlike the blood-sugar level that changes minute by minute, so it can be used as a "quality control" test. Patients with diabetes who do not keep their HbA1C under 7 percent are at risk of developing serious long-term health problems including stroke, heart disease, diabetic retinopathy, blindness, kidney failure, and amputation.

nutritional management of diabetes

PEOPLE WITH DIABETES have been bombarded with nutritional advice for many years. At the beginning of the twentieth century, they were advised to limit all food—not a very happy state of affairs. Later, in the 1920s, they were advised to eat high-fat diets on the basis that fat does not break down to glucose in the blood. In the 1970s and 1980s, the emphasis was on the amount of carbohydrate eaten, regardless of the type, and people with diabetes were advised to eat a set amount of carbohydrate at each meal. Nowadays the differences between types of carbohydrates are more clearly understood, and it is therefore much easier for a diabetic to control their blood glucose through diet, using the Glycemic Index and Glycemic Load.

The Glycemic Index

It used to be thought that carbohydrates were either fast-release or slow-release, that is refined foods such as sugar were thought to release their sugar content rapidly, resulting in a rapid rise in blood glucose, while complex carbohydrates, such as whole grains, would release it more slowly. During the 1980s scientists conducted a series of trials in which volunteers fasted for some hours, then were given a single food to eat. The rise in their blood sugar was then measured over four hours to see the effect of each food on blood glucose. The researchers had two surprises. The first was that all carbohydrates, regardless of quality, cause a peak in blood glucose approximately 30 minutes after being eaten. The second was that some foods cause a much more dramatic rise than others. It was further discovered that some foods cause a higher blood-glucose spike if they are cooked than if they are eaten raw, for example carrots.

Glucose was given a value of 100, and all other carbohydrates were ranked according to their effect on blood-glucose levels. This ranking is known as the Glycemic Index (GI). Carbohydrates that cause a sharp rise in blood glucose have the highest GI, whereas carbohydrates that have a gentler effect on blood glucose have a low GI. Various factors influence the GI value of a food: for example the gelatinization of starch in pasta. If pasta is cooked until it is soft, the starch has had more time to absorb water, and consequently is more gelatinous than if the pasta is cooked "al dente." So the well-cooked pasta will have a higher GI than "al dente" pasta. Similarly, if a food consists of small particles, for example white flour, it is easier for water and digestive enzymes to penetrate the particles, and consequently they will hit the bloodstream sooner than the large particles in stone-ground flour. Therefore, the white flour will have a higher GI. Finally, and perhaps surprisingly, sugar is digested less rapidly than starch and thus has a relatively low GI (60–65). This is because sugar is not pure glucose, but consists of two molecules, one of glucose and one of fructose. Fructose produces a low blood-sugar response, thus mitigating the effect of the glucose in sugar.

A low GI means a smaller rise in blood-glucose levels after meals. A diet featuring low-GI foods can help people lose weight and improve their sensitivity to insulin. Low-GI foods can help refuel carbohydrate stores after exercise, improve diabetes control, keep you feeling fuller for longer and can prolong physical endurance.

rona

RONA IS A qualified nutritionist, recently graduated, and came to her new career largely because of her diabetes that made her interested in the whole topic of blood glucose and how to control it. She comes from a medical background, so when at the age of 22 she began to lose weight and grow very thin, while at the same time suffering from extreme thirst, she readily diagnosed herself as being diabetic. The condition progressed over a period of six weeks or so, during which she was climbing mountains in Scotland, so as she says, her energy appeared not to be unduly affected at that time. She is still puzzled as to why she got diabetes—there was no particular stress in her life that she could think of, except the usual stresses a student might undergo, perhaps exacerbated in her case by a year in France where she had to write a thesis and make presentations in French. There is no diabetes in her family.

When she was finally diagnosed, Rona went into shock and denial about her diabetes. At that time she was injecting insulin, but she refused to test her blood, hoping perhaps that the diabetes would go away if she ignored it. She was helped to accept it by her boss whose son was a diabetic and used an insulin pen. Rona, too, now uses an "Act Rapid" pen, four times a day, with Insulatard at night.

Being nutritionally aware, Rona has learned to manage her diabetes successfully using low-GI foods. She finds lentils and porridge with raisins particularly helpful, and also relies on brown basmati rice and multiseed bread. Interestingly, in spite of their supposedly high GI rating, baked potatoes are still on Rona's menu, and they don't appear to raise her blood sugar unduly. She even eats ice cream sometimes—having discovered the Glycemic Index in the last two years, she was delighted to find that ice cream did not score too highly. She mentioned the GI to her dietitian, who was aware of it, but only had a casual acquaintance with it. Generally, Rona has not been impressed with dietitians and feels they could give more comprehensive and informed advice to people with diabetes. She has, however, had two successful pregnancies since becoming diabetic, and cannot praise more highly the care and monitoring she received while pregnant.

Rona is aware of when she's getting hypoglycemia, and uses sugary sweets to bring her blood-glucose level up quickly if necessary. As she says, "the bottom line is: if you eat more than you inject, your blood sugar will not be controlled."

■ ■ ■

The Glycemic Load

The Glycemic Load takes the concept of GI a step further, in providing a measure of total glycemic response to a food or to a meal. The GL is equivalent to the GI value of a food multiplied by the amount of carbohydrate per serving and divided by 100. One unit of GL is equivalent to the glycemic effect of 1g of pure glucose.

A food with a GL of 20 or more is high, a GL of 11 to 19 inclusive is medium, and a GL of 10 or less is low. Foods that have a low GI invariably have a low GL, while foods with an intermediate or high GI range from a very low to a very high GL. Therefore, you can reduce the GL of your diet by limiting foods that have both a high GI and a high carbohydrate content. A further complication is that acidic foods like lemon juice and vinegar lower the total glycemic load, and fats such as olive oil slow the absorption of carbohydrates.

A meal contains a variety of different foods, so how do you work out the GI or GL value of a whole meal? Briefly, this is done by adding up all the grams of carbohydrate in the meal, working out what percentage each food contributes to the total carbohydrate content, and then multiplying this percentage by the GI value. An exact calculation is difficult and at times impossible, because the GI and GL of all foods have not yet been measured. I have therefore given an approximate guide for each recipe, stating whether a recipe is high, medium, or low. The lists at the back of this book give both GI and GL values for reference. I have used the latest tables available, those published in the *American Journal of Clinical Nutrition* in 2002.[15] However, I would add the caveat that these are approximate only, and that the actual GI value may well be slightly different.

The Glycemic Index and Glycemic Load were never intended to be used in isolation. A food can have a low GI but still be high in saturated fat or have other undesirable qualities. So the recipes in this book have been chosen not only because they have a low GI but also because they are healthy and well balanced.

What Proportion of Carbohydrates?

All food is made up of three macronutrients—protein, fat, and carbohydrate. Because diabetes is a disorder of carbohydrate metabolism, a person with diabetes needs to know what proportion of carbohydrates in the diet will enable them to control their blood sugar most effectively.

The standard dietary advice given by both the American Diabetes Association and American Dietetic Association provides a number of meal-planning approaches, ranging from the simple guidelines of the Food Guide Pyramid or menus to more complex approaches such as carbohydrate counting and use of the exchange lists for meal planning. The dietary recommendations for each individual are based on the person's weight, activity level, diabetes medications, and blood-glucose levels. The ratio of macronutrients ranges from 15–20 percent protein, 50–55 percent carbohydrates, and 30 percent fat. However, it doesn't seem logical to base the diet on carbohydrates, as these are the foods that people with diabetes, by definition, have the most difficulty metabolizing. A high intake of carbohydrates, particularly of high-GI carbohydrates, leads to consistently high blood-glucose levels. The solution would appear to be a lower-carbohydrate diet, replacing carbohydrates not with saturated fat, but with modest amounts of essential fats and more protein. This approach is supported by a recent preliminary study in which people with Type 2 diabetes achieved lower blood glucose and lower blood fats following a lower-carbohydrate, higher-protein diet (30 percent protein, 40 percent carbohydrate, and 30 percent fat) than those on the standard ADA diet. The lower-carbohydrate, higher-protein diet is characterized by a high intake of vegetables, legumes, fruit, and whole grains, and a low intake of red meat, processed meat, high-fat dairy products, and refined grains. It is not the same as the Atkins diet, which contains far less carbohydrate, more protein, and typically a high intake of saturated fat too. The lower-carbohydrate, higher-protein diet is the pattern on which I have based the recipes in this book, although in practice it is quite difficult to achieve that level of protein over the course of a day's menus, particularly if you are avoiding or limiting red meat, which is the richest source of dietary protein. While it is not excessive when compared to the Atkins diet, caution should be taken by those individuals with preexisting renal problems. They should consult their medical practitioner before embarking on a high-protein diet.

Vegetables

It is important to eat a wide variety of vegetables. They are rich in fiber and nutrients and help to protect the cardiovascular system and nerves from glycosylation. Avoid cooked starchy root vegetables especially potatoes and parsnips as they have a very high GI value. **Beets** should be eaten raw, as they contain chromium, as do the beet greens. **Mushrooms** also contain chromium. Certain vegetables are particularly beneficial, such as **onions** and **garlic**, as they are able to reduce blood sugar. They contain active ingredients that appear to increase insulin in the blood by preventing it from being inactivated by the liver.[17] **Jerusalem artichokes**, **broccoli**, **celery**, **cabbage**, **chicory**, **Chinese cabbage**, **zucchini**, **kale**, **radishes,** and **tomatoes** are also among the recommended "nutriceuticals" for diabetes.[18] **Avocados** and **olives** are particularly high in mono-unsaturated fatty acids, and are good choices. Finally, mung beans, usually eaten as **bean**

sprouts, are thought to be beneficial as an antidiabetic, low glycemic-index food, rich in antioxidants.[19] Antioxidants have been found to be very important in relation to the prevention of Type 2 diabetes, particularly vitamin E. In a recent study, researchers found that the highest long-term vitamin E intake was significantly associated with a reduced risk of Type 2 diabetes, compared to subjects with the lowest intake. Good sources of vitamin E include spinach, eggs, meat, poultry, fish, nuts and seeds, avocado and tomatoes. Those with the highest intakes of a carotenoid found in sweet peppers, sweetcorn and watermelon also had a 40 percent reduced risk of Type 2 diabetes.[20]

Fruit

Choose low-GI fruits such as **apples** and **pears** and avoid high-GI fruits such as melon and bananas. **Grapefruit**, which has a very low GI, may be one of the healthiest dietary choices for people with diabetes and for those trying to lose weight, because it contains enzymes that help control insulin spikes that occur after a meal, thus freeing the digestive system to process food more efficiently, with the result that fewer nutrients are stored as fat.

Consumption of fruit should, however, be moderate. One rather startling finding of interest to people with diabetes is that apparently fruit is getting sweeter. Recent American government research found that apples can now comprise up to 15 percent sugar compared with 8 to 10 percent three decades ago. Similar increases have been reported in pineapples, pears, and bananas. It appears that farming techniques have changed to meet consumer demand. For example, in apples this is partly due to new varieties and partly to how they are picked and stored so that they retain more sugar. Most fruit juice provides about 10 grams of sugar per 100 grams—about the same as a cola drink. It is wise to avoid fruit juice for this reason, or to dilute it with water. Vegetable juices are a better choice, and you will find several delicious recipes for vegetable juices in the drinks section.

Protein Foods

Amino acids, the breakdown products of protein foods, are normally considered as the "building blocks" of the body, in that their primary role is that of maintenance and repair. But our bodies will also make glucose from protein. Since glucose, usually sourced from carbohydrates, is what gives us energy, it is important for a person with diabetes who is limiting their carbohydrates to eat enough protein. Protein also has the effect of slowing the absorption of glucose from carbohydrates, so always make sure you eat a small portion of protein at each snack or meal. Choose fish, especially the oily fish such as organic or wild **salmon** and **mackerel**, **yogurt**, **cottage cheese**, **legumes**, **quinoa**, **soy**, and **poultry**, as these are low in saturated fats.

It may be wise to limit the amount of red meat you eat if you have diabetes. A study has indicated that the consumption of red meat, which contains heme iron, is associated with an increased risk of Type 2 diabetes.[21] The findings also revealed that people with hemochromatosis, a disease in which the body takes in too much iron with food, are more likely to develop diabetes. This may be because iron is a catalyst in the formation of dangerous free radicals.

Whole Grains

Although carbohydrates should be limited, they should definitely not be avoided completely. But it is important to choose the right sort of carbohydrates—vegetables, fruit, legumes, and whole grains. Studies have shown that those with the highest intake of whole grains and cereal fiber are less likely to develop metabolic syndrome, which predisposes to diabetes.

One of the most beneficial grains for people with diabetes is **buckwheat**, which is readily available in health-food shops. It is not related to wheat, and is not even, technically, a grain, but a fruit. Several studies have shown that buckwheat may help increase insulin sensitivity. Previous studies have shown how a component of buckwheat called chiro-inositol may prompt cells to become more receptive to insulin. Chiro-inositol is relatively high in buckwheat and rarely found in other foods. Of all the seeds analyzed, only mung beans have more. Some diabetics don't see any change in blood-glucose levels when they consume buckwheat, but it is possible that the compound is still helping their bodies to use glucose more effectively. Also, there are a couple of small studies published in China and India indicating that people with Type 2 diabetes who consumed buckwheat had better glycemic control. The glycemic index of buckwheat has been extensively tested and is about 54, and its glycemic load is 16, which is medium.

In the recipes I have used **buckwheat**, **pearl barley**, **quinoa**, **brown rice**, **polenta**, **whole wheat**, and **amaranth**, as these all have a low GI value. Whole grains contain chromium, needed for carbohydrate metabolism, and lots of minerals and vitamins. Avoid any products made with refined white flour. Not only is it a high GI, but it is almost devoid of nutritional value.

The gluten grains (barley, rye, oats, and wheat) can pose potential problems for people with diabetes, and a small proportion (about 5 percent) of Type 1 diabetics are celiac, which means they cannot digest these grains at all. I have therefore included some gluten-free recipes. However, many people intolerant to wheat but not actually celiac can tolerate oats and barley, though they do contain some gluten.

I have only included one bread recipe, and that is for barley bread, because barley has a relatively low GI. The fiber content of barley accounts for its ability to lower cholesterol and glucose, and the beta-glucan it contains may also reduce appetite by slowing down emptying of the stomach and stabilizing blood sugar. Bread should not really be used as a staple by people with diabetes due to its high carbohydrate content. If you cannot do without bread, it might be worth searching out a whole-grain, multigrain or sourdough bread.

Dairy Products

It appears that dairy products cause an unusual increase in insulin secretion. This may be because cow's milk proteins are designed to stimulate growth in young calves, whose normal growth rate consists of doubling their birth weight within the first month. Insulin does more than drive glucose into the cells—it also encourages the uptake of essential fatty acids and proteins, needed for growth. I therefore do not use cow's milk in the recipes, but substitute **soy milk** or **rice milk**. Butter is acceptable in small amounts as it is nearly all fat and contains virtually no protein. I do use butter in baking and in recipes where the taste of the fat is important, and I also use a little Parmesan and goat cheese for flavor where nothing else can substitute. Yogurt and a little cottage cheese are also acceptable.

Fats and Oils

Fat does not increase blood-glucose levels, but that does not mean that fats can be eaten indiscriminately, for there are good fats and bad fats. It is very important to avoid scrupulously any trans-fatty acids or hydrogenated fats (most cooking fats, margarines and processed foods) and refined oils. A large, long-term study of 84,000 women recently found that trans-fatty acids can raise a woman's risk of Type 2 diabetes, while substituting foods rich in trans fats with those that contain polyunsaturated fats could reduce the risk by about 40 percent.[22]

The monounsaturated fats, such as **extra-virgin olive oil**, and the omega-3 fatty acids found in oily fish and nuts, actually lower serum triglycerides and contribute to glycemic control in people with diabetes. Population studies on the peoples of Greenland have suggested that fish oil might help protect against diabetes. These people, who live on whale blubber, are often overweight and could be expected to have diabetes and heart disease, but they do not. Researchers think this is because of the high proportion of omega-3 fatty acids in their diet.

There are only three fats and oils that should be used for cooking—extra-virgin olive oil, virgin coconut oil, and organic butter. For salad dressings, extra-virgin olive oil or any of the delicious cold-pressed seed or nut oils may be used, such as walnut oil and flaxseed oil (rich in omega-3 fatty acids), avocado oil, or pumpkin-seed oil. For spreading, try almond or hazelnut butter or tahini (sesame-seed paste). Organic butter is also an acceptable choice, as it is a rich source of easily absorbed vitamin A and all the other fat-soluble vitamins (E, K, and D). It is rich in trace minerals, especially selenium, a powerful antioxidant. It has appreciable amounts of butyric acid, used by the colon as an energy source, and lauric acid, a medium-length long-chain fatty acid (MCFA).

Coconut oil has some interesting properties that make it very suitable for people with diabetes. It helps to regulate blood sugar, and it also raises the metabolic rate, causing the body to burn up more calories and thus promoting weight loss. A faster metabolic rate stimulates increased production of insulin and increases absorption of glucose into cells, thus helping both Type 1 and Type 2 diabetics.[23] Coconut oil is composed of about 50 percent lauric acid. Like other MCFAs, lauric acid is digested and processed differently from other fats. It is sent directly to the liver where it is immediately converted into energy—just like a carbohydrate. Numerous studies have shown that replacing long-chain fatty acids with MCFA results in a decrease in body-weight gain and a reduction in fat deposition.[24] Furthermore, reports from India reveal that Type 2 diabetes there has increased as people have abandoned coconut oil in favor of refined vegetable oils.[25] Organic coconut oil is available from Spectrum Naturals.

Acid and Fermented Foods

The acetic acid in vinegar and the citric acid in lemon and lime juice are able to actually reduce blood-glucose levels by slowing the speed at which the stomach empties into the intestine.[26] In one study the glucose response with vinegar was 31 percent lower than without it. In another study vinegar significantly reduced the glycemic index of a starchy meal from 100 to 64.[27] Fermented foods such as pickles and sauerkraut may have the same effect.

Nuts and Seeds

Nuts and seeds are nutrient-dense and contain essential fats, protein, and some fiber. The best nuts are those with a higher proportion of monounsaturated fatty acids, such as **macadamia nuts**, **hazelnuts**, **pecans**, and **almonds**. Almonds are particularly important for people with diabetes or metabolic syndrome. A recent study found that a low-calorie diet supplemented with almonds not only helped people to lose weight but also enabled Type 1 diabetics to reduce their medication.[28] Nuts and seeds are rich in magnesium. Findings from a recent large long-term study suggest a significant inverse association between magnesium intake and diabetes risk. Furthermore, diabetics are usually deficient in magnesium.[29] It is therefore important to increase consumption of major food sources of magnesium, such as whole grains, nuts, seeds, and green leafy vegetables.

Nuts and seeds can be eaten as a snack with a piece of fruit, or ground and added to porridge, yogurt, or vegetable juices to increase fiber intake. Avoid salted or dry roasted nuts.

Sugar and Sweeteners

Sugar consumption and the incidence of diabetes appear to have kept pace with each other in the developing world. However, there is no proof that sugar consumption is the direct cause of diabetes. Indeed, the story is much more complex. It's not sugar that causes diabetes, but rather a combination of genetic and environmental factors, some of which I have outlined earlier. But even if sugar doesn't cause diabetes, should people who have the disease avoid it? In fact, the American Diabetes Association (ADA) stopped recommending that people with diabetes avoid sugar in May 1994. Similarly, other diabetes associations no longer forbid sugar. However, there are plenty of reasons why diabetics, along with everyone else, should avoid refined sugar at all costs. Reducing the amount of sugar in the diet helps to reduce weight, which in turn improves glycemic control.[30]

White sugar is particularly damaging as the B vitamins and trace minerals such as zinc, manganese, chromium, selenium, and cobalt are all removed by the refining process. As these substances are necessary for the body to metabolize sugar, the sugar squanders these nutrients from the body's reserves. Sugar also suppresses the immune system and has a hand in numerous other conditions, such as elevated cholesterol, kidney damage, depression, hormonal imbalance, free radical formation, hypertension, migraines, and osteoporosis.

Unfortunately many doctors and dietitians are still advising people with diabetes to replace sugar with substances that could be even more harmful in the long run—sweeteners. There are five intense (artificial) sweeteners that are permitted for use in the USA: aspartame, saccharin, acesulfame-K, neotame, and sucralose. These sweeteners have their own disadvantages, and should be avoided because they promote a sweet tooth, increase cravings for sweet foods and make it more difficult to lose weight. A possible explanation is that when you eat an artificial sweetener, the body prepares itself to digest carbohydrates that then fail to materialize. When you do subsequently eat some carbohydrate the body compromises by creating a greater than normal rise in blood sugar. Not only that, but some sweeteners have more sinister drawbacks. Aspartame is a neurotoxin.[31] It is processed using methanol, which is highly toxic. Complaints about its effects range from headaches to seizures. Sucralose, which is marketed as Splenda, has no calories and is about 600 times sweeter than sugar. It is produced by chlorinating sugar, which involves chemically changing the structure of the sugar molecules. Sucralose has not been much tested on humans, but one small study of diabetic patients using sucralose showed a statistically significant increase in the long-term blood-glucose marker, HbA1C.

Fructose is the form of sugar found in fruit, as its name suggests. When naturally contained within a whole food, it causes no problems. However, it is commercially extracted and refined from corn, and is often found in processed foods as high-fructose corn syrup.

It does not affect the blood glucose as much as sucrose, but it is thought to lead to the formation of advanced glycation end products (AGEs), which have been implicated in many degenerative diseases such as cataracts. Animal studies have found that fructose consumption contributes to insulin resistance, an impaired tolerance to glucose, high blood pressure, and elevated levels of triglycerides. Although the data in humans is not quite as conclusive as the animal trials, the researchers report that an increased intake of fructose may increase body weight and encourage insulin resistance, both of which are risk factors for Type 2 diabetes. Finally, evidence is mounting that many people who experience irritable bowel syndrome and other gastrointestinal discomfort may be suffering from fructose intolerance.

There are two forms of sweetener that are safer than aspartame and sucralose. The first is FOS (Fructo-oligosaccharides), obtainable from health-food stores. FOS can be used in baking and to sweeten stewed fruit. It is mildly sweet and nourishes the beneficial bacteria in the gut. However, it can cause flatulence and bloating. The second is **stevia**, a member of the chrysanthemum family. This natural sweetener, which comes from Paraguay, has been used for centuries, and is used today in South America, Southeast Asia, and the Far East. However, in the USA, stevia has not yet gained FDA approval as a nonnutritive sweetener—it is approved for use as a "dietary supplement." The EC Scientific Committee on Food (SCF) came to the conclusion that it has the potential to produce adverse effects in the male reproductive system that could affect fertility, and that it could damage DNA. It is therefore highly controversial. Many diabetics do use it, and in recent studies it has proved to have beneficial effects on Type 2 diabetes and high blood pressure.[32]

I think the best approach to sugar and sweeteners is to try to reeducate one's palate, so that one does not crave sweet foods. This is possible, although it takes time. You may be helped by using a supplement containing magnesium, chromium, or glutamine (see pages 32–33). Fresh fruit can fulfill the need for sweetness without the health concerns attached to artificial sweeteners or stevia.

Drinks

Tea, coffee, cola drinks, and chocolate

All these drinks contain stimulants such as caffeine that produce spikes in blood-glucose levels. Preliminary findings from a small study suggest that drinking moderate amounts of coffee may decrease insulin sensitivity in healthy people by as much as 15 percent.[33] The finding may have serious health implications, especially with regard to people who already have Type 2 diabetes, because this effect is the reverse of that of prescription diabetes drugs such as metformin (Glucophage), so that if you take a drug for Type 2 diabetes and wash it down with coffee, you may be cancelling out the effects of the drug.

On the other side of the argument, however, a recent large-scale study revealed that regular daily coffee drinking may *reduce* the risk of developing Type 2 diabetes. Though caffeine appears to be the primary source of benefits, the study's authors suggested that the potassium, magnesium, and antioxidants in coffee might improve the body's response to insulin. The study had limitations, however. The researchers could not be certain that coffee decreases the incidence of Type 2 diabetes, as it could be something else about coffee drinkers that protects them from diabetes.[34] Other studies, from Sweden and Holland, have shown that regular coffee consumption may protect against the development of Type 2 diabetes.[35, 36] However, coffee has other disadvantages, as it may interfere with your body's ability to keep homocysteine and cholesterol levels in check, probably by inhibiting the action of the vitamins folate, B_{12}, or B_6, and it is associated with increased risk of stroke and rheumatoid arthritis. Studies have also shown that the caffeine in coffee can raise blood pressure. It also raises the levels of adrenaline by up to 500 percent, which may be connected to its ability to decrease insulin sensitivity. Since coffee is a stimulant it will only worsen any symptoms of insomnia and anxiety and should definitely be avoided.

Soft drinks and cordials should be avoided as they are high in sugar. Diet drinks contain sweeteners such as aspartame and should also be avoided. This also applies to the currently fashionable flavored waters. Instead, drink **herbal teas**, **water**, **dandelion coffee**, **green** or **jasmine tea**, **hot water** with **lemon** or **ginger**.

Avoid fruit juice—fruit juice is a concentrated form of carbohydrate—the sugars in fruit juice contribute to major distortions of insulin balance.

Alcohol

It appears that moderate alcohol consumption, as opposed to total abstinence, is associated with a decreased incidence of heart disease in people with diabetes, according to a recent review of the scientific literature on the subject.[37] A French study has found that insulin resistance is minimal in individuals with regular mild to moderate alcohol consumption and increases in both heavy drinkers and subjects without any alcohol consumption at all.[38] Moderate alcohol consumption is usually taken to mean not more than one to two alcoholic beverages per day. However, some people should not consume any alcohol because of the medication they take for diabetes or other conditions.

The dangers of heavy drinking are even more acute for people with diabetes than for anyone else. The risks of heavy or continuous alcohol intake include hypoglycemia, glucose intolerance, and ketone and lactate accumulation.[39] The growing alcohol consumption in young people, particularly in young women, may be a risk factor for the development of Type 2 diabetes. A recently completed 10-year study examining the relationship between alcohol consumption and the incidence of Type 2 diabetes in women found that, whereas light alcohol consumption may be associated with a lower risk, this benefit may not persist at higher levels.[40]

Convenience Foods

Convenience foods and conventionally prepared meals should be avoided whenever possible. Read labels carefully to check for saturated fat, fiber, and sugar content. Hidden sugars include corn syrup, high-fructose corn syrup, fructose, and dextrose. Low-fat foods are by default high in carbohydrates and often in sugar too.

Salt

For years doctors have told people to restrict salt, even those who do not have high blood pressure. But a recent study from Columbia University Medical School shows that salt restriction raises blood sugar and insulin levels, while a diet high in salt apparently lowers them. The conclusion of the study was that a high sodium intake may improve glucose tolerance and insulin resistance, especially in diabetic subjects."[41] This was a small preliminary study and should itself be taken with a grain of salt! I would advise very moderate use of salt, and to avoid highly salted foods. I usually use sea salt as it contains some trace minerals and is very concentrated so you need to use less of it.

Herbs and Spices

Several culinary herbs have been shown to help improve the action of insulin in lowering blood-sugar levels. These include coriander, bay, juniper berries, fenugreek seed, cloves, turmeric, and cinnamon, and you will find many uses for these spices in the recipes that follow.

Cinnamon is particularly effective. A recent study reported in *Diabetes Care* found that just 1g (less than half a teaspoon) of cinnamon per day reduced blood-glucose levels by 20 percent, as well as triglycerides, LDL cholesterol, and total cholesterol in 60 people with Type 2 diabetes.[42] In the study, lower blood-glucose levels were maintained for 20 days after stopping the cinnamon capsules. This may mean that it is not necessary to take cinnamon every day to produce a benefit.

The active ingredient in cinnamon is a flavonoid called methylhydroxychalcone polymer (MHCP) which has insulin-like activity. It appears that MHCP works both in synergy with insulin and on its own to regulate glucose metabolism. It would be wise for any diabetic wishing to try cinnamon to work with their doctor or diabetes nurse to monitor progress.

Exercise caution if using large amounts of whole cinnamon. It has both fat-soluble and water-soluble fractions and there is some evidence that high levels of the fat-soluble fractions of cinnamon could be cause for concern if a person is taking 1g per day. One solution is to make an infusion of cinnamon by boiling it in water, then straining the liquid through muslin and discarding the pulp. The liquid, which will contain only the water-soluble fraction, can then be drunk as a tea or used in food.

Snacks

Snacks are very important to people with diabetes, though less so to those who are using a combination of a basal insulin such as Lantus together with a fast-acting insulin at mealtimes. For those who are less able to keep their blood-sugar levels even, snacks should be consumed between meals. But they have to be balanced snacks. A snack consisting solely of carbohydrate will have a marked effect on blood glucose, whereas a combination of protein and a low-GI carbohydrate will keep the blood glucose more even. An exception is when people with diabetes, usually Type 1, experience a hypoglycemic episode, when their blood-glucose level dips below 70mg/dl and they feel shaky and weak, or perhaps start talking incoherently. Then they need a high-GI-carbohydrate snack, and they need it fast, or they are in danger of passing out. Most diabetics have their own personal choice of high-glucose food to raise their blood sugar quickly. Some people use pure glucose tablets, while some use orange juice or sugar cubes.

nutritional supplementation

IT IS A good idea for people with diabetes to boost their diet with nutritional supplements, but this should be done with your doctor's full knowledge and in conjunction with a qualified nutritionist. If you are taking prescribed medication for diabetes, the medication may need adjustment if you start to take natural remedies. This is because some supplements could potentiate the action of the drugs you are taking, i.e., make them more powerful, so you may need less medication.

Multivitamin

It is advisable for people with diabetes to take a good quality multiple vitamin because of their increased risk of cardiovascular disease, nerve and kidney damage and blindness. A small-scale double blind study of older people with Type 2 diabetes has shown that people with diabetes can reduce the risk of infection by supplementing with a multivitamin.[43]

Vitamins C and E

One out of three people with diabetes develops kidney disease in their lifetime. But if the warning signs are noted before kidney function is actually reduced, treatment may prevent further damage. One of the most valuable markers of a diabetic's kidney health is urinary albumin excretion rate (AER). Albumin is a protein synthesized in the liver that works to transport various substances in the blood stream. A Danish study has shown that vitamin C (1250mg/day) and vitamin E (680IU/day) had kidney-protective effects on a group of diabetic subjects with high AER levels. The AER levels decreased significantly in the patients taking the vitamins.

A recent study showed that vitamin C appears to reduce levels of C-reactive protein (CRP), which is an indicator of inflammation. There is a growing body of evidence that chronic inflammation is linked to an increased risk of heart disease and diabetes.[44] Long-term adverse health effects occur when inflammation persists at low levels. This chronic inflammation, with persistent low levels of CRP, has been found among smokers and Type 2 diabetics, as well as among people who are overweight.

Vitamin D

Chronic inflammation and CRP levels, along with associated risk of diabetes and other inflammatory conditions, have been shown to be lowered with vitamin D supplementation.[45]

Vitamin D deficiency has been associated with insulin deficiency and insulin resistance.[46] It has also been hypothesized that vitamin D deficiency may be a major factor in the development of Type 1 diabetes in children.[47] The best dietary sources of Vitamin D are eggs and oily fish. But the best strategy is exposure to sunlight in the summer months, which causes the body to manufacture vitamin D. Between October and March, cod liver oil as a vitamin D supplement of not more than 1,000IU per day may be advisable. Check with your doctor before starting supplementation.

Alpha-Lipoic Acid

Alpha-lipoic acid (ALA) is a powerful antioxidant that can help lower blood sugar, decrease glucose and insulin levels, increase insulin sensitivity, decrease insulin resistance, inhibit glycosylation (HbA1C levels), and help promote and maintain eye health. It has also been shown in studies to alleviate diabetic neuropathy at doses of 600mg a day. It is used in Germany to treat diabetes.

In addition, ALA can create new molecules of vitamins C and E from their molecular building blocks. There is research showing that ALA lowers blood-sugar levels in normal, or nondiabetic, subjects as well as in those with diabetes.

Essential Fatty Acids

Fish oils contain two fatty acids—Eicosapentaenoic Acid (EPA), and Docosahexaenoic Acid (DHA). People with diabetes have been shown to have markedly lower levels of DHA than other people.[48] In one study, three months of daily supplementation with DHA produced a "clinically significant" improvement in insulin sensitivity in overweight people.[49] This study used only DHA, but ideally EPA and DHA should always be taken in a balanced dose. The EPA and DHA probably work by improving the sensitivity of insulin receptors. Not only will this help diabetes, but it will also help control weight. In an encouraging new study, doctors in Denmark have concluded that fish-oil supplementation can help Type 2 diabetics reduce the high levels of fat present in their blood. Study participants who took fish oil lowered their ratio of LDL to HDL by almost one percent. Those taking corn oil, which is largely omega 6, raised their ratio by four percent.[50]

Evening Primrose Oil (EPO) contains Gamma Linoleic Acid (GLA), one of whose functions is to protect the nerves. The body normally makes GLA from alpha-linoleic acid (ALA), but diabetes can reduce the body's ability to produce GLA, and therefore neuropathy, or nerve damage, is a common complication of diabetes. Neuropathy can occur in any part of the body, but in diabetics it is particularly prominent in the legs and feet, causing numbness, tingling, pain, skin ulcers, and other problems.

Diabetics given GLA supplements were proven in a Glasgow study to be totally protected from small blood-vessel damage in the eyes and peripheries, due to improved blood flow. Evening primrose oil supplements reduce elevated total cholesterol levels found in many diabetics, and a recent review of 22 clinical studies of evening primrose oil showed that all but six of the studies confirmed EPO to have a positive effect in treating diabetic neuropathy.

Magnesium

Research suggests that supplementing with magnesium can help promote healthy insulin production. It can also reduce the craving for sweet foods that can contribute to the development of Type 2 diabetes.[51] Researchers have assessed six years of data on more than 12,000 people who participated in the Atherosclerosis Risk in Communities Study. The researchers found no significant correlation between low dietary intake of magnesium and diabetes risk. However, while that might seem at first like a paradox, body stores of magnesium can be depleted by a high intake of starches or alcohol, while diuretics and some prescription drugs can increase urinary excretion of magnesium. Menstruation and stress can also contribute to magnesium depletion. Other studies have shown a clear association between low serum-magnesium levels and an elevated risk of type 2 diabetes. Now a new study has shown that there may even be a correlation between magnesium depletion, Type 2 diabetes, and Alzheimers disease (AD).[52] Some researchers believe that high blood-glucose levels may play a role in the abnormal processing of a protein that prompts the accumulation of destructive peptide tangles in the brain.

Coenzyme Q10

Coenzyme Q10 is a powerful antioxidant that may help to maintain a healthy heart. Those doctors who are inclined toward a more natural approach have been using it successfully for years to help diabetic and prediabetic patients improve their fasting blood glucose and fasting insulin levels.[53] Fifty milligrams a day can be beneficial, but it is an expensive supplement.

Chromium

Chromium appears to be the most useful mineral in preventing Type 2 diabetes for a couple of reasons. It is one of the major components of glucose-tolerance factor, a molecule that improves the ability of insulin to lower blood-glucose levels. In fact, without adequate chromium, insulin cannot be activated and blood glucose goes out of control.[54] Chromium can also significantly reduce sugar cravings. A study in India found that chromium supplementation seemed to improve glycemic control in Type 2 diabetic patients. This effect appeared to be due to an increase in insulin action rather than stimulation of insulin secretion.[55]

Chromium helps stabilize blood-sugar levels and can be beneficial in Type 2 diabetes. It also helps to reduce heart disease due to its effect in improving insulin utilization and decreasing insulin requirements. Precisely because it is effective, however, people with diabetes may have an increased risk of hypoglycemic episodes when taking chromium supplements as self-medication, so blood-sugar levels should be strictly monitored while taking chromium. Chromium is found in brewer's yeast, liver, beef, beets, black pepper, thyme, and mushrooms. It is also found in whole grains, but the refining process removes chromium as it does other minerals, so refined grains lack it.

B-Complex

The entire B-complex is important in blood-sugar metabolism, but make sure that the supplement you choose contains at least 15 to 25 milligrams of niacin and 50 to 100 milligrams of niacinamide (both are forms of vitamin B_3). Niacin is another crucial component of the glucose-tolerance factor. Niacinamide helps protect pancreatic islet cells against the ultimate exhaustion that can be created by years of insulin overproduction.

Vitamin B_6 (pyridoxine)

Along with folic acid and B_{12}, B_6 has been found to help reduce the levels of homocysteine in the blood. Homocysteine is a toxic metabolite of protein digestion, high levels of which are associated with increased risk of heart disease. One study found that high homocysteine levels were associated with diabetic neuropathy.[56] Not only that, but people with diabetes are often deficient in vitamin B_6.

Biotin

It is a good idea to take an additional biotin supplement, even though this nutrient is found in most multivitamins. In order for biotin to really help metabolize blood sugar once it gets into the cells, you should take 1 to 2 milligrams a day—multivitamins don't usually provide nearly enough. B-complex and biotin can help inhibit glycosylation of proteins in diabetics.

Vitamin K

Protecting the body from insulin resistance appears to be one of vitamin K's many roles in the body. Dark green leafy vegetables are excellent sources of vitamin K, so make sure to eat plenty of broccoli and cabbage. It is not usually necessary to supplement vitamin K. If you are on blood thinners such as coumadin, check with your physician before using a vitamin K supplement or increasing your daily intake of vitamin K-containing foods.

Vanadium

Twenty years ago, researchers were finding that small doses of this trace mineral could significantly improve blood-sugar regulation. A word of caution, however: as with many of the trace minerals, there is a very narrow line between the benefits and toxicity of vanadium. While it can be an effective addition to your diabetes prevention and treatment program, more does not necessarily mean better. Vanadium does occur naturally in food, such as pepper, dill, radishes, eggs, buckwheat, and oats. As for supplementing with vanadium, the best plan is to find a multivitamin that contains vanadium as vanadyl sulphate.

Pycnogenol

In a recent study, researchers found that Type 2 diabetes patients had lower blood sugar and healthier blood vessels after supplementing with Pycnogenol, a French maritime pine tree–bark extract. The researchers report that the patients were able to significantly lower their glucose levels when they supplemented with 50–200 mg of the supplement. Pycnogenol has also been shown to improve cardiovascular problems prevailing in diabetics. Studies have found that Pycnogenol reduces high blood pressure, platelet aggregation, and LDL cholesterol and enhances circulation.[57]

herbal supplements

▶ **Ginseng** is believed by the Chinese to stimulate the release of insulin from the pancreas and increase the number of insulin receptors. In one clinical trial quite low doses of Asian ginseng (Panax ginseng) had beneficial blood-sugar lowering effects on Type 2 diabetes.[58]

▶ **Bitter melon** (Momordica Charantia or karela), a fruit indigenous to South America and Asia, has a blood-sugar lowering effect in diabetes and appears to increase the healthy regeneration of insulin-secreting beta cells in the pancreas.[59] Modern science has confirmed that the juice and unripe fruit of this plant have powerful blood-sugar reducing effects, mainly due to two compounds it contains, one of which, momordica, is chemically similar to insulin.

▶ **Gymnema Sylvestre,** a tropical-forest plant from India, is known as "gurmar," which means "sugar-destroyer." It stimulates the pancreas to produce insulin and reduces the craving for sweet foods. It is also reported to assist with beta-cell regeneration. Clinical trials have found it to considerably reduce blood sugar in over 90 percent of patients.[60]

▶ **Guar Gum** can reduce blood-glucose levels if taken in adequate quantities, probably by slowing down the absorption of carbohydrates. It must be accompanied by large quantities of water, however, to prevent constipation, and it can cause flatulence.

▶ **Garcinia cambogia** is a yellowish pumpkin-shaped tropical-tree fruit native to India that contains hydroxycitric acid (HCA), which has been shown to suppress fatty-acid synthesis and food intake, in addition to sparing the use of carbohydrate in the body while causing an increase in fat oxidation. However, these were animal studies, and so far human studies have not confirmed these findings.

▶ **Chinese herbs.** It is estimated that more than 200 species of plants exhibit hypoglycemic properties, including many common plants, such as pumpkin, wheat, celery, and lotus root as well as bitter melon. To date, hundreds of herbs and traditional Chinese medicine formulas have been reported to have been used for the treatment of diabetes.[61]

a note about glucosamine

RECENT ANIMAL STUDIES as well as some anecdotal evidence have suggested that glucosamine might increase insulin resistance and therefore could be harmful to diabetics. It appears that glucosamine may raise blood glucose in about 50 percent of people with diabetes. So if you have Type 2 diabetes and want to take glucosamine and chondroitin to relieve your arthritis symptoms, be sure that the doctor is aware that you're taking it and closely monitors your glucose levels.

exercise

THE SINGLE MOST important factor in controlling (and preventing) insulin resistance and adult-onset diabetes mellitus is exercise. Regular exercise can lower insulin resistance and improve Type 2 diabetes. The Finnish Diabetes Prevention Study (2001) by Tuomilehto and colleagues demonstrated conclusively that lifestyle modification could thwart the development of diabetes. This 10-year study of 522 people with impaired glucose tolerance showed that their risk of developing diabetes was reduced by 80 percent if they lost 22 pounds. A second study showed that people who did some aerobic-type exercise that caused them to "sweat a little" for 30 minutes three times a week cut their risk of going from Metabolic Syndrome (see page 9) to diabetes by nearly 60 percent.

Exercise will decrease blood sugar if the exercise is prolonged and strenuous. Blood sugars should be monitored every 10 minutes when starting an exercise routine to check for hypoglycemia (low blood sugar) and test if the exercise needs to be covered with carbohydrate to compensate for hypoglycemia. Anaerobic exercise (i.e., weightlifting) is ideal for diabetics because it lowers blood sugar more than aerobic exercise (running, biking, swimming, etc.), and it causes insulin to be much more efficient in transporting glucose into the cells.

Perhaps more important, however, exercise improves insulin sensitivity (a major problem in diabetes). Older people hampered by arthritis generally don't exercise enough and often become sedentary. This lack of activity causes insulin resistance, obesity, elevated fasting blood sugar and even elevated cholesterol. One large 16-year longitudinal study of 5,000 men has found that physical activity causes a reduction in insulin resistance. In the study, the risk for Type 2 diabetes decreased progressively with increasing levels of physical activity. The authors maintain that insulin resistance definitely plays an important role in the development of diabetes.[62]

All of the muscles need exercise in order to maximize glucose absorption. There is a difference between aerobic and anaerobic exercise. Anaerobic exercise is done in short sessions and improves muscle tone. Aerobic exercise is usually done in longer sessions and improves heart rate. When it comes to improving insulin sensitivity (reducing insulin resistance), most research supports aerobic activity. Earlier research indicated that only high-intensity aerobic activity reduced insulin resistance, but more recent research indicates that even low-intensity aerobic exercise, such as walking, helps. Only recently has anaerobic exercise been given equal billing with aerobic activity for controlling and managing diabetes.

When should you exercise? Since we expect blood-glucose levels to rise after meals, then diabetics would do well to engage in physical activity after meals. This way, the glucose will enter the muscles (reducing blood-sugar levels in the process) without needing insulin.

Walking briskly for thirty minutes five times a week has been nationally adopted as the minimum requirement for healthy benefits. Thirty minutes spread over the day is equally beneficial and activity within your daily routine can also burn calories and improve metabolic function, such as your body's response to insulin.

self-help

Stress Management. Stress has a part to play in diabetes, both in the inception of Type 2 and in terms of diabetes management. People who suffer from diabetes and who undergo emotional stress such as anxiety or depression tend to have poor glucose control, making them more susceptible to long-term physical complications such as eye, kidney, or nerve disorders. Stress management is therefore very important in the management of diabetes. Patients with Type 2 diabetes who incorporate stress-management techniques into their routine care can significantly reduce their average blood-glucose levels.

Stress-management techniques such as instructions on how to identify everyday-life stressors and how to respond to them with progressive muscle relaxation and breathing exercises have been shown in studies to reduce the HbA1C score by 0.5 percent and the blood-glucose level by 1 percent or more.[63] Although this doesn't sound like much, even a 0.5 percent reduction in HbA1C levels has been shown to produce a significant decrease in diabetic complications.

Acupuncture. The Chinese have long used acupuncture in the treatment of diabetes. Apparently it stimulates the pancreas to make insulin; it increases the number of insulin receptors and it speeds up the body's use of glucose.[64] It often also results in weight loss.

Mind/body techniques, such as thermal biofeedback, have been shown to improve peripheral circulation, pain, neuropathy, ulcers, walking ability and quality of life in people with diabetes.[65]

Sleep. Over time, sleeping five hours or less or nine hours or more each night may increase your risk of developing diabetes. After following more than 70,000 diabetes-free women for a 10-year period, researchers found that women who slept five hours or less every night were 34 percent more likely to develop diabetes symptoms than women who slept for seven or eight hours each night.[66] Comparatively, women who slept nine hours or more each night were 35 percent more likely to develop diabetes symptoms. During the course of the study, which began in 1986, 1,969 women developed diabetes and most showed symptoms of the condition. Researchers were not certain why sleeping too much or too little might be linked to diabetes, though one theory involves leptin, a hormone that may play a role in signaling the body to stop eating. Too little sleep may reduce levels of leptin, possibly causing people to gain weight and develop diabetes. Too much sleep may increase diabetes risk because people who sleep a lot may have sleep apnea, a condition that prevents restful sleep and causes them to sleep more overall due to feeling tired. Independently, sleep apnea may also increase diabetes risk.

Hot Baths. Extraordinary as it may seem, having hot baths may help reduce blood-glucose levels. As heat increases metabolism, it also speeds up glucose regulation. A recent study found that subjects who took a 30-minute hot bath every day for 3 weeks lowered their blood-glucose levels and lost weight into the bargain.[67]

Relaxation and Laughter. People with Type 2 diabetes may be better able to process sugar from meals if they laugh, according to a small study. Researchers are not certain why laughter appears to reduce blood sugar, but suggested that it might increase the consumption of energy by using the abdominal muscles, or might affect the neuroendocrine system, which controls glucose levels in the blood.[68]

breakfasts

apple, pear, and tofu smoothie

■ ■ ■

SERVES 1 ▶ **TIME TAKEN:** 10 minutes

---

*S*moothies are a great way to start the day, particularly if you are in a hurry, as they only take a few minutes to make. If you are using flaxseed, this smoothie thickens on standing, so it needs to be drunk right away.

1 tablespoon mixed seeds (sesame,
    sunflower, or flaxseed)
1 small apple
1 small ripe pear
3 ounces tofu, drained and cut into small cubes
¾ cup soy or rice milk
a few drops of pure vanilla extract

> Protein 20%
> Carbohydrate 48%
> Fat 32%
> GI: medium
> GL: medium

Grind the seeds in an electric grinder. Quarter and core the fruit but do not peel. Place all ingredients in a blender and blend until smooth.

PER SERVING

Calories 336 ▶ Protein 18g ▶ Carbohydrates 43g ▶ Sugar—Total 29g ▶ Fiber 10g ▶ Fat—Total 12g ▶ Saturated Fat 2g ▶ Vitamin C 12mg ▶ Magnesium 92mg

---

▶ Apples and pears are particularly good in the morning because they both have a low GI. The seeds and tofu provide protein, so this smoothie is well-balanced.

tropical tofu smoothie

■ ■ ■

SERVES 2 ▶ **TIME TAKEN:** 5 minutes

This smoothie contains even more tofu than the previous one, combined with fruits that are normally considered too high GI for people with diabetes. However, the addition of soy protein mitigates their effect, and the added flaxseeds provide valuable soluble fiber. The end result is an almost perfectly balanced breakfast.

2 tablespoons flaxseeds
6 ounces tofu, drained and cut into small cubes
1 cup soy or rice milk
1 small, ripe papaya, peeled and chopped
½ mango, peeled and cubed

Protein 26%
Carbohydrate 34%
Fat 40%
GI: low
GL: low

Grind the seeds in an electric grinder. Place all ingredients in a blender and blend until smooth.

PER SERVING
Calories 263 ▶ Protein 18g ▶ Carbohydrates 23g ▶ Sugar—Total 13g ▶ Fiber 7g ▶ Fat—Total 12g ▶ Saturated Fat 2g ▶ Vitamin C 62mg ▶ Magnesium 100mg

▶ Papayas provide valuable amounts of vitamins C and E, both of which are important antioxidants. Mangoes are one of the very best sources of antioxidant carotenes, and all tropical fruit are rich sources of minerals as they are usually grown on mineral-rich soils.

oat and citrus smoothie

■ ■ ■

SERVES 1 ▶ TIME TAKEN: 10 minutes plus soaking

*T*he oats for this smoothie should be soaked overnight to make them more digestible. But if you forget to soak them, use 1½ tablespoons and soak for a few minutes. A spoonful of ground mixed seeds is a good addition.

1 tablespoon rolled oats
2 tablespoons oat milk or water
1 orange, rind and juice
½ grapefruit
⅔ cup plain yogurt
cinnamon

Protein 16%
Carbohydrate 74%
Fat 10%
GI: low
GL: medium

Soak the oats overnight in the oat milk or water. In the morning, finely grate the rind from the orange and squeeze out the juice. Squeeze the grapefruit. Put the soaked oats in the blender with the orange and grapefruit juice, orange rind, and the yogurt. Blend until smooth and serve with a dusting of cinnamon.

PER SERVING
Calories 286 ▶ Protein 12g ▶ Carbohydrates 57g ▶ Sugar—Total 20g ▶ Fiber 10g ▶ Fat—Total 4g ▶ Saturated Fat 2g ▶ Vitamin C 161mg ▶ Magnesium 52mg

▶ Oats are one of the few readily available sources of chromium in our modern diet. We need chromium to help us metabolize the carbohydrate in our food. Grapefruit and oranges are both low GI, and less than half a teaspoon of cinnamon per day has been found in one study to reduce blood-glucose levels by 20 percent in people with Type 2 diabetes.

apricot, soy, and plum smoothie

■ ■ ■

SERVES 1 ▶ **TIME TAKEN:** 5 minutes plus soaking

Apricots, plums, and soy milk are all low GI (soy milk is 43), so this smoothie should help you control your blood glucose. You could substitute yogurt if you prefer.

5 dried apricots
2 tablespoons soy milk
⅔ cup soy yogurt
2 plums, halved and pitted
1 tablespoon sunflower seeds, ground

Protein 12%
Carbohydrate 60%
Fat 28%
GI: low
GL: low

Soak the dried apricots in water overnight, then chop roughly. Place in the blender, together with the soy milk, yogurt, pitted plums, and ground sunflower seeds. Blend until smooth.

— **PER SERVING** —
Calories 321 ▶ Protein 12g ▶ Carbohydrates 45g ▶ Sugar—Total 28g ▶ Fiber 5g ▶ Fat—Total 12g ▶ Saturated Fat 1g ▶ Vitamin C 17mg ▶ Magnesium 16mg

▶ I have included this smoothie because it contains a range of nutrients, including potassium in the apricots to help regulate blood pressure and vitamin E from the sunflower seeds. Vitamin E is important for people with diabetes as it helps to protect the kidneys according to one research study.

rainbow fruit salad

■ ■ ■

SERVES 2 ▶ TIME TAKEN: 15 minutes

*H*ere I've combined all the most colorful fruit I can think of. It isn't just that colorful fruits are good to look at—the deeper the color the more bioflavonoids they contain, and the more antioxidant properties they have. Kiwi fruit is a useful source of vitamin C.

½ cup strawberries
2 kiwi fruit
¼ cup blueberries
4 fresh apricots
10 red or black seedless grapes

Protein 7%
Carbohydrate 87%
Fat 6%
GI: low
GL: very low

Wash all the fruit. Hull the strawberries, cutting in half or quarters if they are very large. Peel and slice the kiwi fruit. Quarter the apricots and remove the stones. Cut the grapes in half if large. Place all the fruit in a bowl and moisten with apple or orange juice if desired.

PER SERVING

Calories 123 ▶ Protein 2g ▶ Carbohydrates 30g; Sugar—Total 23g ▶ Fiber 6g ▶ Fat—Total 1g ▶ Saturated Fat 0g ▶ Vitamin C 99mg ▶ Magnesium 36mg

▶ The strawberries can be replaced with raspberries in season. Other fruit can be added, but keep a good mix of colors to make the fruit salad really appetizing. As with any fruit, serving it on its own for breakfast would raise the blood glucose too high, so accompany with yogurt and some ground seeds, and follow with rye toast or an oat-bran muffin.

marion's breakfast

■ ■ ■

SERVES 1 ▶ **TIME TAKEN:** 15 minutes preparation plus 10 minutes soaking

---

*M*arion is a friend of mine who runs a wonderful bed and breakfast in Aberdovey on the west coast of Wales. This is the breakfast she has every morning before tackling the fried-foods her customers often prefer.

1 cooking apple
1 tablespoon raisins
1 tablespoon concentrated apple juice
1 tablespoon old-fashioned rolled oats
2 teaspoons flaxseeds
2 tablespoons apple juice
To serve: plain or vanilla yogurt

Protein 9%
Carbohydrate 79%
Fat 12%
GI: medium
GL: low

First, make an apple purée: peel and chop the apple roughly, and stew in a tablespoonful of water together with the raisins until the apple is tender and soft. Stir to make a purée, and sweeten with a little concentrated apple juice. Leave to cool overnight.

The next morning, soak the oats and flaxseed in apple juice for 10 minutes or so. Top the oat/flaxseed mixture with apple and raisin purée, and serve with yogurt.

PER SERVING

Calories 286 ▶ Protein 7g ▶ Carbohydrates 60g ▶ Sugar—Total 41g ▶ Fiber 5g ▶ Fat—Total 4g ▶ Saturated Fat 1g ▶ Vitamin C 9mg ▶ Magnesium 28mg

---

▶ Oats are good for the health of the arteries. The soluble fiber they contain helps to reduce harmful levels of cholesterol in the blood. Old-fashioned rolled oats are particularly valuable for people with diabetes as they have been minimally processed and therefore they take longer to digest than quick-cooking oats.

oat and almond muesli

■ ■ ■

MAKES 12 servings ▶ **TIME TAKEN:** 15 minutes plus soaking

*I*t's useful to have some muesli on hand for those days when you are short of time. It is important to soak the muesli, as this makes it more digestible and releases the protein in the oats, nuts, and seeds. However, if you forget to soak it the night before, even a few minutes of soaking helps to break down the fiber.

1 pound rolled oats
1 cup sunflower seeds
2 cups raw almonds, chopped
⅓ cup sesame seeds, lightly crushed
1½ cups unsulphured apricots, chopped
¾ cup raisins

Protein 13%
Carbohydrate 49%
Fat 38%
GI: low
GL: low

Simply mix all the ingredients together and store in an airtight container.

To serve, soak about 3 ounces of muesli per serving overnight in an equal volume of water. In the morning, drain off any excess water and serve with soy, almond, or rice milk. Add grated apple on top.

PER SERVING
Calories 400 ▶ Protein 14g ▶ Carbohydrates 50g ▶ Sugar—Total 16g ▶ Fiber 8g ▶ Fat—Total 18g ▶ Saturated Fat 2g ▶ Vitamin C 3mg ▶ Magnesium 113mg

▶ Oats are a great source of soluble fiber. One serving of this muesli also contains 5 mcg of chromium, a hard-to-get mineral that is good for keeping blood-sugar levels even throughout the morning. The combination of almonds and oats provides an excellent source of magnesium, needed by diabetics for healthy insulin production.

raspberry muesli sundae

■ ■ ■

SERVES 2 ▶ **TIME TAKEN:** 5 minutes

This lovely summery breakfast can be made the night before for a quick getaway next morning. If you don't have raspberries, try other berries such as blueberries or sliced strawberries, or a mixture. There is an unsweetened mixture of frozen "mixed fruits" available in the supermarkets that, when thawed, works very well when berries are out of season.

½ cup fresh or frozen thawed raspberries
⅔ cup vanilla yogurt
3 ounces oat and almond muesli
   (see page 46)

Protein 16%
Carbohydrate 52%
Fat 32%
GI: low
GL: low

Put a tablespoon of raspberries into each of two glass dishes or tall glasses. Top each serving of raspberries with a spoonful of yogurt. Sprinkle a layer of oat and almond muesli onto each serving. Continue the layers until all the ingredients have been used up. Top each serving with a whole raspberry, and refrigerate overnight.

PER SERVING

Calories 266 ▶ Protein 11g ▶ Carbohydrates 36g ▶ Sugar—Total 10mg ▶ Fiber 8g ▶ Fat—Total 10g ▶ Saturated Fat 2g ▶ Vitamin C 16mg ▶ Magnesium 62mg

---

▶ Raspberries contain a little iron together with a lot of vitamin C, which helps your body absorb the iron. Berries cause a slow increase in blood glucose that helps to lead to a feeling of fullness and does not lead to a large release of insulin.

yogurt cheese with apricots and walnuts

■ ■ ■

SERVES 2 ▶ TIME TAKEN: 5 minutes plus overnight soaking

Yogurt cheese, which is simply strained natural yogurt, is a good way to get some quality protein for breakfast. The texture is like that of a soft cheese, and it can be used in savory and sweet dishes. Its taste is a little sharp, which is why I've included some honey in the recipe, but you may find you don't need the honey.

⅔ cup plain yogurt
½ cup unsulphured dried apricots
2 teaspoons honey (optional)
2 teaspoons walnuts, chopped
ground cinnamon, for serving

Protein 12%
Carbohydrate 76%
Fat 12%
GI: low
GL: medium

Spoon the yogurt into a fine-meshed sieve over a bowl and leave to drain overnight in the refrigerator. Put the apricots into a small saucepan, cover with cold water and simmer for 10 minutes or so. Leave covered with water overnight.

Next morning, drain the apricots, chop roughly, and put into a bowl with the honey.

Discard the liquid that has drained off the yogurt, and add the yogurt to the apricot and honey mixture, together with the chopped walnuts. Spoon into two individual serving bowls and sprinkle with cinnamon.

PER SERVING

Calories 212 ▶ Protein 7g ▶ Carbohydrates 41g ▶ Sugar—Total 24g ▶ Fiber 3g ▶ Fat—Total 3g ▶ Saturated Fat 1g ▶ Vitamin C 8mg ▶ Magnesium 4mg

---

▶ Dried apricots have a GI of 30, which is quite low. They are an excellent source of beta-carotene and very high in potassium. They are quite high in fructose, which helps to lower their GI value. Although there are concerns about refined fructose (see pages 26–27), the fructose naturally occurring in fruits is perfectly fine for people with diabetes.

steel-cut oats with cinnamon and raisins

■ ■ ■

SERVES 2 ▶ **TIME TAKEN:** 1½ hours plus soaking

---

*S*teel-cut oats look a little like brown rice grains. They are in fact whole oats that haven't been crushed and rolled. They have to be soaked overnight and cooked for a long time, but they are well worth the trouble.

⅓ cup steel-cut oats
2 cups water
1 teaspoon cinnamon
2 tablespoons raisins
soy or rice milk, to serve

Protein 11%
Carbohydrate 79%
Fat 10%
GI: low
GL: low

Wash the oat groats, then soak for several hours in cold water. I usually do this during the day. When you are ready to cook them, transfer to a saucepan together with the soaking water, and bring to a boil. Lower the heat to a simmer, and cook for 1–1½ hours, or until cooked to your liking, adding more water as necessary. This can be done the night before, then left to cool and reheated at breakfast time.

Alternatively, the groats can be successfully cooked overnight on the low setting of an electric Crock-Pot.

Before serving the groats, stir in the cinnamon and raisins. Serve with milk of your choice.

PER SERVING

Calories 160 ▶ Protein 4g ▶ Carbohydrates 34g ▶ Sugar—Total 9g ▶ Fiber 1g ▶ Fat—Total 2g ▶ Saturated Fat 0g ▶ Vitamin C 1mg ▶ Magnesium 30mg

---

breakfast barley with molasses and pears

SERVES 2 ▶ TIME TAKEN: 1 hour the day before plus 5 minutes reheating

Barley is an underrated grain, in my opinion, usually only making its appearance in soups or stews. It makes a very tasty and sustaining breakfast on a cold morning.

⅓ cup pearl barley
2 cups cold water
2 pears
2 tablespoons blackstrap molasses
soy milk or rice milk, to serve
2 teaspoons sunflower seeds

Protein 7%
Carbohydrate 85%
Fat 8%
GI: low
GL: low

Place the barley in a saucepan and cover with the water. Bring to a boil, then lower the heat and cook, covered, until soft to the bite. This will take 45–60 minutes, and is better done the night before you want to eat it. Cool, covered, overnight. In the morning, add the milk of your choice and the molasses, and simmer. Cook for a few minutes until heated through, then stir in the chopped pears before serving. Sprinkle with sunflower seeds.

PER SERVING
Calories 254 ▶ Protein 5g ▶ Carbohydrates 57g ▶ Sugar—Total 20g ▶ Fiber 9g ▶ Fat—Total 2g ▶ Saturated Fat 0g ▶ Vitamin C 6mg ▶ Magnesium 66mg

▶ Pearl barley is unusual in that, although it is a relatively refined grain, it has a very low GI, probably because it is high in soluble fiber. The sunflower seeds provide a useful amount of vitamin E.

chickpea and tomato frittata

■ ■ ■

SERVES 4 ▶ **TIME TAKEN:** 20 minutes

I'm sure this isn't an authentic Italian frittata, but it came about when I was trying to think of ways to include legumes in the breakfast menu. Chickpeas, aslo called garbanzo beans, are so good for moderating the blood-glucose level, as they provide ready mixed protein and complex carbohydrate, that people with diabetes should incorporate them into their daily eating pattern whenever possible. This frittata is also good eaten cold for lunch.

1 cup cooked chickpeas (or one 14-ounce can, drained and rinsed)
2 large beefsteak tomatoes, peeled, seeded, and diced
2 tablespoons extra-virgin olive oil
6 organic, free-range eggs
sea salt and freshly ground black pepper
2 tablespoons chopped flat-leaf parsley or finely shredded fresh basil

Protein 20%
Carbohydrate 30%
Fat 50%
GI: low
GL: low

Beat the eggs with seasoning to taste, and add half the parsley or basil. Heat the olive oil in a large frying pan over medium heat. Pour the eggs into the pan and then add the chickpeas and diced tomato. Cook until nearly set. If you like your frittata quite firm, preheat the grill while the frittata is cooking, then slip the frying pan under the grill for a minute or two, just to set the top. Serve hot or at room temperature, cut into wedges, with the remainder of the parsley or basil sprinkled over the top.

PER SERVING

Calories 271 ▶ Protein 14g ▶ Carbohydrates 21g ▶ Sugar—Total 4g ▶ Fiber 5g ▶ Fat—Total 15g ▶ Saturated Fat 3g; Vitamin C 21mg ▶ Magnesium 47mg

▶ Tomatoes are a valuable source of lycopene, a powerful antioxidant especially when cooked, and even more so when accompanied by healthy fats, such as those found in olive oil.

baked eggs with mushrooms

■ ■ ■

SERVES 2 ▸ **TIME TAKEN:** 25 minutes

Eggs are a great source of protein for starting the day and keeping your energy levels up. I've baked them on a bed of mushrooms here, but you could substitute lightly cooked spinach or tomatoes if you prefer. Add a teaspoon of miso to each serving for extra flavor and protein. For a balanced meal, precede an egg dish like this with a smoothie or fruit salad.

1 tablespoon extra-virgin olive oil
2 ounces button mushrooms, sliced
freshly grated nutmeg
2 teaspoons miso (optional)
2 organic, free-range eggs
sea salt and freshly ground black pepper to taste

Protein 19%
Carbohydrate 5%
Fat 76%
GI: very low
GL: very low

Preheat the oven to 400°F. Lightly grease 2 ramekins and sprinkle each one with nutmeg.

Heat the oil in a small pan, then add the mushrooms. Sautée on low heat for 5–8 minutes until the juices run. Stir in the miso, if using, and season to taste.

Divide the mushrooms between the ramekins and make a well in the center of each one. Crack an egg into each well. Bake for 10–15 minutes and serve hot.

PER SERVING

Calories 145 ▸ Protein 7g ▸ Carbohydrates 2g ▸ Sugar—Total 1g ▸ Fiber 0g ▸ Fat—Total 12g ▸ Saturated Fat 3g ▸ Vitamin C 1mg ▸ Magnesium 12mg

---

▸ Do not be alarmed at the apparently high proportion of fat in this recipe, most of which comes from the egg yolk. There's as much monounsaturated fat in an egg as there is saturated fat, and it provides so much else—a useful amount of protein, B vitamins, and vitamin E.

poached eggs florentine

■ ■ ■

SERVES 2 ▶ **TIME TAKEN:** 15 minutes

---

*F*lorentine means spinach. Don't throw up your hands in horror at the idea of having spinach for breakfast. These days you can get bags of baby spinach so tender you can eat it raw or very lightly steamed, and it's packed with nutrients. This is a good protein breakfast with which to start your day.

5 cups baby leaf spinach
sea salt and freshly ground black pepper
1 tablespoon melted butter
Freshly grated nutmeg
2 organic free-range eggs

Protein 23%
Carbohydrate 10%
Fat 67%
GI: very low
GL: very low

Wash the spinach and place in a pan with no more water than that clinging to the leaves. Cook briefly—a couple of minutes should do, just until the spinach wilts. Drain and press to remove any excess moisture. Season and stir in the melted butter and nutmeg. Place on individual plates and keep warm.

Meanwhile, poach the eggs: fill a deep saucepan with water, add a couple of tablespoons of vinegar and bring to a boil. Reduce the heat so that the water is just simmering, break the first egg into a cup, stir the simmering water vigorously with a wooden spoon, then slip the egg into the water to poach for about 4 minutes. Lift out with a slotted spoon and drain on paper towels. Repeat with the other egg.

Season the eggs and place on the bed of spinach to serve.

Variations: Add a sprinkling of grated Parmesan or toasted sesame seeds.

PER SERVING

Calories 150 ▶ Protein 9g ▶ Carbohydrates 4g ▶ Fiber 2g ▶ Sugar—Total 1g ▶ Fat—Total 11g ▶ Saturated Fat 5g ▶ Vitamin C 8mg ▶ Magnesium 81mg

---

▶ Spinach provides a useful amount of calcium, needed for bone health, and eggs are one of the few dietary sources of vitamin D, which the body needs to absorb calcium, so the combination of spinach and eggs is especially beneficial for the bones. Calcium and vitamin D in moderation also have a good safety profile and may actually have benefits far beyond bone health. For example, calcium may increase HDL (the good sort of cholesterol), reduce blood pressure, and reduce kidney stone occurrence. Vitamin D may reduce the risk of some cancers and even prevent Type 1 diabetes.

poached eggs with sweet potato cakes

■ ■ ■

SERVES 4 ▶ TIME TAKEN: 45 minutes

*T*his is quite quick if you cook and mash the potato the night before. For a really elegant breakfast, add a slice of smoked salmon and a wedge of lemon. The eggs should be really fresh for poaching—the fresher the egg the better the white coagulates in the poaching water.

2 sweet potatoes, about 10–11 ounces each
1 tablespoon extra-virgin olive oil
½ cup wholegrain or gluten-free flour
freshly grated nutmeg
low sodium salt and freshly ground black pepper
1 teaspoon extra-virgin olive oil, or use an olive-oil spray
4 organic, free-range eggs
2 tablespoons white wine vinegar or cider vinegar,
    for poaching the eggs
8 whole chives, for garnish

Protein 12%
Carbohydrate 59%
Fat 29%
GI: low
GL: medium

First, peel and dice the sweet potatoes, cook them until tender, and mash with the olive oil. Leave to cool.

To make the potato cakes, mix the mashed sweet potato with the flour and season to taste with freshly grated nutmeg, salt, and pepper. The mixture should come together into quite a firm dough—if it is a bit slack, add a little more flour. Roll the dough out on a lightly floured surface to a thickness of about ½ inch. Cut out 8 cakes using a 2½-inch biscuit cutter. Up to here the recipe can be completed the night before, in which case dust the cakes with flour and store in the fridge.

In the morning, heat a nonstick frying pan and spray with olive-oil spray or cover with a film of olive oil. Cook the sweet potato cakes until lightly browned, about 4–5 minutes on each side.

Meanwhile, poach the eggs: fill a deep saucepan with water, add a couple of tablespoons of vinegar and bring to a boil. Reduce the heat so that the water is just simmering, break the first egg into a cup, stir the simmering water vigorously with a wooden spoon, then slip the egg into the water to poach for about 4 minutes. Lift out with a slotted spoon and drain on paper towels. Repeat with the other eggs. Keep warm.

Serve one egg and two potato cakes per person, with two whole chives laid across the top as garnish.

PER SERVING

Calories 367 ▸ Protein 11g ▸ Carbohydrates 54g ▸ Sugar—Total 32g ▸ Fiber 8g ▸ Fat—Total 12g ▸
Saturated Fat 2g ▸ Vitamin C 34mg ▸ Magnesium 43mg

▸ Sweet potatoes have a low GI, which is why I have used them here. They are also a very good source of beta-carotene, calcium, and vitamin C.

▸ Eggs provide not only protein but also choline, one of the B vitamins to help give you energy during the day.

buckwheat pancakes with apple and almond filling

■ ■ ■

SERVES 4 ▶ **TIME TAKEN:** 20 minutes

---

*B*uckwheat is actually a member of the grass family and not a wheat at all, and has therefore the supreme advantage of being gluten-free. You can make these pancakes with all buckwheat flour, but I have added a little mixed gluten-free flour to lighten the mixture.

½ cup buckwheat flour
¼ cup gluten-free flour
1 large, organic free-range egg
1 cup soy or rice milk
3 tablespoons almond butter
2 tablespoons apple, stewed without sugar
1 apple, raw
½ teaspoon ground cinnamon

Protein 15%
Carbohydrate 49%
Fat 36%
GI: low
GL: low

For the pancakes, put the flour, egg, and milk in the blender, and blend until well mixed. Leave the batter to rest while you make the apple/almond filling.

For the filling, mix the almond butter and stewed apple together.

To cook the pancakes, lightly oil a nonstick omelette pan (or use olive-oil spray) and ladle in enough batter just to cover the base of the pan. Cook over medium-high heat until the surface bubbles and starts to dry. Turn and cook the other side until lightly browned. Repeat with the remaining mixture. This should make 8 medium-sized pancakes.

To serve, spread the apple/almond mixture on the pancakes and roll up. Grate raw apple over the top and sprinkle with cinnamon.

PER SERVING

Calories 247 ▶ Protein 9g ▶ Carbohydrates 32g ▶ Sugar—Total 7g ▶ Fiber 5g ▶ Fat—Total 10g ▶ Saturated Fat 1g ▶ Vitamin C 2mg ▶ Magnesium 115mg

---

▶ The combination of buckwheat and almond provides a good level of magnesium, which helps prevent Type 2 diabetes and reduces the craving for sweet foods. And the almond butter provides a rich source of vitamin E.

whole grain and seed muffins

Makes 12 muffins ▶ **TIME TAKEN:** 25 minutes

The natural sweetness in these muffins is provided by the sunflower seeds, which are good sources of essential fatty acids, protein, and magnesium.

1 cup rolled oats
1⅓ cups whole grain pastry flour
¼ cup sunflower seeds
2 tablespoons flaxseed
1½ teaspoons salt-free baking powder
½ teaspoon baking soda
1 organic, free-range egg
4 tablespoons extra-virgin olive oil
½ cup plain or soy yogurt
2 tablespoons soy, rice, or almond milk

Protein 14%
Carbohydrate 40%
Fat 46%
GI: medium
GL: high

Preheat oven to 375°F. Either spray a 12-muffin pan with olive-oil spray, use nonstick muffin pans, or use paper muffin cases, which don't need oiling.

Mix together the oats, flour, seeds, baking powder, and baking soda in a large bowl. In a separate bowl, beat together the egg, oil, yogurt, and your chosen milk. Next, add the egg mixture to the dry ingredients, combining the two mixtures with a few swift strokes to form a fairly stiff dough. Spoon into the prepared muffin pan and bake for 15 minutes in the preheated oven.

Leave in the muffin pan for a few minutes before turning out onto a rack to cool.

PER MUFFIN
Calories 149 ▶ Protein 5g ▶ Carbohydrates 16g ▶ Fiber 3g ▶ Sugar—Total 1g ▶ Fat—Total 8g ▶ Saturated Fat 1g ▶ Vitamin C 0mg ▶ Magnesium 40mg

▶ These muffins are high in both calcium and magnesium. They are good on their own, or try them with a pure fruit spread, such as St. Dalfour or Polaner All Fruit.

breakfast baked beans on rye toast

■ ■ ■

SERVES 4 ▶ TIME TAKEN: 2½ hours plus soaking

Yes, you could open a can of baked beans. But when they're your own baked beans you know what's gone into them, and if it's these baked beans, then they're full of good things. One of my testers commented "this sounds like a lot of work but it's not really—soak it, boil it, bake it." If you wish to use canned beans, use two 14-ounce cans for this recipe, drain the beans and rinse well before proceeding.

1 cup dried haricot beans or other white beans
2 tablespoons extra-virgin olive oil
1 onion, peeled and finely chopped
2¼ cups fresh tomato sauce (see page 234)
   or store-bought passata
1 tablespoon concentrated tomato purée
1 tablespoon blackstrap molasses
1 teaspoon dry mustard powder
¼ cup vegetable stock or water
sea salt and freshly ground black pepper
4 slices rye bread or pumpernickel (or try the barley bread on page 130)

Protein 16%
Carbohydrate 65%
Fat 19%
GI: medium
GL: low

Soak the beans overnight in cold water, then drain, refresh, and cook until tender—about an hour to 1½ hours, depending on the age of the beans—making sure that the beans boil at a good pace for at least ten minutes of that time. Then drain the beans and place in an ovenproof casserole.

Preheat the oven to 350°F.

Sauté the onion in the olive oil until soft but not browned. Add the tomato sauce, tomato purée, molasses, mustard powder, and stock. Pour over the beans in the casserole, cover tightly, and bake for 45 minutes. When cooked, season to taste with salt and pepper.

To serve, toast the bread and spoon over the baked beans.

PER SERVING

Calories 367 ▶ Protein 16g ▶ Carbohydrates 65g ▶ Sugar—Total 14g ▶ Fiber 15g ▶ Fat—Total 9g ▶ Saturated Fat 1g ▶ Vitamin C 42mg ▶ Magnesium 81mg

---

▶ I thought long and hard about whether this recipe should be included, as it's quite high in calories. However, it contains complete protein—the beans and the bread together contain all the essential amino acids—and beans are a good source of iron and fiber. So it's one of those dishes that really works for you—lots of calories, yes, but they're all doing something useful for your body.

snacks
AND drinks

quick sardine pâté

███

SERVES 1 ▶ **TIME TAKEN:** 5 minutes

This easy pâté is delicious spread on rye or pumpernickel bread. As a variation, try it with other canned fish such as mackerel. Smoked mackerel is good too.

1 can of sardines packed in olive oil
1 teaspoon horseradish sauce
1 tablespoon finely chopped onion
1 teaspoon fresh parsley, finely chopped
1 teaspoon fresh lemon juice
paprika, to serve

Protein 43%
Carbohydrate 7%
Fat 50%
GI: low
GL: low

Drain the sardines and mash them, together with the horseradish, in a small bowl. Add the chopped onion and parsley and season to taste with lemon juice.

Serve on pumpernickel or rye toast with a dusting of paprika on top.

───── **PER SERVING** ─────
Calories 137 ▶ Protein 14g ▶ Carbohydrates 2g ▶ Fiber 0g ▶ Sugar—Total 1g ▶ Fat—Total 7g ▶ Saturated Fat 1g ▶ Vitamin C 5mg ▶ Magnesium 26mg

▶ Sardines are a rich source of omega-3 fatty acids, known to help reduce risk of heart disease, high blood pressure, and cancer.

tapenade

This is a delicious, strongly flavored dip or spread from the South of France. Spread it on oat or rye toast, or serve as a dip for raw vegetables such as carrots or celery sticks.

8 ounces black olives, pitted
1 teaspoon lemon juice
2-ounce can of tuna
2-ounce can of anchovy fillets
4 tablespoons capers, rinsed (optional)
2–3 garlic cloves
2 tablespoons extra-virgin olive oil
freshly ground black pepper

Protein 15%
Carbohydrate 10%
Fat 75%
GI: low
GL: low

Put all the ingredients, apart from the olive oil and pepper, into a food processor and blend until smooth. Add the olive oil gradually to make a thick paste.

Season to taste with a little black pepper and store in the fridge, where it will keep for several days.

PER SERVING
Calories 72 ▶ Protein 3g ▶ Carbohydrates 2g ▶ Fiber 0g ▶ Sugar—Total 330mg ▶ Fat-Total 2g ▶ Saturated Fat 0g ▶ Vitamin C 1mg ▶ Magnesium 7mg

▶ Olives are easily digested, and are beneficial for the liver and gall bladder, increasing the secretion of bile. The leaves of the olive tree can be infused in boiling water and drunk as a remedy for high blood pressure, heart disease, and diabetes.

white bean and mint hummus

■ ■ ■

SERVES 2 ▶ **TIME TAKEN:** 50 minutes

*T*his is a delicious variation on traditional hummus, which is made with chickpeas. Do not be put off by the large amount of garlic in this recipe—roasting it first imparts a mellow flavor that is not strong at all. I have suggested canned beans here for convenience, but if you prefer to cook them from scratch, use about ½ half cup of dried beans, which will yield the right amount of cooked beans for this recipe.

1 small head of garlic
1 teaspoon extra-virgin olive oil, for drizzling
2 teaspoons ground cumin
½ teaspoon chili powder (optional)
1 14-ounce can of cannellini beans, haricot beans,
     or butter beans, drained and rinsed
1 handful fresh mint leaves, chopped
½ lemon, juice only
2 tablespoons extra-virgin olive oil
sea salt and freshly ground black pepper to taste

Protein 12%
Carbohydrate 46%
Fat 42%
GI: medium
GL: low

First, roast the garlic. Preheat the oven to 350° F. Cut the top off the head of garlic, place on a baking tray, drizzle with a little olive oil and roast for 35–40 minutes or until soft. Leave to cool, then pop the garlic cloves out of their skins. Even if you don't use all the garlic, it is a good idea to roast it whole—single cloves usually dry up too much when roasted. Any unused roasted garlic cloves make a tasty addition to a sauce or salad dressing.

Dry roast the cumin and chili powder, if using, in a small pan over medium heat until the cumin gives off its aroma.

Place the garlic cloves, drained beans, chopped mint, lemon juice, olive oil, and toasted spices in a food processor and process until smooth. Season to taste and serve at room temperature as a spread or dip.

PER SERVING

Calories 329 ▶ Protein 10g ▶ Carbohydrates 38g ▶ Fiber 9g ▶ Sugar—Total 1g ▶ Fat—Total 15g ▶ Saturated Fat 2g ▶ Vitamin C 17mg ▶ Magnesium 13mg

spicy chickpea snacks

These are terribly easy, and good to have on hand to serve with drinks. Caution—the chickpeas have a tendency to jump about or even explode if the oven is too hot, so if this starts to happen, remove the tray from the oven, cool it a little, then return the tray to finish cooking at a lower temperature.

1 pound dried chickpeas
½ teaspoon sea salt
¼ teaspoon cayenne pepper, or to taste

Protein 21%
Carbohydrate 65%
Fat 14%
GI: low
GL: low

Preheat the oven to 350°F.

Soak the chickpeas overnight in plenty of cold water. The next day, drain thoroughly.

Spread the chickpeas in a single layer on a baking tray or trays. Bake in the preheated oven until crisp and shrunk again to their original size (about 45 minutes).

Toss with sea salt and cayenne pepper while still hot. Taste as you do this as a heavy hand with the seasoning could ruin the effect. Store in an airtight tin and serve cold as a snack with drinks.

Variation: These are also delicious tossed with curry powder. Whichever seasoning you choose, try sprinkling the chickpeas with a few drops of olive oil when you remove them from the oven.

PER SERVING
Calories 96 ▶ Protein 5g ▶ Carbohydrates 16g ▶ Fiber 4g ▶ Sugar—Total 1g ▶ Fat—Total 2g ▶ Saturated Fat 0g ▶ Vitamin C 1mg ▶ Magnesium 28mg

▶ Chickpeas have a low GI—the average of four different studies was 28. Like other legumes, they are digested slowly and are therefore very valuable to people with diabetes. Over the long term they may help to improve blood-glucose control.

granola bars

Makes 12 bars ▶ TIME TAKEN: 1 hour

These bars are quite high in starchy carbohydrate so should be treated with caution. They would be good to have in midafternoon if your blood-sugar levels are getting low, but shouldn't be eaten on a regular basis. They are delicious eaten warm.

1 cup organic wholegrain flour
1 cup organic white self-raising flour
1 teaspoon baking powder
½ teaspoon cinnamon
½ teaspoon ground ginger
1½ cups rolled oats
½ cup raisins
½ cup dried unsulphured apricots, chopped
1 tablespoon sunflower seeds
1 tablespoon sesame seeds
½ cup apple juice
4 tablespoons coconut oil
1 organic, free-range egg
2 organic, free-range egg whites, lightly beaten

Protein 11%
Carbohydrate 62%
Fat 27%
GI: high
GL: medium

Preheat the oven to 350°F. Line a 9 × 12 inch baking tray with greaseproof paper or baking parchment.

Sift the flour, baking powder, cinnamon, and ginger into a large bowl. Stir in the oats, raisins, chopped apricots, sunflower seeds, and sesame seeds.

Beat together the apple juice, coconut oil, and whole egg. Pour into the mixture and stir well. Gently mix in the egg whites and stir to combine.

Press the mixture firmly into the prepared baking tray and smooth the surface. The easiest way to do this is to cover the mixture with a sheet of greaseproof paper and roll it with a rolling pin. Score the surface into 12 bars using a very sharp knife.

Bake in the preheated oven for 20–30 minutes or until lightly browned. Cool and cut into bars. Wrap each bar in greaseproof paper, store in an airtight tin, and consume within one week.

PER BAR

Calories 226 ▸ Protein 6g ▸ Carbohydrates 36g ▸ Fiber 4g ▸ Sugar—Total 10g ▸ Fat—Total 7g ▸
Saturated Fat 4g ▸ Vitamin C 1mg ▸ Magnesium 44mg

▸ I always specify unsulphured apricots in recipes. These are darker in color than the conventionally dried apricots and don't keep as well. However, they are worth searching out as sulphur dioxide is normally added to the fruit as a preservative and to give the dried product a brighter orange color. Sulphur dioxide is a toxic gas that can irritate the respiratory tract especially in asthmatics.

fruit and seed bars

■ ■ ■

Makes 16 bars ▶ **TIME TAKEN:** 1 hour

These gluten-free bars are made with a variety of dried fruit. I chose pears because of their chewy texture and natural sweetness, and unsweetened dried bananas and dried apricots for their potassium content. This makes the bars quite high in concentrated fruit sugars, so, like the previous recipe, they should only be eaten on an occasional basis or after a high-protein meal.

You could vary the fruits, using dried apples, dates, raisins, figs, or whatever you have to hand, but keep the quantities similar.

5½ ounces dried pears, roughly chopped
4 ounces unsweetened sundried bananas, roughly chopped
1½ ounces unsulphured dried apricots, roughly chopped
1½ ounces dried cranberries
1⅔ cups rolled oats
1 cup sunflower seeds
1½ ounces organic puffed-rice cereal (such as Kashi)
2 tablespoons honey
2 organic free-range eggs, lightly beaten
2 tablespoons extra-virgin olive oil
6 tablespoons apple juice

Protein 10%
Carbohydrate 61%
Fat 30%
GI: high
GL: medium

Preheat the oven to 325°F. Oil a 9 × 12 inch baking tray and line with greaseproof paper.

Put the dried fruit, oats, and sunflower seeds in the food processor, and process until the pieces of dried fruit are the size of peas. This might have to be done in two batches. Tip out into a large bowl and add the puffed-rice cereal.

Stir together the honey, beaten eggs, olive oil, and apple juice.

Mix the wet ingredients into the dry ingredients until well amalgamated. Spoon into the prepared baking tray and flatten out the top with the back of a spoon. Score the mixture into sixteen bars with a sharp knife. Cover with a sheet of greaseproof paper to prevent the mixture from getting too brown. Bake in the preheated oven for 30 minutes. Cool and cut into bars. Wrap each bar in greaseproof paper, store in an airtight tin and eat within one week.

PER BAR
Calories 194 ▶ Protein 5g ▶ Carbohydrates 31g ▶ Fiber 4g ▶ Sugar—Total 16g ▶ Fat—Total 7g ▶ Saturated Fat 1g ▶ Vitamin C 2mg ▶ Magnesium 51mg

▶ The organic puffed-rice cereal specified here is available in health-food stores. It is simply brown rice grains puffed with air, and as such is gluten-free. Its GI has not been tested but it is likely to be fairly high as its composition is similar to that of rice cakes (78). Try adding it to muesli or sprinkled with ground seeds.

tamari seeds

███

SERVES 16 ▶ **TIME TAKEN:** 20 minutes

These seeds are quite salty owing to the tamari sauce, so if you're using them as a nibble with a drink, have some water as well. This saltiness is the natural flavor of tamari, which is a wheat-free, naturally fermented Japanese soy sauce. This treatment can also be given to soaked soy beans, but they will need longer in the oven—about 20 minutes.

2 cups sunflower seeds
2 cups pumpkin seeds
4 tablespoons tamari, to taste

Protein 15%
Carbohydrate 14%
Fat 71%
GI: low
GL: low

Preheat the oven to 350° F.

Mix the seeds together in a large bowl and toss with the tamari so that the seeds are well coated. Spread out on baking trays in a single layer and roast for 10–15 minutes, turning from time to time, until the seeds are golden brown. Cool and serve as a snack with drinks.

PER SERVING

Calories 178 ▶ Protein 7g ▶ Carbohydrates 7g ▶ Fiber 2g ▶ Sugar—Total 1g ▶ Fat—Total 15g ▶ Saturated Fat 2g ▶ Vitamin C 1mg ▶ Magnesium 104mg

---

▶ Pumpkin seeds have many virtues, one of which is their high magnesium content. Magnesium is an important mineral for people with diabetes as it can help promote healthy insulin production. It can also reduce the craving for sweet foods, thus helping to prevent Type 2 diabetes.

cinnamon muesli cookies

■ ■ ■

Makes 12 cookies ▶ **TIME TAKEN:** 25 minutes

These cookies are based on oat and almond muesli, but you could use another unsweetened muesli instead. You may have to chop up the fruit and nuts in the muesli to achieve a less chunky texture.

2 tablespoons extra-virgin olive oil
3 tablespoons maple syrup
6 tablespoons apple juice
1 cup oat and almond muesli (see page 46)
2 cups organic self-raising whole wheat flour
1½ tablespoons cinnamon

Protein 10%
Carbohydrate 62%
Fat 27%
GI: high
GL: medium

Preheat the oven to 350°F. Line two baking sheets with greaseproof paper or parchment.

Mix together the olive oil, maple syrup, and apple juice. Stir in the muesli, flour, and cinnamon and stir to make a soft dough.

Roll the dough into 12 equal-sized balls and place well apart on the baking sheets. Flatten into discs using a rolling pin or the back of a spoon.

Bake in the preheated oven for 15–20 minutes until golden brown. Remove from the tray when cooked and cool on a wire rack. The cookies will keep for about 4 days in an airtight tin.

PER COOKIE

Calories 141 ▶ Protein 4g ▶ Carbohydrates 23g ▶ Fiber 4g ▶ Sugar—Total 6g ▶ Fat—Total 4g ▶ Saturated Fat 1g ▶ Vitamin C 0mg ▶ Magnesium 41mg

---

▶ Cinnamon has been shown to reduce blood-glucose levels by 20 percent in people with Type 2 diabetes, as well as triglycerides, LDL cholesterol, and total cholesterol. It is therefore beneficial to include it in your diet at every opportunity. About ½ teaspoon per day has been shown to have a beneficial effect.

apricot and pecan cookies

▪ ▪ ▪

Makes 24 cookies   ▸   **TIME TAKEN:** 35 minutes

These cookies are very "short," i.e. they crumble easily, probably because of the high rice-flour content. To make the cookies easier to handle, flatten them well before baking, otherwise they may fall apart on removal from the oven. I have included them because the combination of apricots and pecans is divine. One of my testers, who couldn't resist waiting for the cookies to cool, tells me that they are delicious warm straight from the oven.

2 cups gluten-free rice flour

1 level teaspoon baking powder

1 cup pecans, chopped

½ cup dried unsulphured apricots, chopped

3 tablespoons honey

7 tablespoons coconut oil

Protein 3%
Carbohydrate 41%
Fat 56%
GI: medium
GL: medium

Preheat the oven to 375°F.

Mix the flour, baking powder, pecans, and apricots in a large bowl. The pecans and apricots should be quite finely chopped as the finished cookies are small. Warm the coconut oil slightly to make it liquid (I do this by putting the bottle in a jug of hot water for a few minutes), then mix with the honey. Add this mixture to the dry ingredients, stirring until evenly mixed.

Place teaspoons of the mixture onto ungreased baking trays and flatten with a rolling pin.

Bake in the preheated oven for 10–12 minutes, until golden brown. Leave to cool on the trays for a couple of minutes, then, using a palette knife, transfer to a wire rack to cool. Store in an airtight tin.

PER COOKIE

Calories 124 ▸ Protein 1g ▸ Carbohydrates 13g ▸ Fiber 1g ▸ Sugar—Total 4g ▸ Fat—Total 8g ▸ Saturated Fat 4g ▸ Vitamin C 1mg ▸ Magnesium 7mg

---

▸ Pecans are bursting with zinc, so they are ideal for those needing to boost their immune system. They have more fiber and less fat than some other nuts, so they are a healthy choice. Dried apricots are a rich source of minerals, particularly potassium, important for helping to control blood pressure.

fruit and nut truffles

■ ■ ■

Makes 24 truffles ▶ **TIME TAKEN:** 20 minutes

---

*S*ometimes you just want a sweet treat, and that's where these come in. Dates are high GI, so they should only be regarded as something to have after a balanced meal rather than eaten on their own. And here their effect on blood sugar is mitigated by the fat and protein in the nuts and seeds.

½ cup dates, pitted
½ cup raisins
3 tablespoons organic cocoa powder
⅔ cup walnuts, chopped
½ cup sunflower seeds

Protein 8%
Carbohydrate 41%
Fat 51%
GI: low
GL: low

Place the dates and raisins in a small saucepan with a little water. Bring to a gentle simmer for about 5 minutes, just to soften them. Drain and cool. Place the dates, raisins, 2 tablespoons of the cocoa powder, walnuts, and sunflower seeds in a food processor, and process until everything is finely chopped and the mixture adheres into a large ball. With your hands, form the mixture into 24 small balls. Roll in the last tablespoonful of cocoa powder. Place truffles in paper cases and refrigerate for a few hours. Serve chilled.

PER TRUFFLE
Calories 66 ▶ Protein 2g ▶ Carbohydrates 7g ▶ Fiber 1g ▶ Sugar—Total 5g ▶ Fat—Total 4g ▶ Saturated Fat 0g ▶ Vitamin C 0mg ▶ Magnesium 16mg

---

▶ If you cannot tolerate cocoa—for instance, if you suffer from migraines—substitute carob powder for the cocoa powder. Carob is a very good source of calcium and has a delicious taste, often indistinguishable from cocoa.

VEGETABLE JUICES ARE an excellent source of vitamins and minerals and other phyto-nutrients that have been shown to combat disease. Because juices are raw, the vitamin C and other water-soluble vitamins and enzymes that are largely lost in cooking are still intact. Juices are easily absorbed and therefore offer instant energy without pushing up your blood glucose. I don't recommend pure fruit juices for people with diabetes, as these contain concentrated fructose and may cause a rapid rise in blood glucose, though adding a little low-GI fruit to a mixed vegetable juice enhances the flavor and should not have too great an effect on blood sugar. The juice of sweeter vegetables, such as carrot and beets, should be treated with caution and only drunk mixed with that of green leafy vegetables such as spinach or watercress.

The preparation of fruit and vegetables for juicing will depend on the kind of juicer you have. All produce should be well washed (and peeled unless it is organic) and cut up to fit the opening of your juicer. If you are using a centrifugal juicer, the juice should be drunk immediately as it will deteriorate quickly. The more expensive masticator type of juicer makes better juice that lasts longer. I have not given a method for the first four of these recipes as it is basically the same for any juice. Just prepare the produce, put it through the juicer, and enjoy.

Here are some ideas, but feel free to make up your own combinations. Use organic produce whenever possible to avoid chemical residues which cannot be washed off. If you can't get organic vegetables, peel or wash them in water acidified with a spoonful of cider vinegar.

juices

spinach, carrot, and beet juice

This juice is utterly delicious and a great way to introduce yourself to vegetable juices.

1 handful spinach leaves

2 large carrots, peeled
   if not organic

1 small cooking apple, quartered and cored

1 small raw beet, scrubbed, with leaves if possible

Protein 10%
Carbohydrate 87%
Fat 3%
GI: medium
GL: low

PER SERVING

Calories 163 ▶ Protein 5g ▶ Carbohydrates 40g ▶ Fiber 0g ▶ Sugar—Total 28g ▶ Fat—Total 1g ▶ Saturated Fat 0g ▶ Vitamin C 39mg ▶ Magnesium 88mg

▶ Lots of valuable nutrients here: the spinach provides vitamin C, folic acid, and vitamin K, the carrots provide a huge amount of beta-carotene and some vitamin C, the beet provides folic acid and the apples vitamin C. All these nutrients are needed for bone health, skin health, heart health, and immunity.

more-than-tomato juice

■ ■ ■

SERVES 1 ▶ **TIME TAKEN:** 5 minutes

T*he addition of watercress makes this juice delightfully peppery.*

5 ripe medium-sized tomatoes
1 bunch watercress, well washed
2 sticks of celery

Protein 16%
Carbohydrate 73%
Fat 11%
GI: low
GL: low

PER SERVING
Calories 148 ▶ Protein 7g ▶ Carbohydrates 32g ▶ Fiber 0g ▶ Sugar—Total 18g ▶ Fat—Total 2g ▶ Saturated Fat 0g ▶ Vitamin C 187mg ▶ Magnesium 87mg

▶ Tomatoes contain an antioxidant called lycopene, good for protecting against free radicals. It is especially important for people with diabetes to eat a diet high in antioxidants as they tend to have low antioxidant levels and are therefore more vulnerable to free-radical damage.

gardener's tonic

■ ■ ■

SERVES 1 ▶ **TIME TAKEN:** 5 minutes

This juice gets its name because you could grow all its ingredients in your own garden, and it's a wonderful pick-me-up tonic.
The cucumber adds a surprisingly strong flavor.

1 large leaf of dark green
   or Savoy cabbage
1 handful of spinach
3 carrots, peeled unless organic
½ cucumber, peeled unless organic
½ red or yellow pepper, deseeded

Protein 13%
Carbohydrate 81%
Fat 6%
GI: medium
GL: low

PER SERVING

Calories 143 ▶ Protein 5g ▶ Carbohydrates 33g ▶ Fiber 0g ▶ Sugar—Total 16g ▶ Fat—Total 1g ▶ Saturated Fat 0g ▶ Vitamin C 267mg ▶ Magnesium 85mg

▶ There is a stunning amount of vitamin C in this juice, mostly due to the red pepper, provided it was picked when ripe and has not been stored for too long. Peppers are actually one of the best sources of vitamin C, but this vitamin is easily damaged by light, air, and storage, so buy your vegetables as fresh as possible, consume them quickly and don't cut them up too soon before eating.

broccoli, tomato, and cucumber juice

SERVES 1 ▶ **TIME TAKEN:** 5 minutes

---

*B*roccoli makes a strong-tasting juice that is best mixed in a ratio of about 1:4 with the juice of milder-tasting vegetables, but its nutritional benefits are so good it is worth getting used to the taste. I cook the broccoli heads and use the thick stems either sliced raw in salads or in juices like this one.

4 ripe medium tomatoes
2 broccoli stems
½ cucumber, peeled
   unless organic

Protein 18%
Carbohydrate 72%
Fat 10%
GI: low
GL: low

PER SERVING

Calories 141 ▶ Protein 7g ▶ Carbohydrates 30g ▶ Fiber 0g ▶ Sugar—Total 18g ▶ Fat—Total 2g ▶ Saturated Fat 0g ▶ Vitamin C 188mg ▶ Magnesium 68mg

▶ Broccoli is an excellent food for people with diabetes for many reasons, one of which is that it is a good source of vitamin K. Protecting the body from insulin resistance appears to be one of vitamin K's many roles in the body.

kale cooler

■ ■ ■

Putting avocado through a centrifugal juicer could clog up the mechanism, so you need to bring the blender into play for this juice. Substitute dark green cabbage leaves or spring greens if you don't have kale.

½ avocado
6 leaves of kale
2 ripe tomatoes
2 stick of celery

Protein 10%
Carbohydrate 38%
Fat 52%
GI: low
GL: low

Whizz the avocado in the blender. Juice all the other ingredients, then pour the juice into the blender and whizz until mixed.

PER SERVING

Calories 251 ▶ Protein 7g ▶ Carbohydrates 27g ▶ Fiber 4g ▶ Sugar—Total 10g ▶ Fat—Total 16g ▶ Saturated Fat 2g ▶ Vitamin C 157mg ▶ Magnesium 94mg

---

▶ Because of the kale, this is a rich source of minerals, especially magnesium.

grape and green

■ ■ ■

SERVES 1 ▶ TIME TAKEN: 10 minutes

*T*his odd-sounding mixture comes from Natalie Savona's inspiring Big Book of Juices and Smoothies. *I would not have thought of combining grapefruit and kale, but it works surprisingly well.*

1 grapefruit
2 handfuls of spinach
2 sticks of celery
4 leaves of curly kale

Protein 16%
Carbohydrate 78%
Fat 6%
GI: low
GL: low

First, juice the grapefruit using a citrus juicer. Then put the rest of the ingredients through the juicer and stir in the grapefruit juice.

───── PER SERVING ─────
Calories 143 ▶ Protein 6g ▶ Carbohydrates 31g ▶ Fiber 0g ▶ Sugar—Total 20g ▶ Fat—Total 1g ▶ Saturated Fat 0g ▶ Vitamin C 186mg ▶ Magnesium 126mg

▶ This juice is particularly good for people with diabetes because grapefruits are a low GI. If you can save some of the white pith of the grapefruit (but not the bitter peel) to put through the juicer, this will give you a shot of bioflavonoids. The kale and spinach provide lots of magnesium, an important nutrient for diabetics.

carob, date, and almond milk

■ ■ ■

SERVES 1 ▶ **TIME TAKEN:** 15 minutes

I love almond milk and often have it on cereal or porridge. Adding carob and dates is simply gilding the lily. If it is too much bother to make your own almond milk, you can purchase it from a good health-food store and blend it with the dates and carob powder. This drink is also delicious made with soaked dried figs.

⅓ cup whole almonds, soaked overnight
3 pitted dates, soaked overnight
¾ cup filtered or bottled water
2 tablespoons carob powder
a few drops of almond extract

Protein 10%
Carbohydrate 40%
Fat 50%
GI: low
GL: low

Blend all the ingredients in a blender on high speed until smooth and creamy. To separate the liquid from the almond skins and pulp, press through a fine metal sieve set over a bowl, using the back of a spoon. Alternatively, you can line the sieve with a piece of clean muslin. This has the advantage that you can squeeze the muslin with your hands to extract as much milk as possible. Serve at room temperature or chilled, and shake well before serving.

PER SERVING

Calories 355 ▶ Protein 10g ▶ Carbohydrates 38g ▶ Fiber 6g ▶ Sugar—Total 18g ▶ Fat—Total 22g ▶ Saturated Fat 2g ▶ Vitamin C omg ▶ Magnesium 17mg

---

▶ Almonds are an excellent addition to the diet for a number of reasons, one of which is that they are the best dietary source of calcium. They are also a rich source of vitamin E, needed especially by people with diabetes.

fresh ginger mint tea

■ ■ ■

SERVES 2 ▶ TIME TAKEN: 10 minutes

Homemade herbal teas are much more vibrant and zingy than those bought in sachets. Try this one in the summer when mint grows like a weed.

2-inch piece of fresh root ginger
1 small handful fresh sprigs
  of mint, washed
2 cups filtered or bottled water

Protein 17%
Carbohydrate 72%
Fat 11%
GI: low
GL: low

Peel and slice or grate the ginger into a teapot or other heatproof receptacle. Add the sprigs of mint. Boil the water and pour over the ginger and mint. Stir and cover. Leave to steep for at least 5 minutes before straining and drinking hot or warm.

Variation: fresh lemon and ginger tea can be made substituting lemon slices for the mint.

PER SERVING

Calories 5 ▶ Protein 0g ▶ Carbohydrates 1g ▶ Fiber 0g ▶ Sugar—Total 0g ▶ Fat—Total 0g ▶ Saturated Fat 0g ▶ Vitamin C 1mg ▶ Magnesium 8mg

▶ There is some evidence that ginger can help stabilize insulin levels if taken 40 minutes before a meal,[69] and this tea is a delightful way to test this theory.

spicy ginger and fennel tea

■ ■ ■

SERVES 2 ▶ TIME TAKEN: 15 minutes

This tea is very soothing to the digestive tract, and is good drunk before, with, or after a meal.

2 inches piece of fresh root ginger
1 tablespoon fennel seeds
1 cinnamon stick
2 cloves
2 cups filtered or bottled water

Protein 13%
Carbohydrate 64%
Fat 23%
GI: low
GL: low

Peel and grate the ginger. Crush the fennel seeds in a mortar and pestle. Break up the cinnamon stick. Put all the spices in a teapot or other heatproof receptacle. Boil the water and pour over the spices. Stir, cover, and allow to stand for 10 minutes. Strain and drink hot.

PER SERVING
Calories 17 ▶ Protein 1g ▶ Carbohydrates 3g ▶ Fiber 0g ▶ Sugar—Total 0g ▶ Fat—Total 0g ▶ Saturated Fat 0g ▶ Vitamin C 1mg ▶ Magnesium 13mg

▶ Fennel seeds are gently tonic and diuretic. Their main use is for digestive problems, such as poor digestion, bloating, nausea, and flatulence. This is a very good tea to drink if you are feeling a bit queasy.

fenugreek tea

■ ■ ■

SERVES 2 ▶ **TIME TAKEN:** 5 minutes plus 3 hours soaking

This tea may be drunk several times a day to help lower blood glucose. If you can't find fenugreek seeds, substitute with powdered fenugreek.

1 tablespoon fenugreek seed
2 cups filtered or bottled water

Soak the seeds in the water for three hours, then strain. Reheat to serve, or drink the tea iced.

Protein 24%
Carbohydrate 61%
Fat 15%
GI: low
GL: low

PER SERVING
Calories 36 ▶ Protein 3g ▶ Carbohydrates 6g ▶ Fiber 3g ▶ Sugar—Total 0g ▶ Fat—Total 1g ▶ Saturated Fat 0g ▶ Vitamin C 0mg ▶ Magnesium 24mg
---

▶ Fenugreek seeds are a traditional Indian remedy, recently confirmed by Western scientists. Studies have shown that active ingredients in the seeds raise HDL (the "good" cholesterol) and lower blood glucose. The unique fiber composition and high saponin content in fenugreek appears to be responsible for these therapeutic properties.[70]

juniper berry wine

■ ■ ■

Makes 15 servings ▶ **TIME TAKEN:** 5 minutes plus 1 week standing

*T*his idea comes from Food Is Medicine *by Pierre Jean Cousin, a Frenchman who makes looking after your health sound like going out for a restaurant meal. The recommended dose for people with diabetes is 2 ounces per day.*

3 cups white wine
2½ ounces juniper berries, crushed
2 teaspoons lemon zest from organic lemons

Protein 1%
Carbohydrate 5%
Fat 0%
Alcohol: 94%
GI: high
GL: low

Decant the wine into a container that can be sealed. Add the juniper berries and lemon zest to the wine. Seal tightly and leave for a week. Strain through muslin and store in a tightly sealed bottle.

PER SERVING
Calories 102 ▶ Protein 0g ▶ Carbohydrates 1g ▶ Fiber 0g ▶ Sugar—Total 0g ▶ Fat—Total 0g ▶ Saturated Fat 0g ▶ Vitamin C 1mg ▶ Magnesium 15mg

▶ Juniper was traditionally used in the treatment of diabetes in the days before insulin was available. In a recent study the blood-sugar-lowering effect of juniper was tested on mice, together with that of various other herbs such as agrimony, alfalfa, coriander, eucalyptus, and others. The results suggested that these traditional plant treatments for diabetes, including juniper, could retard the development of diabetes in mice.[71]

soups
AND starters

cream of avocado soup with coconut milk

■ ■ ■

SERVES 4 ▶ **TIME TAKEN:** 10 minutes

*T*his absurdly easy but sophisticated soup comes from the days I spent cooking on yachts in the Caribbean. It was ideal for catering at sea because it was quick and foolproof. The quantities are not large, but it is very rich, so you don't need much.

2 large avocados
½ teaspoon sea salt
1 cup coconut milk
1 lime, juice only
2 cups vegetable stock (see page 229)
1 tablespoon dry sherry (optional)
dash of hot sauce, such as Tabasco
slices of lime and coriander leaves, for garnish

Protein 8%
Carbohydrate 17%
Fat 75%
GI: low
GL: low

Cut the avocados in half. Remove the seeds and scoop out the flesh. Place the avocado flesh, salt, coconut milk, and lime juice in a blender or food processor. Blend to a smooth purée. Heat the vegetable stock to boiling point. With the machine running, slowly add the hot stock to the purée. Stir in the sherry, if using, and a dash of hot sauce to taste. This soup may be served hot or cold.

If serving hot, heat but do not let it boil. If serving cold, refrigerate for several hours and serve in cold bowls. Garnish each serving with a thin slice of lime and a couple of whole coriander leaves.

PER SERVING

Calories 269 ▶ Protein 4g ▶ Carbohydrates 12g ▶ Sugar—Total 3g ▶ Fiber 9g ▶ Fat—Total 24g ▶ Saturated Fat 13g ▶ Vitamin C 9mg ▶ Magnesium 34mg

▶ I'm glad to say that avocados are back on the menu these days, having fallen out of favor. The fat they contain is nearly all oleic acid, a monounsaturated fat, and they are a very good source of vitamin E, an important nutrient for people with diabetes.

sweet potato and coconut soup with lime

■ ■ ■

SERVES 4 ▶ **TIME TAKEN:** 45 minutes

---

*T*his soup is pretty and delicious and full of good things. What more could you ask for?

1 tablespoon coconut oil
1 onion, peeled and chopped
1 clove garlic, peeled and crushed
1 inch piece of ginger root, peeled and chopped
1 small fresh red chili, deseeded and finely chopped
1½ pounds sweet potatoes, peeled and chopped
1 tablespoon fresh lemon grass, chopped
2 cups vegetable stock (see page 229)
1½ cups coconut milk
sea salt and freshly ground black pepper to taste
2 organic limes, finely grated zest and juice

Protein 5%
Carbohydrate 35%
Fat 60%
GI: medium
GL: medium

Heat the oil in a large saucepan and gently fry the onion, garlic, ginger, and chili for about 5 minutes until tender. Add the sweet potatoes and lemongrass and cook for a further 3 minutes.

Add the stock and bring to a boil. Reduce the heat and simmer, covered, for 20 minutes until the vegetables are tender.

Cool the soup slightly, then purée with half of the coconut milk and process until smooth. Return the soup to the saucepan, and gradually add the remaining coconut milk, tasting as you go. You don't want the flavor of coconut to overwhelm the sweet potato, so you may not need all the coconut milk. Season to taste. Heat through without allowing the soup to boil, and add the lime juice. Ladle the soup into bowls and garnish with the lime zest.

PER SERVING

Calories 450 ▶ Protein 6g ▶ Carbohydrates 49g ▶ Fiber 7g ▶ Sugar—Total 23g ▶ Fat—Total 28g ▶ Saturated Fat 24g ▶ Vitamin C 65mg ▶ Magnesium 58mg

---

▶ Sweet potatoes are a rich source of three important antioxidants: vitamins C and E and beta-carotene. They are thus protective both of the heart and of the eyes. Since diabetes is a risk factor for cardiovascular diseases and eye problems, these are important nutrients for people with diabetes.

broccoli soup with horseradish

■ ■ ■

SERVES 4 ▶ TIME TAKEN: 50 minutes

*T*he horseradish in this soup provides a pleasant "bite." If you can't find fresh horseradish, substitute 2–3 teaspoons of creamed horseradish and omit the yogurt. You could try this soup using cauliflower instead of broccoli, as cauliflower would stand up to the horseradish equally well, and has a similar nutritional profile to broccoli.

2 tablespoons extra-virgin olive oil
1 small onion, peeled and finely chopped
1 small potato, peeled and diced
1½ cups broccoli, roughly chopped
3½ cups vegetable stock (see page 229)
1 organic lime, juice and finely grated zest
1 tablespoon fresh parsley, chopped
1 tablespoon fresh chives, chopped
2 tablespoons plain yogurt
2 teaspoons freshly grated horseradish
sea salt and freshly ground black pepper to taste

Protein 11%
Carbohydrate 40%
Fat 49%
GI: medium
GL: low

Heat the oil in a large pan and sauté the chopped onion and potato over gentle heat until softened but not brown. Add the vegetable stock, lime zest and juice, bring to a boil and simmer for 30 minutes, until the vegetables are soft.

Meanwhile, steam the broccoli in another pot until just tender but still green—about 8 minutes. As soon as it is cooked, plunge into cold water to set the color. Drain well and set aside.

When the potato and onion mixture is cooked, take off the heat, cool a little and then blend to a smooth consistency in the blender or food processor. Add the cooked broccoli and blend again briefly—there should still be recognizable pieces of broccoli. Return to a clean saucepan and stir in the chopped herbs, yogurt, grated horseradish, and seasoning to taste. Reheat without boiling, check seasoning and serve piping hot in heated bowls.

PER SERVING
Calories 150 ▶ Protein 4g ▶ Carbohydrates 15g ▶ Sugar—Total 4g ▶ Fiber 5g ▶ Fat—Total 8g ▶ Saturated Fat 1g ▶ Vitamin C 80mg ▶ Magnesium 29mg

▶ I have come to regard broccoli as something of a superfood, and I think we should all be eating it at least once a day. It is ranked first in the US National Cancer Institute's list of all-round anticancer vegetables as it is rich in several potential anticancer substances such as indoles, glucosinolates, beta-carotene, and vitamin C. Not only that, but it is one of the richest sources of iron in the vegetable world and contains a significant amount of magnesium.

jerusalem artichoke soup
with lemon and saffron

SERVES 4 ▶ TIME TAKEN: 1 hour

*J*erusalem artichokes were a part of my childhood as we always had a row of the huge green plants growing right at the back of the vegetable garden. Gardeners say that the only way to get rid of them is to move away as any little bit of root left in the ground will sprout. They discolor very quickly, so when you are peeling them, keep the peeled ones in water acidulated with a few drops of lemon juice or vinegar.

2 tablespoons extra-virgin olive oil
1 small onion, peeled and chopped
2 sticks celery, chopped
1½ cups celeriac, peeled and cut into chunks
1 pound Jerusalem artichokes, peeled and cut into chunks
   (keep in cold acidulated water until needed)
3½ cups vegetable stock (see page 229)
½ teaspoon saffron threads
½ organic lemon, finely grated zest and juice
2 tablespoons soy cream or plain yogurt
a few leaves of flat-leaf parsley

Protein 7%
Carbohydrate 60%
Fat 33%
GI: medium
GL: low

Heat the olive oil in a large saucepan and soften the onion and celery in it for 5 minutes, keeping the heat fairly low. Next, drain the artichokes and add them to the pan, along with the sweet potatoes. Keeping the heat low, cover and let the vegetables sweat for 15 minutes.

Add the stock and saffron, stir well, put the lid back on and simmer, very gently, for a further 20 minutes, or until the vegetables are soft. Cool a little, then puree the soup in a blender. This may have to be done in two batches. Return the soup to the pan, add the lemon juice, season to taste, and reheat gently. Serve hot, garnishing each serving with a swirl of soy cream or yogurt and a few leaves of flat-leaf parsley.

PER SERVING
Calories 220 ▶ Protein 4g ▶ Carbohydrates 34g ▶ Sugar—Total 12g ▶ Fiber 4g ▶ Fat—Total 8g ▶ Saturated Fat 1g ▶ Vitamin C 25mg ▶ Magnesium 24mg

The stored carbohydrate of the artichoke is inulin, which differs from the starch of the potato. If you are not used to it, your stomach will rumble. The consolation is that inulin has been found to increase the levels of beneficial bacteria in the colon and helps to normalize bowel function if you are constipated.

gazpacho with eggplant croûtons

■ ■ ■

SERVES 4 ▶ TIME TAKEN: 20 minutes plus 2 hours resting

This is a raw soup. There are huge advantages to eating raw food—none of the nutrients are lost in cooking, and the plant enzymes are for the most part still intact. Gazpacho is normally bulked out with white bread crumbs, but I use ground almonds to boost the protein and fatty acid content and reduce the carbohydrate load.

4 tablespoons ground almonds
2 garlic cloves, peeled and crushed
1 tablespoon red wine vinegar
1 tablespoon extra-virgin olive oil
1 green pepper, coarsely chopped
1 onion, coarsely chopped
5 very ripe tomatoes, peeled, seeded
    and coarsely chopped
1 cucumber, peeled and coarsely chopped
1 tablespoon tomato purée
sea salt, to taste

Protein 8%
Carbohydrate 34%
Fat 58%
GI: low
GL: low

for the eggplant croûtons:
2 tablespoons extra-virgin olive oil
½ medium eggplant

Put the ground almonds and garlic in a small bowl. Add the vinegar and olive oil. Mix well, cover and set aside for a couple of hours to let the flavors combine. Put the green pepper, onion, tomatoes, cucumber, tomato purée, and almond mixture in a blender or food processor. Process briefly, until vegetables are just chopped. You may have to do this in two batches. Transfer the mixture to a large chilled bowl and stir in enough very cold water to give the soup a creamy consistency. Season to taste and refrigerate until ready to serve.

To make the croûtons, heat the olive oil in a frying pan or wok over high heat. Add the eggplant cubes and stir fry over high heat until they are browned. Drain well on kitchen paper.

It makes an interesting contrast with the chilled soup if you can serve the croûtons very hot, but if not, room temperature is fine.

PER SERVING

Calories 208 ▶ Protein 4g ▶ Carbohydrates 19g ▶ Sugar—Total 9g ▶ Fiber 5g ▶ Fat—Total 14g ▶
Saturated Fat 2g ▶ Vitamin C 62mg ▶ Magnesium 48mg

▶ This soup depends largely on the quality of the tomatoes used. It is worth searching out tomatoes that have been ripened on the vine, thus allowing them to
develop not only a depth of flavor but also more nutritional value. Fruit and vegetables that have been harvested before they are ripe are nutritionally depleted.

smoked haddock and cabbage soup

■ ■ ■

SERVES 4 ▶ TIME TAKEN: 40 minutes

This is a lovely comforting fishy stewlike soup from Scotland. It is normally made with cream, but I use a spoonful of yogurt instead, to keep the fat content down. I feel the butter is needed for its rich taste, but you could substitute olive oil in order to reduce saturated fat.

2 fillets of naturally smoked haddock, flaked
4 tablespoons butter
2 onions, peeled and finely chopped
2 garlic cloves, peeled and chopped
½ savoy cabbage, shredded
4 tablespoons white wine
3½ cups vegetable stock (see page 229)
4 tablespoons plain or soy yogurt
2 tablespoons chopped parsley

Protein 26%
Carbohydrate 29%
Fat 45%
GI: low
GL: low

First, place the smoked haddock in a frying pan with water to cover. Bring to a simmer, then immediately turn off the heat and leave to cool. Drain the fish and roughly flake the flesh, removing any skin and bones.

Melt the butter in a saucepan over medium heat. Add the onion and garlic and sauté for 2 minutes. Add the cabbage and sauté for 1 minute. Add the white wine and stir well to collect the cooking juices. Pour in the vegetable stock. Add the smoked haddock flakes and allow the soup to simmer for 5 minutes. It is important not to overcook at this stage as the cabbage needs to retain some crunch. Stir in the yogurt at the last minute and heat without allowing the soup to boil. Serve in very hot bowls with a sprinkling of chopped parsley on top.

PER SERVING
Calories 269 ▶ Protein 18g ▶ Carbohydrates 18g ▶ Sugar—Total 8g ▶ Fiber 5g ▶ Fat—Total 14g ▶ Saturated Fat 8g ▶ Vitamin C 24mg ▶ Magnesium 63mg

▶ Any way we can encourage ourselves to eat cabbage is worth pursuing. Cabbage, like broccoli, is a superfood. It contains lots of minerals such as calcium and magnesium, and is full of antioxidants such as vitamins C and E, which protect the kidneys—vital for those with diabetes. Smoked haddock is less of a superfood—smoked foods do contain carcinogens, but unless large amounts are eaten regularly, the risks associated with eating smoked foods are not very great.

fish and watercress soup with ginger

■ ■ ■

SERVES 4 ▶ **TIME TAKEN:** 40 minutes

½ ounce dried shiitake mushrooms
½ cup hot water
2 teaspoons extra-virgin olive oil
1 teaspoon oriental (toasted) sesame oil
2 scallions, finely chopped
2 garlic cloves, peeled and finely chopped
1-inch piece of ginger root, peeled and finely chopped
2½ cups chicken stock (see page 230)
2 tablespoons thai fish sauce
1 tablespoon dry sherry (optional)
1 tablespoon tamari sauce
½ pound white fish, such as cod, cut into ¾-inch cubes
3 bunches watercress, washed and chopped

> Protein 31%
> Carbohydrate 15%
> Fat 54%
> GI: low
> GL: low

Soak the mushrooms in a little hot water until softened, about 20 minutes. Drain them, reserving soaking liquid. Squeeze out excess moisture. Thinly slice the caps and discard the stems.

Heat the olive and sesame oils in a heavy large saucepan over medium heat. Add the scallions, garlic, and ginger and sauté until just tender, about 3 minutes. Add the sliced mushrooms and sauté until mushrooms are tender, about 3 minutes. Add the chicken stock, the mushroom soaking liquid, Thai fish sauce, sherry (if using), and tamari sauce. Bring to a boil. Stir in the fish and watercress and boil until the fish is just cooked through, about 2 minutes. Do not cook any longer as the watercress will lose its bright green color. Serve immediately in hot bowls.

PER SERVING
Calories 156 ▶ Protein 12g ▶ Carbohydrates 5g ▶ Sugar—Total 1g ▶ Fiber 2g ▶ Fat—Total 9g ▶ Saturated Fat 1g ▶ Vitamin C 16mg ▶ Magnesium 41mg

▶ Like broccoli, watercress is a superfood and should be eaten regularly. It is a particularly good vegetable source of calcium, which is important for bones, healthy muscles and nerves, and the beta-carotenes it contains are protective of eye health. The peppery taste is caused by a mustard oil, which is a powerful natural antibiotic.

roasted garlic and onion soup

■ ■ ■

SERVES 6 ▶ **TIME TAKEN:** 1 hour 50 minutes

*R*eading *this recipe might make you think that this soup will be very fiercely flavored, but roasting the onions and garlic brings out their essential sweetness, and the result is deeply flavored without being overpowering.*

6 medium onions
3 whole heads of garlic, unpeeled
2 tablespoons extra-virgin olive oil
5 cups chicken stock (see page 230)
1 sweet potato (about 10 ounces), peeled and chopped
1 tablespoon fresh thyme leaves
freshly ground black pepper

Protein 13%
Carbohydrate 57%
Fat 30%
GI: medium
GL: low

for the Parmesan crisps:
6 tablespoons Parmesan cheese, finely grated

Preheat the oven to 375°F.

Cut the onions in half, without peeling, and place in a roasting pan together with the whole heads of garlic. Sprinkle with olive oil and bake for 50–60 minutes until the vegetables are soft and browned.

While the onions and garlic are roasting, make the Parmesan crisps. On the underside of a piece of baking parchment draw four 4-inch circles, leaving at least 1 inch between each. Place the parchment on a baking sheet with the drawn side down. Sprinkle 1 tablespoon of the grated Parmesan in each circle, spreading evenly. Bake in a preheated oven for approximately 5–8 minutes or until they are light golden brown. Remove from the oven and cool—they will become crisp as they cool. Gently lift off the parchment paper using a metal spatula and use immediately.

Now remove the onions and garlic from the oven, cool a little, then slip them out of their skins. Chop the onion and garlic flesh quite finely and put in a saucepan with the chicken stock, sweet potatoes, thyme leaves, and pepper. Bring to a boil, then turn down the heat and cook for 20–30 minutes until the soup has reduced and thickened a little. Transfer some or all of the soup to a blender and purée if you prefer a smoother texture. If you do this, return to the pan to reheat. Ladle into bowls and serve very hot, accompanied by Parmesan crisps.

PER SERVING

Calories 211 ► Protein 7g ► Carbohydrates 31g ► Fiber 4g ► Sugar—Total 12g ► Fat—Total 7g ►
Saturated Fat 2g ► Vitamin C 23mg ► Magnesium 24mg

► Not only are onions full of nutrients that support the liver and help to prevent cancer, they are also a very rich source of chromium, vital for blood-glucose control. There are 29mcg of chromium in each serving of this soup—that's more than any other recipe in this book.

butter bean soup with parsley pesto

■ ■ ■

SERVES 4 ▶ **TIME TAKEN:** 3 hours

I've used butter beans in this soup, but you could substitute any pale colored bean, such as white haricot beans, cannellini beans, or flageolet beans. I love the contrast of the white soup and the dark green pesto, not to mention the delicious flavor. The addition of ginger seems to help counteract the unfortunate tendency of beans to cause flatulence in some people.

1⅓ cups butter beans, soaked overnight in water
1 thumb-sized piece of root ginger, peeled
2 tablespoons extra-virgin olive oil
1 large onion, chopped
2 sticks celery, chopped
3½ cups chicken stock (see page 230)
sea salt and freshly ground black pepper to taste

Protein 20%
Carbohydrate 52%
Fat 28%
GI: low
GL: low

for the parsley pesto:
1 small bunch flat leaf parsley, roughly chopped
1 clove garlic, crushed
2 tablespoons parmesan cheese, finely grated
2 tablespoons extra-virgin olive oil
sea salt and freshly ground black pepper to taste
lemon juice, to taste

Drain the butter beans and cover with clean cold water. Add the ginger, bring to a boil and cook at a rolling boil for 10 minutes, skimming off any foam as it boils. Reduce the heat, cover and simmer until the beans are tender. This depends on their age, and can take anything from 1–2 hours. When they are soft, remove from the heat, drain the beans and discard the piece of ginger.

Heat the olive oil in a large pan and sauté the onion and celery over gentle heat until softened but not browned. Add the drained beans, chicken stock, and seasoning, bring to a boil and cook for another 30–40 minutes until the beans and vegetables are really soft. Cool a little, then blend in the blender or food processor, and check for seasoning. Return the soup to the pan and reheat.

While the soup is cooking, make the parsley pesto: place the chopped parsley into a food processor with the garlic and Parmesan. Process until smooth. With the motor still running, slowly add the olive oil and a squeeze of lemon juice. Season with salt and pepper.

Serve the soup very hot with a swirl of parsley pesto in each bowl.

Variations: The pesto can be made with any strongly flavored herb, such as coriander or the traditional basil.

PER SERVING

Calories 282 ▸ Protein 14g ▸ Carbohydrates 37g ▸ Sugar—Total 8g ▸ Fiber 12g ▸ Fat—Total 9g ▸ Saturated Fat 2g ▸ Vitamin C 26mg ▸ Magnesium 80mg

---

▶ At 31, the GI of butter beans is very low. They have other beneficial properties, too. Like all legumes, they are a combination of protein and carbohydrate and an extremely good source of soluble fiber. This means that they are digested slowly and so are naturally good for balancing blood glucose.

june's spicy chana dal soup

■ ■ ■

SERVES 5 ▶ **TIME TAKEN:** 1¾ hours

T his soup comes from June Marriott, my sister-in-law and a gifted cook. She makes it with chickpeas, but chana dal cooks in the same way as chickpeas and tastes quite similar while having a far lower GI, so it is invaluable for people with diabetes. I've also replaced June's crème fraîche with yogurt to reduce the fat.

1¼ cups chana dal, soaked overnight in
   twice their volume of water
3 tablespoons butter
1 tablespoon coriander seeds
1 tablespoon cumin seeds
6 garlic cloves, peeled and finely chopped
2 small red chilies, halved, deseeded and finely chopped
1 organic lemon, grated zest and juice
3 tablespoons fresh coriander, leaves and stalks separated
1 cup plain yogurt
sea salt and freshly ground black pepper to taste

> **Protein 15%**
> **Carbohydrate 46%**
> **Fat 39%**
> **GI: very low**
> **GL: low**

Drain the chana dal, rinse and boil in 5 cups of water until tender and squashy (about one hour).

Dry roast the coriander and cumin seeds for 2–3 minutes, then crush them in pestle and mortar.

Melt the butter over gentle heat, add the crushed spices, garlic, and half the chopped chilies and cook for 5 minutes. Add the turmeric, stir and heat gently, then remove from the heat.

Drain the chana dal, drain over a bowl and reserve the cooking liquid.

Blend the chana dal with some of the cooking water and purée until fine and smooth.

Add the lemon zest, coriander stalks, and spices with more cooking liquid and blend until smooth.

Put everything back into the pan with the remainder of the cooking water. Bring to a boil, turn down the heat and simmer for about 30 minutes, stirring from time to time. Season to taste.

When ready to serve, add half the yogurt and the lemon juice.

Serve the soup in hot bowls with the rest of the yogurt swirled in and scatter with the remainder of the chopped chilies and the coriander leaves.

PER SERVING

Calories 245 ▸ Protein 9g ▸ Carbohydrates 30g ▸ Sugar—Total 2g: Fiber 8g ▸ Fat—Total 11g ▸ Saturated Fat 5g ▸ Vitamin C 47mg ▸ Magnesium 62mg

---

▸ I was first alerted to the nutritional benefits of chana dal by David Mendosa. David, who is a health journalist and a diabetic himself, operates a Web site at www.mendosa.com that is the most valuable resource for people with diabetes. Because chana dal has such a low GI (11), David devotes a whole section of his Web site to recipes using chana dal. Chana dal can be obtained from Asian shops and larger supermarkets and is not to be confused with split peas, which have a higher GI.

two-lentil soup with coriander

■ ■ ■

SERVES 4 ▶ **TIME TAKEN:** 1 hour

This is a lovely, comforting winter soup and has an interesting texture because the brown lentils are left whole while the red lentils and vegetables are puréed. It's a good idea to make double quantities and freeze some to have on hand when you don't feel like making soup.

⅓ cup brown lentils
½ cup split red lentils
2 tablespoons extra-virgin olive oil
1 large onion
2 sticks celery
1 large carrot
½ red pepper
2 garlic cloves
3 cups vegetable stock (see page 229)
1 bay leaf
1 organic lemon, grated zest and juice
1 tablespoon concentrated tomato purée
1 bunch fresh coriander
sea salt and freshly ground black pepper

Protein 21%
Carbohydrate 61%
Fat 18%
GI: low
GL: low

Wash the lentils. Put the brown lentils in a saucepan, cover with cold water, bring to a boil and cook for 30 minutes until tender. Drain well and set aside.

Meanwhile, roughly chop the onion, celery, carrot, red pepper and garlic. Gently heat the olive oil in a large saucepan, and sauté the chopped vegetables in the oil, covered, for about 10 minutes over a low heat. Add the stock, bay leaf, lemon zest (keep the juice aside for later), tomato purée, and red lentils, bring to a boil and simmer over low heat for 35–40 minutes or until the vegetables are tender and the lentils have disintegrated. Remove the bay leaf and cool a little.

Wash the bunch of coriander, cutting off most of the stalks, and reserve four of the best leaves for garnish. Roughly chop the coriander and add to the cooled soup, then blend in a blender. If you prefer a smooth texture, rub through a sieve into a clean pan. Otherwise, return to the pan without sieving. Add the lemon juice, tasting to make sure you don't overdo it, and season to taste. Stir in the cooked brown lentils, and reheat the soup gently. Serve in heated bowls, each serving topped with a coriander leaf.

PER SERVING

Calories 224 ▸ Protein 12g ▸ Carbohydrates 36g ▸ Sugar—Total 10g ▸ Fiber 11g ▸ Fat—Total 5g ▸ Saturated Fat 1g ▸ Vitamin C 67mg ▸ Magnesium 55mg

▶ There are lots of good reasons to increase our intake of lentils. They are a very good source of complex carbohydrates and protein, they contain a good level of B vitamins, and may help reduce "bad" cholesterol.

fennel and spinach soup

■ ■ ■

SERVES 4 ▶ TIME TAKEN: 40 minutes

Fennel has a delicate flavor whereas that of spinach is quite robust, so you need to taste this carefully to get the balance right. I find that organic fennel has a much more pronounced aniseed taste than nonorganic, and is worth seeking out for that reason.

1 tablespoon extra-virgin olive oil
1 small onion, peeled and finely chopped
1 garlic clove, peeled and finely chopped
1 stick celery, finely chopped
1 large fennel bulb, preferably organic,
    trimmed and very finely sliced
2 cups vegetable stock (see page 230)
4 cups baby spinach leaves
1 tablespoon chopped fresh dill or chopped fennel tops
½ lemon, juice only
sea salt and freshly ground black pepper to taste
plain or soy yogurt, to serve

Protein 14%
Carbohydrate 48%
Fat 37%
GI: low
GL: low

Heat the olive oil in a large pan and gently sauté the chopped onion, celery, and fennel until soft but not brown. Add the stock, bring to a boil, then lower the heat, cover and simmer for 10–15 minutes, until the fennel is tender. Add the spinach, bring to a boil again, then remove from the heat and let stand for 5 minutes. The spinach should cook in the residual heat.

Cool a little, then put in the blender and blend until smooth. Return to the pan and add the chopped dill, lemon juice, salt, and pepper to taste. Reheat gently and serve immediately.

If you don't plan to serve this soup right away, don't put the lemon juice in until you reheat it, otherwise it will lose its lovely green color.

─── PER SERVING ───
Calories 97 ▶ Protein 4g ▶ Carbohydrates 13g ▶ Fiber 4g ▶ Sugar—Total 3g ▶ Fat—Total 4g ▶ Saturated Fat 1g ▶ Vitamin C 15mg ▶ Magnesium 47mg

▶ Fennel and spinach are both useful sources of beta-carotene and folate, and spinach contains lutein, which is important for eye health, and therefore of special interest to people with diabetes. In addition, fennel is particularly good for the liver.

roasted fennel and red peppers with tapenade

■ ■ ■

SERVES 4 ▶ TIME TAKEN: 40 minutes

Strong colors and strong flavors make this a good dish to eat out of doors in the summer, perhaps with a glass of wine. Tapenade is a delicious olive paste sold in small jars.

2 large red peppers
2 fennel bulbs
2 tablespoons extra-virgin olive oil
1 tablespoon lemon juice
sea salt and freshly ground black pepper
4 tablespoons tapenade
2 tablespoons pine nuts
torn fresh basil, for garnish

Protein 9%
Carbohydrate 23%
Fat 68%
GI: low
GL: low

Preheat the oven to 400°F.

Quarter the peppers and take out the seeds, then cut the quarters in half lengthwise. Trim the fennel and cut downward into quarters, then slice these in half, so that each piece is still attached at the root end. You should now have 16 pieces of each vegetable.

Place the pepper and fennel pieces on an oiled baking tray and sprinkle with the olive oil, lemon juice, and seasoning. Bake the vegetables for 25–30 minutes, or until beginning to char slightly. Meanwhile, toast the pine nuts in a dry pan in the oven for no more than 5 minutes, stirring once or twice so that they are evenly browned.

To serve, place a spoonful of tapenade in the center of each of four individual serving plates. Arrange the fennel and peppers around the tapenade like the spokes of a wheel. Sprinkle with pine nuts and torn basil leaves, and serve hot or at room temperature.

PER SERVING
Calories 288 ▶ Protein 7g ▶ Carbohydrates 17g ▶ Fiber 7g ▶ Sugar—Total 2g ▶ Fat—Total 23g ▶ Saturated Fat 4g ▶ Vitamin C 86mg ▶ Magnesium 41mg

▶ Both peppers and fennel are said to stimulate the appetite, so that's a good enough reason to have them as a starter. Red peppers are also a rich source of vitamin C and bioflavonoids.

chili mussels with garlic rye toast

■ ■ ■

SERVES 4 ▶ **TIME TAKEN:** 15 minutes

This is a twist on the classic Moules Marinières. *The addition of rye toast gives this dish an almost perfect nutritional balance.*

5 pounds mussels (debearded and rinsed in cold water)
2 tablespoons extra-virgin olive oil
3 tablespoons white wine
3 shallots, finely chopped
freshly ground black pepper
1 red chili, chopped finely
1 garlic clove, crushed
3 tablespoons soy cream
2 tablespoons fresh parsley, chopped

Protein 32%
Carbohydrate 31%
Fat 37%
GI: low
GL: low

for the garlic rye toast:
4 slices dark rye bread or pumpernickel
1 garlic clove
extra-virgin olive oil, for drizzling

Put the cleaned mussels, olive oil, white wine, shallots, seasoning, chili, and garlic into a large pan with a close-fitting lid. Put on a high heat. Once the liquid comes to a boil and the mussels start to open, add the soy cream. Continue to steam until the shells have all opened. Discard any that do not open.

For the garlic rye toast, toast the slices of rye bread, then rub with the raw garlic clove on both sides and drizzle with a few drops of olive oil.

Serve the mussels and any liquid in hot deep bowls and sprinkle generously with chopped parsley. Pass the garlic rye toast separately.

PER SERVING
Calories 340 ▶ Protein 27g ▶ Carbohydrates 25g ▶ Sugar—Total 7g ▶ Fiber 2g ▶ Fat—Total 13g ▶ Saturated Fat 2g ▶ Vitamin C 45mg ▶ Magnesium 53mg

pan-fried scallops
with cabbage and juniper

███

SERVES 4 ▶ **TIME TAKEN:** 20 minutes

The most widely available scallops are the large sea scallops, which I have used here. If, however, you are using bay scallops, which are smaller and cheaper, allow 5–6 per person.

2 tablespoons butter
1 medium onion, chopped
1 garlic clove, crushed
6 juniper berries, lightly crushed
3 cups savoy or other dark green cabbage, finely shredded

for the scallops:
8–12 large whole scallops
2 tablespoons extra-virgin olive oil
sea salt and freshly ground black pepper

Protein 18%
Carbohydrate 17%
Fat 65%
GI: low
GL: low

First, prepare the cabbage: melt the butter in a large saucepan. Add the onion, garlic, and juniper berries and lightly cook for 5 minutes, until the onion is soft. Add the cabbage and stir until well coated with butter. Cover and cook the cabbage in its own juices for 6–7 minutes, stirring occasionally. The cabbage should be slightly crunchy and not soft.

To prepare the scallops, slice them in half horizontally if the scallops are very large. To cook the scallops, heat the oil in a small frying pan. Pan-fry the scallops for 1–2 minutes on each side until cooked through and golden. Season to taste.

Serve the scallops on a bed of juniper cabbage.

PER SERVING

Calories 192 ▶ Protein 9g ▶ Carbohydrates 8g ▶ Sugar—Total 3g ▶ Fiber 3g ▶ Fat—Total 14g ▶ Saturated Fat 5g ▶ Vitamin C 23mg ▶ Magnesium 12mg

---

▶ Juniper is a fragrant spice used to make gin. Juniper berries are good for the digestion and have antiseptic qualities as they contain a powerful antibacterial essential oil. They are also recommended for diabetes because they stimulate the pancreas.

grilled polenta with rosemary and anchovy sauce

■ ■ ■

SERVES 4 ▶ TIME TAKEN: 40 minutes plus cooling time

---

*T*his is an elegant but easy hot starter. A word of warning, though: this recipe has strong flavors and is not for the fainthearted. The polenta can be made in advance and need only be grilled just before serving. If you are really feeling lazy, try a ready-cooked organic polenta. You would need to use one 18-ounce package for 4 people. See also: Crispy Polenta with Wild Mushrooms and Coriander Pesto (page 134) and Creamy Baked Polenta with Roasted Vegetables (page 136)

3½ ounces polenta, dry
1 2-ounce can of anchovies in olive oil
2 teaspoons chopped fresh rosemary
2 tablespoons lemon juice
2–3 tablespoons extra-virgin olive oil
To serve: mixed salad greens

Protein 10%
Carbohydrate 29%
Fat 61%
GI: medium
GL: low

To make the polenta, bring 1½ cups water to a boil in a medium saucepan. Pour in the polenta gradually, stirring all the time. Reduce the heat and cook, stirring constantly with a wooden spoon until the polenta comes away from the sides of the pan. This will take about 20 minutes. Alternatively you can use instant polenta, which only takes about 5 minutes to cook. Spread the polenta onto a flat surface to a depth of ¾ inch and let it rest until cold, then cut into slices.

Drain the anchovies but reserve the olive oil in which they were canned. For the sauce, chop the anchovies and mix with the rosemary in a bowl. Slowly add the lemon juice and blend to a paste. Make the reserved olive oil from the anchovies up to 4 tablespoons by adding extra-virgin olive oil. Beat the olive oil into the anchovy and rosemary mixture a little at a time.

Heat the grill until very hot. Brush the polenta with olive oil and grill for 3 or 4 minutes on each side until lightly charred. Arrange the salad greens on 4 individual plates, place the polenta on the salad and pour over the sauce.

PER SERVING

Calories 223 ▶ Protein 5g ▶ Carbohydrates 16g ▶ Sugar—Total 0g ▶ Fiber 2g ▶ Fat—Total 15g ▶ Saturated Fat 2g ▶ Vitamin C 6mg ▶ Magnesium 16mg

---

▶ Polenta is useful for people with diabetes because, for a grain, it has a relatively low GI, and because corn is a gluten-free grain. A small proportion (about 5 percent) of Type 1 diabetics are celiac, which means they cannot digest gluten. Corn is also reputed to be a gentle moderator of the thyroid gland.

zucchini timbale with tomato coulis

■ ■ ■

SERVES 4 ▶ **TIME TAKEN:** 40 minutes

This is a very light starter based on one by Pierre Jean Cousin in his book Food Is Medicine.

1 pound zucchini, roughly chopped
2 organic free-range eggs, lightly beaten
2 tablespoons yogurt cheese
sea salt and freshly ground black pepper
½ yellow or red pepper, finely chopped
1 tablespoon Parmesan cheese, finely grated

Protein 16%
Carbohydrate 29%
Fat 54%
GI: low
GL: low

for the tomato coulis:
2 large ripe beefsteak tomatoes
1 teaspoon tomato purée
2 tablespoons extra-virgin olive oil
sea salt and freshly ground black pepper
To serve: Basil leaves

Preheat the oven to 325°F.

Steam the zucchini for 5 minutes, just to take the raw edge off them. Cool a little, then put in the food processor together with the eggs, yogurt cheese, and seasoning. Process until the zucchini is chopped but not too finely. Stir in the chopped pepper and Parmesan. Lightly grease four individual ramekins and divide the mixture between them. Place the ramekins in a roasting pan and fill half of the pan with hot water. Bake in the preheated oven for 30 minutes.

While the timbales are cooking, make the tomato coulis. Score the tops of the tomatoes with a knife and plunge into boiling water for a couple of minutes, then skin them and chop roughly. Put the chopped tomatoes, tomato purée, olive oil, and seasoning in the blender and blend until the mixture looks like a chunky soup. Then pass through a sieve to achieve a smooth texture.

When the timbales are ready, run the tip of a knife around the inside of each ramekin and carefully turn the timbales out onto heated plates, drizzle round a little tomato coulis and garnish with whole basil leaves.

Calories 164 ▸ Protein 7g ▸ Carbohydrates 13g ▸ Fiber 4g ▸ Sugar—Total 7g ▸ Fat—Total 11g ▸
Saturated Fat 2g ▸ Vitamin C 63mg ▸ Magnesium 59mg

▶ Zucchini are easy to digest, mildly laxative, and diuretic. They are also useful for the relief of bladder and kidney infections, and are recommended for people with diabetes.

buckwheat blinis
with guacamole and salsa

■ ■ ■

SERVES 4 ▶ TIME TAKEN: 1¾ hours

*B*linis are little yeast pancakes, traditionally eaten in Russia with sour cream and caviar. This recipe may be less luxurious, but it's very good all the same.

for the blinis:
1 teaspoon fresh yeast (or ½ teaspoon dried)
1 cup mixed soy milk and water, lukewarm
¼ cup buckwheat flour
¼ cup brown-rice flour
pinch sea salt
1 organic free-range egg, separated
1 tablespoon extra-virgin olive oil

for the guacamole:
1 large avocado
½ small onion
1 garlic clove
½ lime, juiced
sea salt and freshly ground black pepper

for the salsa:
2 tomatoes, skinned and chopped
1 small onion, chopped finely
½ teaspoon ground cumin
½ lime, juiced
2 tablespoons chopped fresh coriander
pinch sea salt
Tabasco sauce to taste
4 sprigs fresh coriander to garnish

Protein 10%
Carbohydrate 41%
Fat 49%
GI: medium
GL: medium

Dissolve the yeast in the soy milk and water and leave for 10 minutes or so to activate. If using dried yeast, follow the manufacturer's instructions. Sift the two flours and salt together in a bowl. Pour in the yeast mixture, egg yolk, and olive oil and mix well. Cover and leave in a warm place to proof for about an hour, until risen and bubbly.

While the batter is rising, make the guacamole: chop the onion and garlic finely together. Mash the avocado and add the remaining ingredients.

To make the salsa, put all the ingredients in a bowl and stir to combine.

When the batter has risen, whisk the egg white and fold it into the batter. Then, heat a little olive oil in a small frying pan and make 8 pancakes, using about 2 tablespoons batter for each, frying them for about 3 minutes each side. Keep warm.

To serve, put 2 blinis per person on individual plates with a dollop of guacamole on each and a spoonful of salsa on the side. Garnish each serving with a sprig of coriander.

PER SERVING

Calories 258 ▶ Protein 7g ▶ Carbohydrates 28g ▶ Sugar—Total 5g ▶ Fiber 6g ▶ Fat—Total 15g ▶ Saturated Fat 2g ▶ Vitamin C 26mg ▶ Magnesium 53mg

---

▶ Buckwheat is beneficial for people with diabetes for a number of reasons. It has a low GI (although buckwheat flour is higher than whole buckwheat grains), and it contains chiro-inositol, which appears to prompt cells to become more insulin-sensitive. It also contains rutin, which aids circulation. Avocado is a good source of the fat-soluble vitamin E.

chicory, apple, and crab with a lime dressing

■ ■ ■

SERVES 4 ► TIME TAKEN: 15 minutes

This recipe was inspired by a delicious salad served to me at the Penhelig Arms in Aberdovey, Wales, where I wrote much of this book. White crab meat comes from the claw of the crab and is tastier than the brown crab meat that comes from the crab's body. You can sometimes get red chicory these days, which would be especially pretty in this salad.

6 ounces cooked white crab meat
2 crisp green apples, such as Granny Smiths
2 heads chicory

for the lime dressing:
1 lime, grated rind and juice
2 tablespoons extra-virgin olive oil
1 teaspoon concentrated apple juice
1 teaspoon wholegrain mustard
sea salt and freshly ground black pepper
whole coriander leaves for garnish

Protein 27%
Carbohydrate 31%
Fat 42%
GI: low
GL: low

Pick over the crab meat. Quarter and core the apples, and cut into thin slices. Separate the chicory leaves. Arrange the chicory leaves like the spokes of a wheel on four individual plates. Arrange the sliced apples attractively on top, and scatter the crab meat over. For the dressing, mix together all the ingredients in a screw top jar and shake well to emulsify. Pour over the salads and serve immediately.

PER SERVING
Calories 161 ► Protein 11g ► Carbohydrates 13g ► Sugar—Total 8g ► Fiber 3g ► Fat—Total 8g ►
Saturated Fat 1g ► Vitamin C 10mg ► Magnesium 8mg

► Chicory contains inulin, which helps in the regulation of blood-sugar levels. It is cleansing to the liver and gallbladder, and beneficial for digestion, the circulatory system, and the blood. It is a good source of calcium, vitamin A, and potassium. As for crab, it contains lots of magnesium, zinc, and copper, all of which are crucial for the formation of many enzymes in the body.

beans
AND grains

chili tofu and coconut stew

■ ■

SERVES 6 ▶ **TIME TAKEN:** 20 minutes

Tofu, being a curd made from soy beans, has its place here in the beans chapter. This recipe is a good introduction to tofu as it contains a variety of tastes and textures in which no single ingredient dominates, though the amount of chili might be too strong for some palates. If you do not like hot food, seek out mild chilis and only use one.

for the coconut broth:
2 cups coconut milk
2 cups vegetable stock (see page 230)
1 lime, grated rind only
1 pound sweet potato, peeled and sliced
1 pound bok choy, sliced

Protein 16%
Carbohydrate 26%
Fat 58%
GI: low
GL: low

for the tofu:
2 red chilies, seeded and chopped
3 tablespoons shoyu sauce
1 tablespoon grated root ginger
1 tablespoon concentrated apple juice
2 tablespoons lime juice
1 pound tofu, drained, pressed and cut into small cubes
3 tablespoons thai basil leaves, or ordinary
    basil leaves, torn

To make the coconut broth, put the coconut milk, vegetable stock, and grated lime rind in a large pan over medium heat. Add the sweet potato and cook, covered, for 10 minutes. Add the bok choy and cook for a further 4–5 minutes, or until the vegetables are tender. Keep warm.

Cook the tofu at the same time. Place the chilies, shoyu, ginger, concentrated apple juice, and lime juice in a frying pan over medium heat and cook for 3 minutes. Add the cubed tofu to the pan and cook for one minute on each side or until coated with the chili sauce.

To serve, spoon the coconut broth, sweet potato, and bok choy into deep bowls. Top with the chili tofu and sprinkle with basil leaves.

▶ There are various kinds of soy sauce on the market. The only two I use are shoyu and tamari, both of which are naturally brewed. Shoyu contains wheat and is a little lighter ▸ it also stands up better to cooking than tamari, which has a stronger taste. I use tamari at the end of a dish as a condiment rather than as a cooking ingredient. Avoid commercial soy sauces altogether—these often have added salt or monosodium glutamate.

tofu fajitas

■ ■ ■

SERVES 6 ▶ TIME TAKEN: 1 hour

*Y*ou can buy ready-made flour tortillas, but make sure they are made from whole wheat flour and not refined white flour. If you can't find ready-made ones, it's not difficult to make your own, just a bit time-consuming.

for the tortillas:
¾ cup organic whole wheat flour
pinch of sea salt
2 tablespoons extra-virgin olive oil
5 tablespoons warm water

Protein 20%
Carbohydrate 30%
Fat 50%
GI: medium
GL: medium

for the filling:
2 tablespoons extra-virgin olive oil
1 large onion, sliced
1 red pepper, seeded and sliced thinly
1 green pepper, seeded and sliced thinly
1 hot chili pepper, seeded and finely diced
4 ounces mushrooms, sliced
1 pound tofu, drained and pressed to extract excess moisture
sea salt

any of the following as a garnish:
plain or soy yogurt
chopped fresh coriander
chopped fresh tomatoes
sliced avocado
scallions

For the tortillas, combine the flour and salt in a bowl. Add the oil, and gradually add enough water to make a soft dough. Divide the dough into 6 pieces. Shape each piece into a small, smooth ball. Flatten the balls with a rolling pin, and roll each one out on a lightly floured surface to a circle about 7 inches in diameter. Roll out no more than two at a time to prevent their drying out. Cook in an ungreased heavy frying pan or direct on a hot griddle until the top is bubbled and the underside flecked with brown. Turn it over and cook the other side. Stack the cooked tortillas in a warm place and cover with a cloth.

Heat the olive oil in a large frying pan over medium-high heat, then add the onions. Sauté, stirring, until the onions are translucent. Stir in the peppers and mushrooms and sauté until the vegetables begin to soften, about 5 minutes. Add the tofu and stir-fry for 5 minutes more. Season with salt to taste and serve in the tortillas.

Serve the fajitas with yogurt, chopped coriander, chopped fresh tomatoes, avocado, scallions, or a combination of these.

PER SERVING (WITHOUT GARNISH)
Calories 383 ▸ Protein 20g ▸ Carbohydrates 30g ▸ Fiber 6g ▸ Sugar—Total 5g ▸ Fat—Total 22g ▸ Saturated Fat 4g ▸ Vitamin C 113mg ▸ Magnesium 85mg

▸ A number of studies have confirmed that 25–50 g soy protein, such as that found in tofu, eaten daily for four weeks, can decrease LDL, the "bad" cholesterol, by as much as 10–20 percent in people with raised blood cholesterol.

black bean cakes
with tomato and orange salsa

■ ■ ■

SERVES 6 ▶ TIME TAKEN: 2 hours plus soaking

*B*lack turtle beans are actually a small variety of black haricot beans, worth searching out as they have a delicious taste and keep their shape well when cooked. They are not the same as Asian black beans, which are actually a type of soybean fermented with salt and used as a flavoring. These spicy bean cakes are typical of Caribbean and Central American cuisine. They would traditionally be fried, but I bake them to cut down on fat. The orange gives an unusual sweetness to the salsa.

1 cup black turtle beans, soaked overnight
1 thumb-sized piece of ginger root, peeled

for the salsa:
1 orange, peeled, sliced, and cut into small pieces
2 large tomatoes, peeled and diced
2 scallions, finely chopped
1 tablespoon torn basil leaves
1 garlic clove, finely chopped
1 lime, juice only
1 tablespoon extra-virgin olive oil
1 small fresh chili, finely chopped
sea salt to taste

for the bean cakes:
2 organic free-range eggs
½ cup ground almonds
1 tablespoon extra-virgin olive oil
1 medium onion, finely chopped
2 garlic cloves, finely chopped
1 stick celery, thinly sliced
2 teaspoons ground cumin
1 teaspoon ground allspice
pinch of cayenne pepper, or to taste
sea salt and freshly ground black pepper

Protein 18%
Carbohydrate 44%
Fat 38%
GI: low
GL: low

First, cook the beans. Drain them of their soaking water, cover with fresh water, and add the ginger. Bring to a boil, then simmer steadily for about 1¼ hours until the beans are tender. Drain, discard the piece of ginger and leave the beans to cool.

Meanwhile, for the salsa, combine all the ingredients in a bowl. Taste and adjust seasoning as necessary. Set aside for the flavors to mingle while you prepare the bean cakes.

Mash the beans coarsely with a potato masher until they start sticking together. Alternatively you could purée them in the processor, but if you do this only purée about a quarter of the beans and leave the rest whole. Put the mashed beans in a large bowl and add the beaten eggs and ground almonds.

Heat the olive oil in a pan over medium heat. Add the onion, garlic, and celery and sauté until very tender and beginning to brown, about 10 minutes. Stir in the cumin, allspice, and cayenne, and cook for another minute or two.

Stir the sautéed vegetables into the bean mixture and season to taste. Stir to mix well.

Preheat the oven to 375°F. Lightly oil a baking sheet. Using your hands, form the bean mixture into 12 round cakes, flattening them with a palette knife, and place on the baking sheet. Bake in the preheated oven for 10 minutes, then take them out, turn them over and bake for 10 more minutes. Serve the bean cakes with salsa on the side.

PER SERVING

Calories 288 ▸ Protein 14g ▸ Carbohydrates 33g ▸ Fiber 11g ▸ Sugar—Total 8g ▸ Fat—Total 12g ▸ Saturated Fat 2g ▸ Vitamin C 44mg ▸ Magnesium 110mg

▶ All of this dish, except the final baking, can be prepared in advance. Serve the bean cakes and salsa with a large green salad.

butter beans with fennel

■ ■ ■

SERVES 6 ▶ **TIME TAKEN:** 2 hours

I've come quite late to butter beans, having been force-fed them as a child, but now regard them as one of my favorite beans. They must be cooked well, until they melt in the mouth but still hold their shape. This dish could be served as an accompaniment to fish or chicken, or as a light meal in its own right.

1½ cups butter beans, soaked overnight
1 thumb-sized piece of ginger root, peeled
3 tablespoons extra-virgin olive oil
2 tablespoons fennel seeds
3 garlic cloves, chopped
2 large onions, cut into wedges
2 fennel roots, trimmed and cut into wedges through the root
1 lemon, juice only
sea salt and freshly ground black pepper
2 tablespoons fresh parsley, chopped
1 tablespoon fresh chives, chopped
1 tablespoon fresh dill, chopped

Protein 17%
Carbohydrate 56%
Fat 27%
GI: low
GL: low

Drain the butter beans of their soaking water and put in a large pan with cold water to cover. Add the ginger. Bring to a boil, reduce the heat, cover, and cook for 1–1½ hours, or until tender. Drain, reserving 1½ cups of the cooking liquid.

Heat 2 tablespoons of the olive oil in a large pan over gentle heat. Add the fennel seeds, garlic and onions, and sauté for 5–10 minutes until softened. Add the fennel together with the reserved cooking liquid, and cook for 10–15 minutes, until the fennel is tender but still has some "bite." There should still be a little liquid left.

Add the drained beans, the remainder of the olive oil, lemon juice, and seasoning. Reheat until piping hot and serve sprinkled liberally with the fresh herbs.

PER SERVING

Calories 254 ▶ Protein 11g ▶ Carbohydrates 37g ▶ Fiber 12g ▶ Sugar—Total 7g ▶ Fat—Total 8g ▶ Saturated Fat 1g ▶ Vitamin C 16mg ▶ Magnesium 74mg

---

▶ Butter beans are believed to neutralize acidity in the stomach that arises from a meat-rich diet. Like all beans, they have cholesterol-lowering and blood pressure-lowering properties as well, probably as a result of the protein and fiber they contain.

chana dal with spinach

■ ■ ■

SERES 4 ▶ TIME TAKEN: 1¼ hours

*T*his recipe comes from Jane Sen, who is the Dietary Advisor to the Bristol Cancer Help Centre, where I have attended a course in nutrition for cancer. Jane uses yellow split peas, but the substitution of chana dal makes this dish very low GI and therefore even more suitable for people with diabetes.

1¼ cups chana dal, washed and soaked overnight
4 cups vegetable stock (see page 229)
1 teaspoon turmeric
2 tablespoons extra-virgin olive oil
2 bay leaves
1 teaspoon black mustard seeds
1 teaspoon cumin seeds
1 cinnamon stick
4 whole cloves
1 inch fresh ginger root, peeled and grated
3 cups spinach leaves, washed and roughly chopped

Protein 21%
Carbohydrate 53%
Fat 26%
GI: very low
GL: very low

Drain the chana dal. Put it in a large pan with the stock. Bring to a boil over medium heat. Add the turmeric. Reduce the heat and simmer, covered, for an hour until the dal is tender. Remove from the heat.

Heat the oil in a large pan, add the bay leaves, mustard seeds, cumin seeds, cinnamon, and cloves and cook until the spices release their aroma. Add the grated ginger and chopped spinach. Stir to coat with the oil and spices. When the spinach has wilted, stir in the chana dal. Reduce the heat and cook for 3 minutes or so, then serve hot with brown basmati rice.

PER SERVING

Calories 295 ▶ Protein 16g ▶ Carbohydrates 40g ▶ Fiber 16g ▶ Sugar—Total 8g ▶ Fat—Total 9g ▶ Saturated Fat 1g ▶ Vitamin C 15mg ▶ Magnesium 121mg

chana dal with coconut and whole spices

■ ■ ■

SERVES 4 ▶ **TIME TAKEN:** 1¼ hours plus soaking

---

*T*his is a delicious Bengali dish that I have adapted from diabetes journalist David Mendosa's comprehensive list of chana dal recipes. It is quite sweet, due to the raisins and coconut, but not cloying. Please don't be put off by the long list of ingredients. It really is worth using whole spices here instead of a premixed curry powder. You can buy chana dal in Asian shops or try the gourmet aisle of your local supermarket.

1½ cups chana dal, washed, then soaked overnight
1 teaspoon turmeric
1 thumb-sized piece of ginger root, peeled
1 whole fresh green chili
½ teaspoon sea salt
3 teaspoons ground cumin
3 tablespoons raisins
2 tablespoons coconut oil
1 bay leaf, crumbled
1 whole dried red chili
6 cardamon pods
1 cinnamon stick
4 whole cloves
½ teaspoon black mustard seeds
1 tablespoon chopped fresh green chili (or to taste)
3 tablespoons dried coconut
1 teaspoon garam masala
lemon wedges and whole coriander leaves, to serve

Protein 17%
Carbohydrate 50%
Fat 34%
GI: very low
GL: very low

Drain the chana dal. Put it in a large pan with 5½ cups water. Bring to a boil over medium heat. Add the turmeric, ginger, and whole green chili. Simmer, covered, for an hour or until the dal is very tender and breaks easily when pressed between thumb and index finger. Stir the dal often, adding 1 to 2 tablespoons of hot water if it starts to stick to the bottom. Discard the whole chili and ginger. Add salt and cumin and remove from the heat.

Purée a cupful (about 6 ounces) of the dal mixture in a blender, adding a little water if necessary. Return to the pan and add the raisins. Bring to a simmer, then keep warm.

Heat the coconut oil in a small pan over medium low heat. Add the bay leaf and red chili and cook until the chili darkens. Add the cardamom, cinnamon, and cloves and fry for 5 seconds. Add the black mustard seeds and fry for another few seconds. Turn the heat to low, add the chopped green chili and coconut and cook for a few seconds, stirring constantly. Remove from the heat. Add this spice mixture to the dal and simmer for 2 to 3 more minutes. Remove from the heat and stir in the garam masala. Garnish with lemon wedges, sprinkle with whole coriander leaves, and serve hot.

PER SERVING

Calories 384 ▸ Protein 17g ▸ Carbohydrates 50g ▸ Sugar—Total 12g ▸ Fiber 19g ▸ Fat—Total 15g ▸ Saturated Fat 12g ▸ Vitamin C 28mg ▸ Magnesium 82mg

▸ David Mendosa suggests serving this over a bed of half rice and half pearl barley, accompanied by chutney.

lentil and sweet potato curry
with broccoli

■ ■ ■

SERVES 4 ▶ **TIME TAKEN:** 1 hour

*U*se green or brown lentils for this dish. The red lentils disintegrate on cooking whereas
you want the lentils to stay intact. This curry is quite substantial—more of a main meal
than a side dish.

⅔ cup green or brown lentils

2 tablespoons extra-virgin olive oil

1 onion, peeled and thinly sliced

2 garlic cloves, peeled and finely chopped

1 inch fresh ginger root, peeled and finely chopped

½ fresh green chili, seeded and finely chopped

1 teaspoon cumin seeds

1 teaspoon coriander seeds, lightly crushed

½ teaspoon turmeric

2 sweet potatoes, peeled and cut into chunks

sea salt to taste

2 14-ounce cans chopped tomatoes

1 cup broccoli, broken into small florets and lightly steamed

> Protein 21%
> Carbohydrate 53%
> Fat 26%
> GI: medium
> GL: low

Wash the lentils, put them in a pan and cover with cold water. Bring to a boil, reduce the
heat, and simmer until tender—about 20 minutes. Drain and reserve.

Heat the oil in a large pan, and sauté the onion, garlic, ginger, and chili over a low heat
until softened but not browned—5–8 minutes. Add the spices and cook for another 3
minutes or so, stirring from time to time, until the spices release their aroma. Add the
sweet potatoes and a little sea salt, and stir. Then add the chopped tomatoes and their
juice, bring to a boil, cover, and simmer for 20 minutes, or until the sweet potato is
nearly tender. Now add the reserved cooked lentils and cook for another 5 minutes. Stir
in the steamed broccoli florets, cover again and leave on a low heat for another couple
of minutes until the broccoli has warmed through. Stir well and serve hot.

PER SERVING

Calories 305 ▶ Protein 13g ▶ Carbohydrates 50g ▶ Fiber 14g ▶ Sugar—Total 10g ▶ Fat—Total 8g ▶
Saturated Fat 1g ▶ Vitamin C 89mg ▶ Magnesium 101mg

▶ Lentils are a valuable food for people with diabetes because they contain both soluble and insoluble fiber that helps to stabilize blood-glucose levels and lower raised blood fats. Their GI is low at 29–30.

fassolada

SERVES 6 ▶ **TIME TAKEN:** 2 hours plus soaking

---

*T*his dish could belong as well in the soup chapter as here. It is a wonderfully comforting winter soup/stew from Greece, where I spent one winter in the 1970s as the guest of a family in Athens. Fassolada (or Fassolatha—the "d" is soft) is typical of the food I ate there in the winter when the Meltemi, the bitter north wind, blew. This makes a large quantity, but you will easily eat it all—it tastes even better the second day.

1½ cups haricot beans or butterbeans, soaked overnight
1 large onion, finely sliced
2 tablespoons extra-virgin olive oil
3 carrots, peeled unless organic, and sliced thickly
4 celery sticks, sliced
3 tablespoons celery leaves, chopped
3 large ripe tomatoes, skinned and chopped
sea salt and freshly ground black pepper

to serve:
6 lemon wedges
2 tablespoons extra-virgin olive oil

Protein 15%
Carbohydrate 54%
Fat 31%
GI: low
GL: low

Drain the beans, rinse well, and put in a large pan with cold water to cover. Bring to a boil, boil hard for 5 minutes, then drain again and throw the water away. (This is the way my Greek hostess dealt with the unfortunate digestive effect beans can sometimes produce.)

Add the onion, carrots, celery, and the chopped leaves, and olive oil. Cover with water. Bring to a simmer and cook for about 1½ hours, adding more water if necessary.

After an hour, add the chopped tomatoes and seasoning. Continue cooking until the beans are tender and the liquid has reduced to a thick sauce.

Adjust the seasoning and serve piping hot in wide shallow bowls with a wedge of lemon and an extra drizzle of olive oil.

PER SERVING

Calories 284 ▶ Protein 11g ▶ Carbohydrates 40g ▶ Fiber 12g ▶ Sugar—Total 10g ▶ Fat—Total 10g ▶ Saturated Fat 1g ▶ Vitamin C 25mg ▶ Magnesium 83mg

---

▶ Haricot beans are a particularly good source of soluble fiber. They also contain more calcium than any of the other legumes.

lentils with olives and anchovies

▪ ▪ ▪

SERVES 4 ▸ **TIME TAKEN:** 30 minutes

---

entils are a versatile and widely used bean. They have a wonderful earthy taste, and go well with the strong flavors of olives and anchovies—truly a taste of the warm South. This dish can be served hot or at room temperature, and is even better the next day.

2 cups brown lentils
2 garlic cloves, peeled
2 2-ounce cans of anchovies, drained and rinsed
6 tablespoons extra-virgin olive oil
½ lemon, juice only
freshly ground black pepper
18–24 black olives, preferably Kalamata
2 tablespoons fresh flat leaf parsley, chopped
2 tablespoons fresh coriander, chopped

Protein 20%
Carbohydrate 38%
Fat 42%
GI: low
GL: low

Wash the lentils and put in a pan with cold water to cover. Bring to a boil and cook for about 20 minutes until tender but still retaining their shape.

Put the garlic and half the anchovies in the blender with the olive oil and blend to a smooth purée. Chop the remaining anchovies and tip into a small saucepan together with the garlic and anchovy purée. Heat gently.

When the lentils are cooked, drain and put in a serving bowl. Add the anchovy mixture and toss well. Add the lemon juice and pepper and taste—you may require more lemon juice. Mix in the olives and chopped parsley and coriander, and serve hot.

PER SERVING
Calories 566 ▸ Protein 27g ▸ Carbohydrates 54g ▸ Fiber 13g ▸ Sugar—Total 4g ▸ Fat—Total 27g ▸
Saturated Fat 3g ▸ Vitamin C 6mg ▸ Magnesium 17mg

▶ Both lentils and anchovies are very good sources of iron. Anchovies contain more protein, gram for gram, than any other oily fish, together with loads of calcium and vitamin B_{12}. This is important as vitamin B_{12} is needed for the production of red blood cells and DNA and is involved in maintaining the health of the nervous system.

barley bread

■ ■ ■

Makes 1 loaf, approximately 15 slices

*B*arley flour is low in gluten, so that a loaf made with all barley flour will be dense and heavy, and its earthy flavor is an acquired taste. However, I have found by experimenting that using about a ratio of 2:1 wheat and barley flour together with some soaked pearl barley results in a flavorsome loaf with a relatively low glycemic index (for bread, that is). There is no fat in this loaf so it should be eaten fresh the day it is made, though it's fine for toast the next day.

3½ ounces pearl barley (10½ ounces cooked)
¾ cup lukewarm water
1 teaspoon honey
2 teaspoons active dry yeast
4½ ounces organic strong white bread flour
4 ounces barley flour
4½ ounces organic stoneground whole grain pastry flour
1½ teaspoons sea salt
1 tablespoon organic barley flakes, for the topping

Protein 14%
Carbohydrate 82%
Fat 4%
GI: medium/high
GL: medium

First, cook the barley for about one hour, until nearly tender but still with some bite. Drain and cool.

Put half the water and the honey into a small bowl. Sprinkle in the yeast and leave in a warm place for 5 minutes. Stir to dissolve.

Mix the three flours and salt in a large bowl. Stir in the soaked and drained pearl barley. Pour in the yeast mixture and most of the rest of the water. Stir well to mix, then add the rest of the water as needed to make a sticky dough.

Turn out the dough onto a work surface sprinkled with barley flour. Knead until smooth. This will take at least 10 minutes.

Place the dough in an oiled bowl and cover with a tea towel. Leave in a warm place to rise until doubled in size, about 2 hours. Turn out and knead again to knock back the dough. Form into a loaf and place in an oiled 1-pound loaf pan. Cover again and leave to proof in a warm place until again doubled in size. The proofing should be quicker this time—about 30–40 minutes.

Preheat the oven to 400°F.

Brush the loaf with water and sprinkle on some barley flakes. Bake for one hour or until the loaf is golden and the base sounds hollow when tapped. Turn out and cool on a wire rack.

Calories 106 ▶ Protein 4g ▶ Carbohydrates 23g ▶ Fiber 4g ▶ Sugar—Total 1g ▶ Fat—Total 1g ▶
Saturated Fat 0g ▶ Vitamin C 0mg ▶ Magnesium 6mg

▶ This bread can also be made successfully in a bread machine, using instant yeast and no honey. Check your bread machine for the proper setting, I use the whole wheat setting on my machine for this bread. Whenever possible, use organic flours for baking. Arrowhead Mills has a variety of organic flours to choose from, and can be found in the baking section of your supermarket or local health-food store.

rye crispbread

Makes 24 crispbreads

This is based on a Swedish recipe for Knäckebröd, which are round fat-free crispbreads, usually made with whole rye grain and wheat flour. Knäckebröd is normally baked at a very high temperature for a short time and then left until thoroughly dry before storing. In Sweden crispbread is often used as a basis for Smørrebrød—Swedish open sandwiches.

12 ounces organic whole rye flour
4 ounces organic rye flakes
1 teaspoon instant yeast
2 tablespoons sesame seed
1 teaspoon sea salt
1 cup lukewarm water

Protein 18%
Carbohydrate 71%
Fat 11%
GI: medium
GL: medium

Place the flour, rye flakes, yeast, sesame seed, and salt in a bowl. Stir in the water until a stiff dough is formed, then turn out onto a floured surface and knead well. Rye dough is hard to knead, but persevere until the dough feels smooth and no longer sticky. Place in an oiled bowl and leave in a warm place until the dough has risen slightly—about one hour.

Turn out the dough and knead again. Roll out as thinly as possible and cut into rectangles or discs. Place these on oiled baking trays and poke holes in the crispbreads with a fork. Cover with a cloth and leave to rise in a warm place for half an hour.

Preheat the oven to its highest setting: 450°F.

Bake the crispbreads for 3–4 minutes, then turn over and bake the other side for a further 2–3 minutes.

Cool on a wire rack and store in an airtight tin.

PER SLICE

Calories 69 ▸ Protein 3g ▸ Carbohydrates 13g ▸ Fiber 3g ▸ Sugar—Total 0g ▸ Fat—Total 1g ▸ Saturated Fat 0g ▸ Vitamin C 0mg ▸ Magnesium 3mg

BY THEIR VERY nature, grains are high in carbohydrate, so it's very difficult to make a grain-based dish yield much less than 50 grams of carbohydrate per serving. However, I have used low-GI grains such as pearl barley, brown rice, and polenta; or foods which are not grains at all, though they cook like grains and are commonly classified as such. These are quinoa, amaranth, wild rice, and buckwheat. Buckwheat in particular has the added advantage of actually increasing insulin sensitivity in people with diabetes. Therefore none of the recipes that follow should have an undue effect on blood glucose. Most of the recipes are designed as light meals for 4 people, but could stretch to feeding 6 people as a side dish.

grains

crispy polenta with wild mushrooms and coriander pesto

◼ ◼ ◼

SERVES 4 ▶ **TIME TAKEN:** 20 minutes plus cooling and drying

---

I think that this is absolutely the best way to serve polenta. Don't worry if you can't find wild mushrooms. You can use any variety of mushrooms instead, or even ordinary white ones. If you use dried wild mushrooms, reconstitute them in hot water as directed on the packet, then use the soaking water instead of vegetable stock.

7 ounces instant polenta
2 tablespoons extra-virgin olive oil
8 ounces mixed wild mushrooms, cleaned and sliced
1 teaspoon chopped fresh rosemary
2 teaspoons chopped fresh thyme
2 garlic cloves, peeled and crushed
freshly ground black pepper
½ cup vegetable stock (see page 229)
3 tablespoons soy cream

Protein 8%
Carbohydrate 13%
Fat 79%
GI: medium
GL: medium

for the coriander pesto
large handful packed fresh coriander leaves
6 tablespoons extra-virgin olive oil
1 garlic clove
¾ cup pine nuts, almonds, or cashews
2 tablespoons lemon juice

Bring 2½ cups of water to boil in a medium saucepan. Pour in the polenta gradually, stirring with a wooden spoon as you do so. Reduce the heat to medium, and cook, stirring constantly, for 5 minutes, until thick. 10 × 12 inch baking sheet, then pour in the cooked polenta so that it makes a layer about ¼ inch thick. Leave to cool completely.

When the polenta is cold, cut it into 12 squares or circles about 3 inches in diameter. Place in a very low oven—150°F—and leave for several hours or overnight to dry out completely. It should become quite crisp.

For the mushrooms, heat the olive oil in a wok or large pan, add the mushrooms, rosemary, thyme, garlic, and seasoning, and stir-fry for 3–4 minutes. Pour in the stock and continue cooking until the stock has reduced by half. Stir in the soy cream and simmer for another 3–4 minutes until thick and creamy.

For the coriander pesto, put the coriander and olive oil in a blender and process until the coriander is finely chopped. Add the rest of the ingredients and process until you have a lumpy paste (you may have to add a little hot water and scrape down the sides of the blender). This can be done in advance.

To assemble the dish, warm the polenta slices, then spread them with coriander pesto. Layer on individual plates with the mushroom mixture and serve warm.

PER SERVING

Calories 406 ▶ Protein 7g ▶ Carbohydrates 14g ▶ Fiber 3g ▶ Sugar—Total 2g ▶ Fat—Total 37g ▶ Saturated Fat 5g ▶ Vitamin C 8mg ▶ Magnesium 52mg

---

▶ The recipe for coriander pesto comes from Karen Watkins of Mineral Check, a company that analyzes hair samples for toxic minerals and trace minerals. Coriander contains selenium and selenium opposes mercury, so Karen recommends that anyone who is found to have high mercury levels should eat two tablespoons a day of this delicious pesto.

creamy baked polenta with roasted vegetables

■ ■ ■

SERVES 6 ▶ **TIME TAKEN:** 1 hour

This is a way to cook polenta that doesn't involve lots of stirring. Don't use the instant polenta for this, but the old-fashioned slow-cook variety. It may take longer to cook, but this way it only requires stirring twice in the hour or so it takes to cook, and it comes out of the oven deliciously creamy.

7 ounces polenta, preferably coarse-ground
3½ cups vegetable stock (see page 229)
2 tablespoons extra-virgin olive oil
1 onion, peeled and chopped
sea salt and black pepper to taste
1 tablespoon fresh flat-leaf parsley, finely chopped
1 tablespoon fresh rosemary, finely chopped
1 tablespoon fresh thyme, finely chopped
3 tablespoons soy cream

for the roasted vegetables:
1 eggplant, sliced
2 medium zucchini, sliced
1 red or yellow pepper, deseeded and cut into chunks
2 tomatoes, quartered
2 garlic cloves, peeled and halved
2 tablespoons extra-virgin olive oil

Protein 7%
Carbohydrate 52%
Fat 41%
GI: medium
GL: medium

Preheat the oven to 350°F.

Mix the polenta and the stock together in a shallow casserole dish, stirring to break up any dry lumps. Bake in the preheated oven for about 40 minutes, then remove from the oven and stir up. It should be soft but fairly thick.

While the polenta is cooking, heat the olive oil in a pan and cook the chopped onions over medium heat, stirring often, until soft and golden brown. When the polenta comes out of the oven, add the onion and stir through, along with the herbs and soy cream.

Return the polenta to the oven for about 10 minutes, then give it one more stir. Adjust the seasoning if necessary, then ladle into bowls or plates.

While the polenta is cooking, prepare the roasted vegetables. Place the eggplant, zucchini, peppers, and garlic in a roasting pan and drizzle with olive oil. Bake in the oven for the same length of time as the polenta.

Serve the polenta straight from the oven with the roasted vegetables on top or on the side.

PER SERVING
Calories 351 ▸ Protein 6g ▸ Carbohydrates 47g ▸ Fiber 7g ▸ Sugar—Total 8g ▸ Fat—Total 16g ▸ Saturated Fat 2g ▸ Vitamin C 50mg ▸ Magnesium 22mg

▶ Corn, from which polenta is made, is suitable for people with gluten intolerance. It is said to be a gentle moderator of the thyroid gland, too.

barley and spring vegetable risotto

■ ■ ■

SERVES 6 ▶ **TIME TAKEN:** 1¼ hours

I have used Parmesan in this risotto, because it does enhance the flavor. If, however, you are avoiding all dairy products, toasted sesame or sunflower seeds make a good and tasty alternative.

2 tablespoons extra-virgin olive oil
1 large onion, peeled and finely chopped
1 garlic clove, finely chopped
1½ cups pearl barley
2 cups white wine
2 cups vegetable stock (see page 229)
¾ cup peas, fresh or frozen
2 small zucchini, thinly sliced
1 bunch of asparagus, trimmed and chopped into ½-inch lengths
    (set aside the asparagus tips)
2 medium tomatoes, peeled, deseeded and chopped
3 tablespoons mint leaves, finely chopped
2 tablespoons parsley, finely chopped
2 tablespoons parmesan cheese, finely grated
sea salt and freshly ground black pepper

Protein 16%
Carbohydrate 59%
Fat 25%
GI: low
GL: low

to serve:
1 tablespoon parmesan, shaved
4 tablespoons pine nuts, lightly toasted
asparagus tips (reserved) blanched in boiling water for 1 minute
1 tablespoon fresh basil leaves, torn

Place the olive oil in a large saucepan over a medium heat. When the oil is hot add the onion and cook until transparent. Add the garlic and barley to the pan and cook, stirring frequently, for 2–3 minutes. Add the white wine and continue to cook and stir until the wine has evaporated.

Meanwhile bring the stock to a boil in a separate saucepan.

Gradually stir a cupful of boiling stock into the barley mixture. Bring the stock to a steady simmer and cook for 50 minutes stirring it regularly, adding the hot stock cupful by cupful until almost all of it has been absorbed. By this time the barley should be tender with a little bite to it. If it is still firm add a little more stock or water and allow it to cook for a further 5–10 minutes.

Stir in the peas, sliced zucchini and chopped asparagus and cook them with the barley for 5–8 minutes until the vegetables are tender.

Remove the risotto from the heat and stir in the mint, parsley, tomatoes, seasoning and Parmesan, and mix it until well distributed.

To serve, spoon the risotto into heated serving bowls and garnish with the reserved asparagus tips, pine nuts, basil, and Parmesan shavings.

PER SERVING

Calories 347 ▶ Protein 12g ▶ Carbohydrates 54g ▶ Fiber 12g ▶ Sugar—Total 8g ▶ Fat—Total 9g ▶ Saturated Fat 2g ▶ Vitamin C 26mg ▶ Magnesium 85mg

▶ Pearl barley is not a whole grain, as the husk has been removed. However, it is extremely useful for people with diabetes as it has a low GI—at 25, it is the lowest of all grains.

barley pilaf with shiitake mushrooms

■ ■ ■

SERVES 4 ▶ **TIME TAKEN:** 1½ hours

*S*hiitake mushrooms have special qualities, being reputed to strengthen the immune system. However, if you can't find them, substitute any fresh mushrooms.

1 cup pearl barley
1 tablespoon extra-virgin olive oil
1 onion, peeled and finely chopped
5 ounces fresh shiitake mushrooms, stemmed and diced
2½ cups japanese stock (see page 232)
1 teaspoon ground cumin
1 tablespoon shoyu
2 tablespoons pine nuts, lightly toasted
2 tablespoons fresh parsley, finely chopped

Protein 12%
Carbohydrate 70%
Fat 18%
GI: medium
GL: medium

for the sauce:
2 cups Japanese stock (see page 232)
3 tablespoons tamari
1 inch piece of ginger root, peeled and grated
2 tablespoons cornstarch

Heat the olive oil in a large saucepan over medium heat and add the chopped onion and shiitake mushrooms. Sauté the vegetables for 2 to 3 minutes. Add the stock and bring to a boil, then add the barley, cumin, and shoyu. Turn the heat down and simmer until the liquid is absorbed and the barley is tender. This will take about 1¼ hours.

To prepare the sauce, place the stock, shoyu, and ginger in a medium saucepan and bring to a boil. Lower the heat. Mix the cornstarch with cold water, and add to the sauce. Stir until the mixture thickens and becomes shiny, about 30 seconds.

Toss the cooked barley with pine nuts and parsley. To serve, pack each serving into a teacup, unmold onto individual plates, and surround with a pool of shiitake mushrooms sauce.

PER SERVING

Calories 314 ▶ Protein 10g ▶ Carbohydrates 57g ▶ Fiber 10g ▶ Sugar—Total 3g ▶ Fat—Total 7g ▶ Saturated Fat 1g ▶ Vitamin C 4mg ▶ Magnesium 76mg

---

▶ This dish is very beneficial for your health for a number of reasons. Shiitake mushrooms are used in Japan to prevent heart disease, build resistance against viruses and disease, and to treat fatigue and viral infections, while the kombu in the Japanese-style stock helps to lower blood pressure and reduce cholesterol levels.

quinoa pilaf with green leaves

■ ■ ■

SERVES 4 ▶ TIME TAKEN: 30 minutes

If you can't find quinoa, you could substitute pearl barley in this pilaff, but it would need considerably more cooking time—about 1¼ hours.

1 cup quinoa
2 cups vegetable stock (see page 229)
3 tablespoons extra-virgin olive oil
4 teaspoons cumin seeds
1 cinnamon stick
1 onion, peeled and finely chopped
1 pound green leaves, such as Swiss chard, beet leaves,
    spring greens, spinach or dark green cabbage leaves, finely shredded
4 tablespoons raisins
sea salt and freshly ground black pepper
1 lemon, finely grated rind and juice
1 large carrot, peeled if not organic, and grated
2 tablespoons fresh coriander, chopped

Protein 11%
Carbohydrate 58%
Fat 31%
GI: medium
GL: medium

Wash the quinoa well as it is coated with a natural substance called saponin, which may taste bitter. Drain thoroughly, then put in a saucepan with the stock. Bring to a boil, lower the heat, cover, and simmer for 15 minutes until nearly tender and most of the liquid is absorbed.

Meanwhile, heat the olive oil in a pan over medium heat and add the chopped onion, cumin seeds, and cinnamon stick. Sauté gently for 5–8 minutes until the onion is soft but not browned. Add the onion, spices, and oil to the simmering quinoa and stir.

Add the shredded green leaves, raisins, seasoning, lemon rind, and juice to the pan, cover tightly and continue cooking for another 5 minutes. When the quinoa is tender and there is no liquid left, stir in the grated carrot, adjust the seasoning, and serve sprinkled with chopped coriander.

PER SERVING
Calories 412 ▶ Protein 11g ▶ Carbohydrates 62g ▶ Fiber 8g ▶ Sugar—Total 13g ▶ Fat—Total 15g ▶
Saturated Fat 2g ▶ Vitamin C 29mg ▶ Magnesium 226mg

▶ Quinoa is not officially a grain at all, but a seed. It is extremely high in fiber, low in fat, and very high in protein. It contains the correct balance of amino acids. The combination of quinoa and greens makes this recipe the richest source of magnesium in the book.

amaranth and lentil cakes

■ ■ ■

SERVES 4 ▶ **TIME TAKEN:** 1 hour

T his dish is based loosely on a traditional Armenian recipe, though traditionally bulgur wheat would have been used rather than amaranth. The cakes go well with a fresh tomato sauce such as that on page 234.

½ cup red lentils
2 cups water
½ cup amaranth
4 tablespoons extra-virgin olive oil
1 medium onion, peeled and finely chopped
½ red pepper, seeded and finely chopped
½ green pepper, seeded and finely chopped
6 scallions, finely chopped
2 tablespoons fresh flat leaf parsley, finely chopped
1 teaspoon paprika
2 tablespoons fresh mint, chopped
sea salt and freshly ground black pepper
olive oil spray for frying

Protein 13%
Carbohydrate 45%
Fat 42%
GI: medium
GL: medium

Put the lentils, amaranth, and water into a large saucepan. Bring to a boil, then lower the heat and simmer for 20 minutes until the lentils and amaranth are tender and the water has been absorbed. Stir in two tablespoonfuls of olive oil and set aside.

Heat the remaining olive oil in a frying pan and sauté the chopped onion for about 10 minutes, until golden, stirring frequently. In a large bowl, mix together the lentils, amaranth, and onions. Add the red and green peppers, scallions, parsley, paprika, mint and seasoning. Mix well with your hands, then form the mixture into 12 equal-sized patties.

Spray a large frying pan with olive-oil spray and fry the patties over moderate heat, turning once, until golden.

PER SERVING

Calories 327 ▶ Protein 11g ▶ Carbohydrates 37g ▶ Fiber 9g ▶ Sugar—Total 4g ▶ Fat—Total 16g ▶ Saturated Fat 2g ▶ Vitamin C 49mg ▶ Magnesium 71mg

▶ Amaranth was a staple in the diets of pre-Columbian Aztecs, who believed it had supernatural powers and incorporated it into their religious ceremonies. Amaranth has a "sticky" texture that contrasts with the fluffier texture of most grains and care should be taken not to overcook it as it can become gummy. Amaranth seed is high in protein (15–18 percent) and contains respectable amounts of lysine and methionine, two essential amino acids that are not frequently found in grains. It is high in fiber and contains calcium, iron, potassium, phosphorus, and vitamins A and C. The fiber content of amaranth is three times that of wheat and its iron content, five times more than wheat. It contains twice as much calcium as milk

Amaranth also contains tocotrienols (a form of vitamin E), which have cholesterol-lowering activity.

wild and brown rice with whole spices

SERVES 6 ▶ **TIME TAKEN:** 1 hour 20 minutes

⅓ cup wild rice
3 tablespoons extra-virgin olive oil
2 onions, peeled and chopped
1½ cups brown rice
1 cup cashew nuts, roughly chopped
3 garlic cloves, peeled and crushed
1 inch fresh ginger root, peeled and grated
fresh red chili, deseeded and finely chopped
2 teaspoons coriander seeds, lightly crushed
1 teaspoon cumin seeds
6 whole cloves
1 stick of cinnamon, broken into 2 or 3 pieces
½ teaspoon turmeric
2½ cups vegetable stock (see page 229)
2 cups French beans, halved
large bunch of coriander, chopped
freshly ground black pepper

to serve:
6 wedges of lemon, grilled
plain or soy yogurt

Protein 10%
Carbohydrate 55%
Fat 35%
GI: medium
GL: medium

Wash the wild rice and put in a pan with water to cover. Bring to a boil, reduce to a simmer and cook, covered for about 30 minutes until just tender. Drain and set aside.

Meanwhile, heat the olive oil in a large heavy pan. Add the onions and fry gently until golden. Stir in the brown rice, cashews, garlic, and all the spices, and cook, stirring, for 2–3 minutes, until the rice starts to look transparent and everything is coated with olive oil.

Add the stock and bring to a boil. Reduce the heat, cover tightly, and cook gently for about 30 minutes until the rice is tender and all the stock has been absorbed. Add the French beans, the drained wild rice and most of the coriander and cook for a further 5–6 minutes, until the beans are tender. Season to taste and serve garnished with the remaining coriander, grilled slices of lemon, and yogurt on the side.

PER SERVING
Calories 423 ▶ Protein 11g ▶ Carbohydrates 60g ▶ Fiber 7g ▶ Sugar—Total 6g ▶ Fat—Total 17g ▶ Saturated Fat 3g ▶ Vitamin C 25mg ▶ Magnesium 147mg

▶ At 57 and 55 respectively, wild rice and brown rice are medium-GI grains (though wild rice is not really a grain, or even a kind of rice, but is actually the seed of an annual aquatic grass). The highly nutritious characteristics of the grain are consistent throughout the kernel, rather than being contained only in the outer layer of bran. Brown rice in particular supplies potassium, which is needed for retaining water balance and keeping blood pressure down. Although neither wild nor brown rice contain any sodium, or very little, this dish should need no added salt because of the strong flavor of the spices.

buckwheat with roasted eggplant

■ ■ ■

SERVES 4 ▶ **TIME TAKEN:** 1 hour, 10 minutes

*K*asha or buckwheat comes as small triangular-shaped grains, and is actually a member *of the grass family and not a wheat at all, and has therefore the supreme advantage of being gluten-free. You can buy buckwheat roasted or unroasted. I usually buy the unroasted sort, which is a greenish color, and roast it myself. If you buy the roasted kind, you do not need to sauté it first, but just wash it and put in the pan with the stock, garlic, and bay leaf.*

1 large eggplant, cut in half vertically
1 red pepper, deseeded and cut in half vertically
3 tablespoons extra-virgin olive oil
1 cup buckwheat
2 garlic cloves, peeled and finely chopped
2¼ cups vegetable stock (see page 229)
1 bay leaf
1 lemon, juice only
1 teaspoon chopped fresh sage
1 teaspoon chopped fresh thyme
2 tablespoons torn fresh basil leaves

Protein 12%
Carbohydrate 62%
Fat 26%
GI: medium
GL: medium

Preheat the oven to 400°F.

Put the halved eggplant and pepper on a baking sheet. Sprinkle with one tablespoon of olive oil, then bake in the preheated oven for 25–30 minutes, or until just starting to char. Take out of the oven and put the vegetables into a paper bag, fold to seal, and set aside.

In a large frying pan, heat the oil over medium heat. Add the buckwheat and sauté for about five minutes, until fragrant. Add the garlic, stock, and bay leaf, then cover and simmer until all the liquid is absorbed—this should take about 15 minutes.

Add the lemon juice, sage, and thyme to the buckwheat and stir well.

Remove the pepper and eggplant from the bag and remove the charred skins with your fingers. Chop the vegetables, add them to the buckwheat and stir well.

Remove the bay leaf, then place the mixture in a serving dish and serve warm sprinkled liberally with the torn basil leaves.

▸ Buckwheat is one of the most beneficial grains for people with diabetes. It is not related to wheat, and is not even, technically, a grain, but a fruit. Several studies have shown that buckwheat may help increase insulin sensitivity. A component of buckwheat called chiro-inositol, which is relatively high in buckwheat but rarely found in other foods, appears to prompt cells to become more insulin-sensitive. In animal studies it has been shown to lower blood-glucose levels, and it has the added benefit of containing good levels of B vitamins and omega-3 fatty acids, as well as acting as a prebiotic, encouraging the growth of "friendly" bacteria in the digestive tract.

buckwheat noodles with tofu, tahini sauce and vegetables

■ ■ ■

SERVES 4 ▶ TIME TAKEN: 1 hour 10 minutes

Like amaranth, buckwheat is not strictly a grain or cereal at all, but the seed of a flowering thistle. However, because its consistency and nutrient content is similar to a cereal, it is treated like one.

½ pound tofu

1 piece of fresh ginger root, about 1 inch,
    peeled and grated

2 tablespoons tamari

1 tablespoon rice vinegar

8 ounces soba noodles (buckwheat noodles)

1 tablespoon extra-virgin olive oil

1 medium onion, peeled and finely chopped

2 carrots, peeled unless organic, and sliced thinly

1 garlic clove, finely chopped

2 small zucchini, sliced thinly

2 tablespoons fresh coriander leaves, chopped

for the sauce:
2 tablespoons tahini
2 tablespoons tamari

Protein 22%
Carbohydrate 53%
Fat 25%
GI: medium
GL: low

First, marinate the tofu: drain, rinse, and press it dry, then cut into ½-inch cubes and place in a bowl. Mix together the grated ginger, tamari, and rice vinegar and pour over the tofu, stirring gently to coat. Leave to marinate for at least 30 minutes.

Heat the olive oil in a wide pan, and sauté the onion for 5–8 minutes until soft but not browned. Add the carrot and garlic and continue to sauté for another 3 minutes. Add the zucchini and cook for another minute or two.

Finally, stir in the chopped coriander. Keep warm.

Drain the tofu and discard the marinade. Grill the tofu under a hot grill, turning once or twice, until golden.

For the sauce, mix together the tahini, tamari, and 6 tablespoons of water in a small bowl.

Cook the soba noodles according to the directions on the packet—they need considerably less time that wheat pasta—about 5–6 minutes. Be careful not to let them overcook or they can become gummy. Drain well, then return to the pan and stir in the tahini sauce, the grilled tofu cubes, and the vegetables. Serve in heated bowls.

PER SERVING

Calories 407 ▶ Protein 23g ▶ Carbohydrates 57g ▶ Fiber 5g ▶ Sugar—Total 5g ▶ Fat—Total 12g ▶ Saturated Fat 2g ▶ Vitamin C 9mg ▶ Magnesium 73mg

▶ This is the highest protein grain dish in this section, mainly due to the combination of tofu and buckwheat. If you do not like tofu, substituting cubed skinless chicken breast would have the same effect.

buckwheat pancakes with ratatouille

■ ■ ■

SERVES 4 ▶ TIME TAKEN: 1¼ hours

*T*hese pancakes are extremely versatile; they can be served with a savory accompaniment as here, or with some guacamole or salsa, or at breakfast time rolled round some poached apple and a sprinkling of cinnamon. They can be made with all buckwheat flour, but I have added a little mixed gluten-free flour to lighten the mixture.

There are almost as many versions of ratatouille as there are cooks. This is my current favorite in which the vegetables are roasted first.

for the pancakes:
¾ cup buckwheat flour
¼ cup unbleached white flour or gluten-free flour
1 large, organic free-range egg
1 tablespoon flaxseeds, ground finely
1 cup soy, almond or rice milk

Protein 13%
Carbohydrate 54%
Fat 33%
GI: low
GL: medium

for the ratatouille:
1 large onion, peeled and sliced downward, from stem to root
1 medium eggplant, cut into ¾-inch chunks
1 sprig fresh rosemary
2 tablespoons extra-virgin olive oil
1 garlic clove, peeled and chopped
3 small zucchini, sliced into ½-inch slices
1 red pepper, cored, deseeded and cut into ¾-inch squares
1 pound fresh ripe tomatoes, peeled, deseeded and chopped
sea salt and freshly ground black pepper to taste
torn fresh basil leaves and 4 sprigs of basil, for garnish

First, mix the batter for the pancakes. Put all the ingredients into the blender and blend to mix, scraping down the sides of the goblet to make sure the mixture is well amalgamated. Set aside for at least half an hour, then give another whiz before using.

Meanwhile, make the ratatouille. Preheat oven to 400°F.

Spray a roasting pan with olive oil and place the onion and eggplant in it. Strip the rosemary leaves off their stem and add to the pan. Sprinkle a little olive oil over the vegetables, then roast for 10 minutes. Add the zucchini and peppers and roast for another 15 minutes.

Put the chopped tomatoes in a pan and add the roasted vegetables. Season to taste, then cook for 15 minutes over a low heat.

For the pancakes, heat a heavy bottomed frying pan, then oil lightly. I find my olive-oil spray invaluable for this, as it uses the minimum of oil. Pour a little batter into the pan and swirl around until the bottom is entirely covered. Cook until a few bubbles appear on the surface, then flip it over and cook the other side for a couple of minutes. Stack the pancakes on a warm plate and cover with a tea towel while you make the remaining pancakes.

To serve, fold the pancakes into quarters to make a cone shape, then fill the cone with ratatouille. Serve sprinkled with torn basil leaves and a sprig of basil.

PER SERVING

Calories 304 ▸ Protein 11g ▸ Carbohydrates 44g ▸ Fiber 8g ▸ Sugar—Total 12g ▸ Fat—Total 12g ▸ Saturated Fat 2g ▸ Vitamin C 83mg ▸ Magnesium 129mg

amaranth with spinach, tomato, and mushroom sauce

▪ ▪ ▪

SERVES 4 ▶ TIME TAKEN: 30 minutes

*A*nother *amaranth dish, which I usually serve as an all-in-one accompaniment to fish or chicken. As it contains grain, vegetables, and sauce, you don't really need to add anything else.*

8 ounces amaranth

2 cups water

1 tablespoon extra-virgin olive oil

5 cups spinach

1 medium onion, peeled and finely chopped

1 garlic clove, peeled and finely chopped

2 ripe tomatoes, skinned and coarsely chopped

8 ounces chestnut mushrooms, sliced

1 teaspoon dried basil

sea salt and pepper to taste

Protein 16%
Carbohydrate 62%
Fat 22%
GI: high
GL: medium

Add amaranth to boiling water, bring back to a boil, reduce heat, cover, and simmer for 18–20 minutes.

While the amaranth is cooking, stem and wash the spinach, and cook in the water still clinging to the leaves until wilted. Drain and cool. Heat the olive oil in a frying pan over medium heat and add the garlic and onion. Sauté until soft but not browned. Add the chopped tomatoes, mushrooms, dried basil, and seasoning. Cook for 20 minutes or so until the tomatoes have cooked down, stirring occasionally. Chop the drained spinach and add to the tomato mixture. Continue cooking for another few minutes.

Serve the amaranth hot with the sauce spooned on top or stirred in.

PER SERVING

Calories 293 ▶ Protein 12g ▶ Carbohydrates 47g ▶ Fiber 11g ▶ Sugar—Total 5g ▶ Fat—Total 8g ▶ Saturated Fat 1g ▶ Vitamin C 22mg ▶ Magnesium 204mg

---

▶ The GI of amaranth has not yet been tested. However, popped Indian amaranth, eaten with milk, has been found to have a GI of 97, so it should be treated with caution until you know how it affects your own blood glucose. It is probably wise to eat it as a side dish with, say, grilled fish, rather than trying it on its own.

poultry
AND **fish**

chicken in coconut milk

■ ■ ■

SERVES 4 ▶ **TIME TAKEN:** 25 minutes

I always insist on organic, free-range chicken. There are so many questionable practices in the poultry industry that it is worth paying the extra for good quality and peace of mind, even if it means you don't eat chicken as often as you have been used to.

4 organic chicken breasts, skinned and sliced diagonally
1 tablespoon coconut oil
1 inch piece of ginger root, peeled and cut into fine julienne
1 fresh red chili, seeded and finely chopped
1 garlic clove, peeled and finely chopped
1½ cups coconut milk
1½ cups chicken stock (see page 230)
1 large handful fresh basil, torn
1 cup fresh mung bean sprouts, washed

Protein 60%
Carbohydrate 8%
Fat 32%
GI: low
GL: low

Heat the coconut oil in a wok or large frying pan over medium heat. Toss in the sliced chicken and stir-fry until sealed. Remove the chicken and set aside. Add the ginger, chili, garlic, coconut milk, and chicken stock and bring to a boil. Turn down the heat and simmer for 5 minutes.

Return the chicken to the pan and cook for another 5 minutes, or until the chicken has cooked through. Stir in the torn basil leaves. Put the bean sprouts into heated serving bowls and spoon the chicken and coconut milk sauce over the top. Serve very hot.

PER SERVING

Calories 197 ▶ Protein 29g ▶ Carbohydrates 4g ▶ Fiber 1g ▶ Sugar—Total 1g ▶ Fat—Total 7g ▶ Saturated Fat 4g ▶ Vitamin C 33mg ▶ Magnesium 58mg

▶ Mung bean sprouts are thought to be beneficial as an antidiabetic, low–glycemic index food, rich in antioxidants.

chicken-in-yogurt
and pumpkin-seed sauce

■ ■ ■

SERVES 4 ▶ TIME TAKEN: 30 minutes

This dish started out using ground almonds, but it occurred to me that pumpkin seeds would make an interesting and nutritious alternative. It is difficult to grind them quite fine enough in a domestic grinder, though. It might be best to grind them in two batches.

4 organic chicken breasts, skinned
2 tablespoons extra-virgin olive oil
1 onion, peeled and finely chopped
1 large garlic clove, peeled and finely chopped
1¼ cups plain or soy yogurt
1 tablespoon tahini
2 heaping tablespoons pumpkin seeds, ground in an electric grinder
sea salt and freshly ground black pepper

Protein 39%
Carbohydrate 10%
Fat 51%
GI: low
GL: low

Slice the chicken into ½-inch strips. Heat the oil in a shallow frying pan, add the onion and garlic and cook gently until soft.

Increase the heat, add the chicken and cook, stirring frequently, until the chicken has slightly colored, about 3 minutes.

Turn the heat down and stir in the yogurt, tahini, and ground pumpkin seeds. Simmer for 8–10 minutes. Season to taste and serve at once, with a salad or fresh vegetables.

PER SERVING
Calories 369 ▶ Protein 35g ▶ Carbohydrates 10g ▶ Fiber 1g ▶ Sugar—Total 2g ▶ Fat—Total 21g ▶ Saturated Fat 5g ▶ Vitamin C 2mg ▶ Magnesium 67mg
---

▶ Pumpkin seeds are a rich source of zinc, iron, and selenium, as well as protein and essential fatty acids. Grinding them makes these nutrients more available.

grilled chicken with quinoa and lemons

■ ■ ■

SERVES 4–5 ▶ **TIME TAKEN:** 45 minutes

The chicken can be cooked on the barbecue or under a grill, but I always take the precaution of baking the chicken first to make sure it is cooked through to the middle without being burnt. Use capers only if you like them—they are an acquired taste.

1 organic or free-range chicken or
   chicken-fryer pieces weighing about 3 pounds
3 tablespoons extra-virgin olive oil
2 tablespoons lemon juice
1 garlic clove, crushed
2 teaspoons dijon mustard
sea salt and freshly ground black pepper
½ cup quinoa
1 cup chicken stock (see page 230)
1 tablespoon finely grated lemon rind
1 tablespoon capers, rinsed (optional)
3 tablespoons sage leaves, finely sliced
1 tablespoon slivered almonds
2 whole lemons

> Protein 30%
> Carbohydrate 17%
> Fat 53%
> GI: low
> GL: low

Preheat the oven to 400°F.

If using a whole chicken, joint the chicken into eight pieces. Cut off the wing tips and discard. Place the chicken pieces in an ovenproof dish. Whisk together two tablespoons of olive oil, the lemon juice, crushed garlic, mustard, and seasoning. Pour over the chicken, making sure it is all well coated. Bake in the preheated oven for ten minutes, then turn over and bake on the other side for another ten minutes.

Meanwhile, wash the quinoa, drain thoroughly, then put in a saucepan with the stock. Bring to a boil, lower the heat, cover, and simmer for 20 minutes until tender and the liquid is absorbed. You may have to add a little more stock or water to prevent it drying out.

Heat the rest of the olive oil in a large frying pan over medium heat. Add the grated lemon rind, capers (if using), sage leaves, and slivered almonds, and cook for 5 minutes or until the almonds are just beginning to turn color. Add this mixture to the quinoa and mix together well. Keep warm while you finish off the chicken.

Preheat the grill. Transfer the chicken pieces to the grill, draining off any fat that has accumulated. Cut the lemons in half and add them to the grill. Grill the chicken and lemons until crisp, turning once. Be careful not to let the chicken burn.

Serve the chicken pieces on a bed of lemon quinoa, and garnish with the grilled lemon halves.

PER SERVING

Calories 510 ▸ Protein 38g ▸ Carbohydrates 21g ▸ Fiber 3g ▸ Sugar—Total 1g ▸ Fat—Total 30g ▸ Saturated Fat 7g ▸ Vitamin C 19mg ▸ Magnesium 85mg

▸ Quinoa is not only delicious but a rich source of protein and minerals, especially magnesium and calcium. However, you could substitute barley or brown rice for the quinoa.

roast chicken with walnut sauce

■ ■ ■

SERVES 4 ▶ TIME TAKEN: 1½ hours

This walnut sauce is based on those used in Iranian and other Middle Eastern cuisines, but without using hard-to-find ingredients. If you prefer a gamey flavor, try substituting guinea fowl in place of the chicken.

1 organic or free-range chicken, about 3½ pounds
sea salt and freshly ground black pepper
2 tablespoons extra-virgin olive oil
½ cup walnuts
1 cup soy, rice or almond milk
1 teaspoon cornstarch
1 small onion, peeled and finely chopped
3 garlic cloves, peeled and finely chopped
½ cup dry white wine
freshly grated nutmeg
1 teaspoon fresh thyme leaves
4 tablespoons plain yogurt

Protein 36%
Carbohydrate 11%
Fat 53%
GI: low
GL: low

Preheat the oven to 400°F.

Lightly season the chicken with salt and pepper, place in a roasting pan on its side and pour over the olive oil. Roast for 20 minutes, then turn over and baste the other side and roast for another 20 minutes. Then turn the bird breast up and cook for another 20 minutes. Remove from the oven and leave to cool on a plate. Set aside the roasting pan and its juices.

Meanwhile, chop the walnuts roughly and put in a small bowl. Heat the milk and pour over the walnuts. Leave to infuse for half an hour, then strain and set the walnuts aside. Mix the milk with the cornstarch and set that aside too.

When the chicken has cooled sufficiently to handle, joint it into four pieces and place the pieces in a baking dish. Return to the oven for ten minutes while you prepare the sauce.

For the sauce, pour off the fat from the roasting pan, leaving a couple of spoonsful of juices. Set over a gentle heat and cook the chopped onion and garlic until tender but not browned. Add the white wine and continue cooking, scraping up any bits from the bottom of the pan. Finally add the milk and cornstarch mixture, and cook, stirring, until the sauce has thickened. Add the nutmeg and thyme and adjust the seasoning if necessary.

Cook for a further 5 minutes, then add the chopped soaked walnuts. Off the heat, stir in the yogurt.

Serve the chicken either with the sauce poured over, or handed round separately, accompanied by a selection of green vegetables.

PER SERVING

Calories 368 ▸ Protein 31g ▸ Carbohydrates 8g ▸ Fiber 1g ▸ Sugar—Total 3g ▸ Fat—Total 21g ▸ Saturated Fat 3g ▸ Vitamin C 4mg ▸ Magnesium 62mg

▶ Any nuts could be used here in place of the walnuts. Try ground almonds or cashews.

poached chicken in ginger sauce

■ ■ ■

SERVES 4 ▶ TIME TAKEN: 30 minutes

This recipe is easy, quick, very low in fat, and delicious. What more could you want?

2 tablespoons fresh ginger root, peeled and cut into fine julienne strips
6 scallions, chopped
2 star anise
2 tablespoons shoyu
2½ cups chicken stock (see page 230)
4 organic chicken breasts, skinned
2 cups French beans, or sugar snap peas,
    washed and trimmed
1 teaspoon cornstarch

Protein 25%
Carbohydrate 69%
Fat 6%
GI: low
GL: low

Put the ginger, scallions, star anise, shoyu, and chicken stock in a wide shallow pan or wok over medium to high heat, bring to a boil and boil hard for 3–4 minutes.

Reduce the heat to a simmer and slip the chicken breasts into the broth. Cook for 12–15 minutes, turning once, until cooked through. Remove from the broth and keep warm. Now cook the green vegetable of your choice in the same broth until tender but still bright green. The length of time depends on which vegetable you choose—sugar snap peas take only take a couple of minutes, while French beans may take 4–5 minutes. Remove the vegetables and keep warm.

Mix the cornstarch with a tablespoonful of cold water, then stir into the broth. Bring to a boil and cook until glossy and thickened slightly.

To serve, put a portion of vegetables in each of four shallow bowls, slice the chicken breasts diagonally and arrange on the beans, then pour over the ginger sauce. Serve hot.

PER SERVING

Calories 74 ▶ Protein 5g ▶ Carbohydrates 13g ▶ Fiber 4g ▶ Sugar—Total 6g ▶ Fat—Total 0g ▶ Saturated Fat 0g ▶ Vitamin C 11mg ▶ Magnesium 9mg

▶ Ginger is a potent anti-inflammatory, and is therefore useful for conditions such as rheumatoid arthritis, an inflammatory disease. It is also good for the digestion. My tip is to peel it as soon as you buy it and freeze lumps of the peeled root. It is quite easy to grate it when it's frozen. For a dish like this, where you need julienne strips, you might have to let it thaw a little before slicing.

juniper chicken

SERVES 4 ▸ TIME TAKEN: 50 minutes

*J*uniper is most usually used as a flavoring for game and pork (and, of course, gin), but I thought I'd try it with chicken, and it works very well. Don't be tempted to use more than 3 juniper berries per person, though, or the juniper will mask the flavor of the chicken.

4 skinless, boneless organic chicken breasts
4 large Savoy cabbage leaves
12 juniper berries, lightly crushed
sea salt and freshly ground black pepper
4 sprigs Fresh thyme
½ cup chicken stock (see page 230)
4 tablespoons dry white wine

Protein 73%
Carbohydrate 6%
Fat 18%
GI: low
GL: low

Preheat the oven to 375°F.

Cut out the tough stems of the cabbage leaves and blanch in boiling water for one minute just to soften slightly. Refresh under cold running water and dry on kitchen paper.

Place each chicken breast in a cabbage leaf, season lightly and add 3 crushed juniper berries to each parcel. Wrap tightly and place in an ovenproof casserole with a lid. Pour over the chicken stock and white wine, cover tightly and bake in the preheated oven for 30 minutes.

Remove the chicken parcels from the casserole. Pour the remaining cooking liquid into a small pan and boil hard to reduce by half. Slice the chicken breasts diagonally and place on individual plates. Pour over the reduced sauce and serve hot.

PER SERVING
Calories 160 ▸ Protein 28g ▸ Carbohydrates 2g ▸ Fiber 1g ▸ Sugar—Total 1g ▸ Fat—Total 3g ▸ Saturated Fat 1g ▸ Vitamin C 12mg ▸ Magnesium 30mg
---

▶ Juniper has been shown to help improve the action of insulin in lowering blood sugar in people with diabetes.

colombo de poulet
with fresh mango relish

■ ■ ■

SERVES 8 ▶ **TIME TAKEN:** 1 hour

This is a French West Indian version of chicken curry. In the markets in Martinique and Guadeloupe you might see mysterious little twists of brown paper, which contain "poudre de colombo"—the local curry powder. Fortunately, you don't have to go to the West Indies for an approximation of the taste, for here it is.

1 large organic or free-range chicken (about 4 pounds),
   skinned and jointed into 8 pieces
2 tablespoons extra-virgin olive oil
2 onions, peeled and chopped
½ teaspoon turmeric
1 teaspoon ground coriander
1 teaspoon mustard seed, ground
¼ teaspoon ground black pepper
3 garlic cloves
1 fresh hot chili pepper, seeded and chopped finely
1 tablespoon tamarind pulp (optional)
1 green (underripe) mango, peeled and chopped
1 large eggplant, peeled and sliced
1 large green papaya (underripe), peeled and sliced
1 cup coconut milk
1 lime, juice only
low-sodium salt to taste

Protein 23%
Carbohydrate 21%
Fat 56%
GI: low
GL: low

for the fresh mango relish:
2 green (underripe) mangoes
1 small onion, peeled and finely chopped
hot pepper sauce to taste
1 tablespoon extra-virgin olive oil
low-sodium salt and freshly ground black pepper to taste
2 tablespoones chopped parsley

Heat the oil in a large frying pan over medium heat and sauté the chicken pieces until browned all over. Remove and place in a casserole. Sauté the onions in the same frying pan until soft. Mash together the spices, crushed garlic, and chopped chili pepper, then add to the onions and sauté for a few minutes, stirring constantly. Put into the casserole with the chicken. Add all the other ingredients, cover, and simmer for half an hour or until the chicken is tender.

For the mango relish, peel and roughly chop the mangoes. Put the chopped flesh, onion, hot sauce, and olive oil into the blender and blend very briefly—the mixture should be slightly chunky. Stir in the chopped parsley and chill before serving.

Serve the chicken colombo with brown rice and pass the mango relish separately.

PER SERVING

Calories 479 ▸ Protein 27g ▸ Carbohydrates 26g ▸ Fiber 4g ▸ Sugar—Total 18g ▸ Fat—Total 30g ▸ Saturated Fat 12g ▸ Vitamin C 74mg ▸ Magnesium 61mg

▸ Mangoes are usually considered to be a high-GI fruit. However, here they are used green, so the GI will be lower. Also any high-GI effect would be mitigated by the presence of protein and fat, so there's no need to deprive yourself of mangoes served this way.

cinnamon smoked duck

■ ■ ■

SERVES 4 ▶ **TIME TAKEN:** 1 hour 20 minutes

This is the Chinese method for home smoking, and is surprisingly straightforward, though it can create a lot of smoke in your kitchen, so turn on the exhaust fan before you start. Smoked food is thought to be carcinogenic, but the duck is smoked for quite a short time just to impart flavor, and because you use only the duck breasts, the smoking takes much less time than if you were smoking a whole duck. Although there is white rice and sugar in the recipe, you don't eat them, so it's a good way to get rid of these nutrient-poor foods that you may have in your store cupboard.

4 duck breasts
1 teaspoon coarse sea salt
1 teaspoon szechuan peppercorns
½ cup uncooked white rice
½ cup sugar
2 cinnamon sticks, broken up into small pieces
3 star anise
2 tablespoons chinese black tea leaves, such as Lapsang Souchong
6 bok choy, halved
2 tablespoons tamari
2 teaspoons oriental sesame oil

Protein 46%
Carbohydrate 3%
Fat 51%
GI: very low
GL: very low

Wipe the duck breasts and prick them two or three times with a sharp fork. Crush the salt and Szechuan pepper and toast them in a wok. Cool, then rub all over the duck breasts.

Fill the wok about one third full with water and place a rack over it. Put the duck breasts on the rack, cover, and steam for 20–30 minutes, depending on the thickness of the breasts.

To prepare the wok for smoking, wash it out, dry, and line with a double thickness of foil. Mix together the rice, sugar, cinnamon, star anise, and tea leaves and spread in the bottom of the wok. Place the rack on top and arrange the duck breasts on it. Put the lid on and seal the edge with a strip of foil. Turn the heat to medium-high and place the wok on the heat. Once it has begun to smoke, which you will smell rather than see, resist the temptation to have a look, and leave the wok on the heat for 10–15 minutes. Remove from the heat and leave to stand for another 15 minutes.

While the duck is standing, steam the bok choy over boiling water for 5 minutes. Place on individual plates. Remove the duck from the wok, slice each breast diagonally into three or four slices and arrange on the bed of bok choy. Sprinkle with tamari and oriental sesame oil.

The smoked duck breasts can also be served cold or at room temperature, thinly sliced.

PER SERVING

Calories 279 ▸ Protein 32g ▸ Carbohydrates 2g ▸ Fiber 1g ▸ Sugar—Total 0g ▸ Fat—Total 15g ▸ Saturated Fat 4g ▸ Vitamin C 25mg ▸ Magnesium 13mg

---

▶ Duck is known to be a fatty meat, but the initial pricking of the skin and steaming renders quite a lot of the fat, and if you are concerned you can always discard the skin before eating. Interestingly, nearly half the fat in duck skin is of the monounsaturated variety, so it may be less harmful than is generally supposed. Duck meat supplies some "heme" iron, which is easily absorbed, useful for those who do not eat red meat, the other good supplier of heme iron.

turkey with fennel and cashew cream

■ ■ ■

SERVES 4 ▶ TIME TAKEN: 1¼ hours

*T*his smooth creamy sauce gives the turkey an unusual aniseed flavor. Celery is a good substitute if you can't find fennel. This dish is a good balance of protein, carbohydrate, and fat. Serve it with vegetables on the side, such as carrots and cabbage.

1 tablespoon extra-virgin olive oil
12 ounces turkey meat, breast or thigh, cut into 1-inch cubes
1 small onion, sliced
1–2 fennel bulbs, sliced horizontally,
    reserving the fronds for garnish (about 1 cup)
1 tablespoon plain or gluten-free white flour
¾ cup chicken stock (see page 230)
1 teaspoon fresh thyme leaves, chopped
sea salt and freshly ground black pepper to taste
½ cup cashew nuts
scant ½ cup water

Protein 44%
Carbohydrate 19%
Fat 37%
GI: low
GL: low

Preheat the oven to 325°F.

Heat the oil in a frying pan over a medium heat, add the turkey and cook quite briskly until brown all over. Using a slotted spoon, transfer to an ovenproof casserole. Add the onion and fennel to the pan and cook for about 10 minutes, stirring occasionally.

Stir in the flour, then gradually add the stock, stirring all the time. Bring to a gentle boil, add the thyme, salt, and pepper. Pour over the turkey. Cover and cook in the oven for 30 minutes. Meanwhile chop the fennel fronds for use as a garnish. Blend the cashew nuts and water together until smooth to make a thick cream.

Take the casserole out of the oven, stir in the cashew cream, cover and continue cooking for about 15–20 minutes, or until the turkey is tender. Serve sprinkled with the chopped fennel fronds.

PER SERVING

Calories 254 ▶ Protein 28g ▶ Carbohydrates 12g ▶ Fiber 3g ▶ Sugar—Total 2g ▶ Fat—Total 11g ▶ Saturated Fat 2g ▶ Vitamin C 9mg ▶ Magnesium 59mg

▶ Fennel contains the antioxidant flavonoid quercetin. It can also be useful for indigestion and spasms of the digestive tract. It also helps expel phlegm from the lungs.

AS A NUTRITIONAL therapist, I find myself constantly advising people to eat more fish, and specifically oily fish. The dilemma is: which fish is it safe and/or environmentally friendly to eat? My answer is that as far as white fish are concerned, our cod stocks are now seriously depleted, and it is better to substitute hake or haddock, both of which appear to be in better supply. As for oily fish, the large carnivorous fish such as tuna and swordfish at the top of the food chain tend to have accumulated more mercury than smaller fish such as mackerel and sardines, so I would opt for the latter. As for salmon, farmed salmon is now very polluted, due to overcrowding and poor farming practices. Yet I still feel that if you cannot afford organic or wild salmon, both of which are very expensive, eating farmed salmon once a week or so is better than eating no oily fish at all. Canned salmon is an option, as it is usually wild oceanic salmon. Another solution may be to choose rainbow trout, which, although it contains less omega-3's in it than salmon, is generally farmed in cleaner conditions than salmon.

fish

coconut fish curry

*M*onkfish works best in this curry, as it has a good, firm texture and does not fall apart as easily as other white fish.

2 teaspoons cumin seeds
2 teaspoons coriander seeds
½ teaspoon fenugreek seeds
1 tablespoon coconut oil
1 cinnamon stick
1 star anise
2 organic limes, finely grated zest and juice
1 can coconut milk
1½ pounds firm white fish, such as monkfish, hake, or haddock,
   cut into 1-inch cubes
fresh coriander leaves, for garnish

Protein 57%
Carbohydrate 12%
Fat 31%
GI: low
GL: low

In an electric grinder, grind the cumin seeds, coriander seeds, and fenugreek seeds to a powder. Heat the coconut oil in a large frying pan over medium heat. Add the ground spices, cinnamon stick, star anise, and the grated lime zest. Cook, stirring, for a couple of minutes until the spices start to release their fragrance. Pour in the coconut milk, bring to a boil, then reduce the heat and simmer for 5 minutes to allow the flavors to meld.

Add the fish to the coconut sauce and simmer for about 8 minutes or until cooked through. Remove the cinnamon stick and star anise, and stir in the lime juice. You may not need all of it, so taste as you go—the lime and coconut should balance each other.

Serve garnished with coriander leaves and accompanied by brown rice or barley.

PER SERVING
Calories 227 ▶ Protein 32g ▶ Carbohydrates 7g ▶ Fiber 2g ▶ Sugar—Total 1g ▶ Fat—Total 8g ▶ Saturated Fat 4g ▶ Vitamin C 15mg ▶ Magnesium 99mg

▶ This recipe contains coconut oil, cinnamon, and fenugreek, all ingredients known to be beneficial for people with diabetes.

fish and spinach parcels
with herb vinaigrette

■ ■ ■

SERVES 4 ▶ TIME TAKEN: 35 minutes

As for the preceding recipe, the best fish for this is monkfish because it has a firm texture, but it is expensive. Other firm-fleshed fish will work well too, such as halibut or hake.

5 cups large spinach leaves
2 tablespoons dry white wine
1 tablespoon lemon juice
1 small onion, peeled and finely chopped
4 thick white fish fillets, about 6 ounces each
sea salt and freshly ground black pepper
1 tablespoon fresh tarragon, chopped
1 tablespoon fresh parsley, chopped
1 tablespoon fresh dill, chopped
1 teaspoon Dijon mustard
1 tablespoon white wine vinegar
3 tablespoons extra-virgin olive oil

Protein 48%
Carbohydrate 7%
Fat 45%
GI: low
GL: very low

Steam the spinach over boiling water for 30 seconds only. Refresh under cold water, drain and dry on kitchen paper.

Put the wine, lemon juice, and chopped onion in a small pan, and cook over very low heat for 5 minutes, until the onion is soft and the liquid has evaporated.

Spread the spinach leaves out on a chopping board, and cut out the tough stems. Top each fish fillet with a spoonful of the cooked onion, season lightly, and wrap the fillets in 3–4 spinach leaves so that they are completely enclosed.

Put the fish parcels in the steamer over simmering water, cover tightly with a lid, and steam for 15 minutes or until the fish is firm.

For the vinaigrette, whisk or shake all the ingredients together and season to taste. Serve the fish parcels surrounded by a drizzle of herb vinaigrette.

PER SERVING
Calories 287 ▶ Protein 33g ▶ Carbohydrates 4g ▶ Fiber 2g ▶ Sugar—Total 1g ▶ Fat—Total 14g ▶ Saturated Fat 2g ▶ Vitamin C 15mg ▶ Magnesium 91mg

▶ Wrapping fish preserves its moisture and flavor, as well as making a neat presentation. As a variation, you could try using cabbage leaves or vine leaves instead of spinach.

salmon with minted pea purée and asparagus

■ ■ ■

SERVES 4 ▶ TIME TAKEN: 45 minutes

This is a dish with which to celebrate the arrival of summer.

1 leek, well washed and thinly sliced
1 tablespoon organic unsalted butter
¾ cup vegetable stock (see page 229)
4 fillets of wild or organic salmon, about 1½ pounds
2½ cups peas, frozen or freshly shelled
6 mint leaves, chopped
sea salt and freshly ground black pepper
12 asparagus tips

Protein 46%
Carbohydrate 17%
Fat 37%
GI: medium
GL: low

Place the leek, butter, and stock in a saucepan over medium heat. Bring to a simmer, cover with a lid and cook over very low heat for 20 minutes, stirring once or twice.

Meanwhile, place each salmon fillet in a piece of foil, top each with a slice of lemon and a sprig of parsley, and wrap loosely, making sure that all the edges are sealed. Place under a hot grill for 15–20 minutes, depending on thickness, turning once.

While the salmon is cooking, add the peas and chopped mint to the leek mixture, cover and cook for 5 minutes. Remove the lid, and continue to cook until the peas are tender, about another 5 minutes. Drain, reserving the cooking liquid. Leave to cool a little, then tip into a blender or food processor together with about 3 tablespoons of the reserved liquid. Process until smooth, then season to taste, and return to the pan to reheat gently.

Steam the asparagus tips over boiling water until done—6 minutes if they are small.

To serve, place the pea purée on individual plates, unwrap the salmon and place on the purée. Garnish with the asparagus tips.

PER SERVING
Calories 426 ▶ Protein 49g ▶ Carbohydrates 18g ▶ Fiber 5g ▶ Sugar—Total 6g ▶ Fat—Total 17g ▶ Saturated Fat 4g ▶ Vitamin C 18mg ▶ Magnesium 103mg

▶ Fresh peas are a good source of vitamin C and they also supply iron, carotenes, and B vitamins. Try them raw in salads when they are very small—delicious. Asparagus is a natural detoxifier and is rich in potassium, a trace element needed for good water balance in the body. Asparagus has also been used in folk medicine to help restore failing eyesight, so it may be helpful for people with diabetes.

thai-style salmon fishcakes
with cucumber salad

■ ■ ■

SERVES 4 ▶ **TIME TAKEN:** 45 minutes

Thai fish cakes are normally served as a starter, but the quantity here is rather more substantial. The chili-flavored cucumber salad makes a pleasantly sharp accompaniment.

for the salad:
2 cucumbers

2 teaspoons sea salt

1 fresh red or green chili, deseeded and finely chopped

6 scallions, chopped

small handful of fresh coriander leaves, chopped

1 lime, juice only

freshly ground black pepper

Protein 44%
Carbohydrate 20%
Fat 36%
GI: low
GL: low

for the salmon cakes:
1½ pounds skinless, boneless fillet of organic or wild salmon, roughly cubed

2 egg whites from organic free-range eggs

4 tablespoons rice flour

2 organic limes, finely grated and juice

1 tablespoon fresh ginger root, peeled and grated

1 teaspoon wasabi paste

4 tablespoons chopped fresh coriander

1 tablespoon coconut oil

4 tablespoons tamari sauce

1 tablespoon honey

First, "degorge" the cucumbers to soften them. With a vegetable peeler, peel lengthwise strips off the cucumbers to achieve a striped effect. Cut them in half lengthwise and scoop out the seeds. Cut the flesh into ½-inch slices. Place in a colander, sprinkle with sea salt, and leave to drain while you prepare the salmon cakes.

Make sure there are no bones in the salmon. Put the salmon, egg white, rice flour, lime zest, ginger, wasabi paste, and chopped coriander in the food processor, and process until combined into a solid mass, but be careful not to overprocess into a paste. Turn the mixture out into a bowl and form into 12 or 16 flat cakes.

Heat the coconut oil in a large heavy frying pan over medium-high heat and fry the salmon cakes for a minute each side. Drain on kitchen paper and keep warm while you fry the rest of the cakes.

For the dipping sauce, mix together the lime juice, tamari sauce, and honey.

Finish off the salad: Rinse the cucumber and dry on kitchen paper. Put in a bowl with the chopped chili, scallions, coriander leaves, lime juice, and black pepper. Toss to mix.

Serve the salmon cakes with the cucumber salad and pass the dipping sauce separately.

─── **PER SERVING** ───
Calories 446 ▸ Protein 49g ▸ Carbohydrates 23g ▸ Fiber 3g ▸ Sugar—Total 6g ▸ Fat—Total 18g ▸ Saturated Fat 5g ▸ Vitamin C 48mg ▸ Magnesium 104mg

▶ Wasabi paste is made from a kind of Japanese horseradish, and is very strong and pungent. If you cannot find it, use creamed horseradish instead.

flounder fillets with tapenade and tomato dressing

■ ■ ■

SERVES 4 ▶ TIME TAKEN: 45 minutes

This recipe has undergone many transformations since I first ate roast cod with capers, olives and anchovies at the Penhelig Arms in Aberdovey where I was living while writing this book. First I substituted flounder for the cod, then I realized that most of the ingredients were already assembled in tapenade, and from there it was a short step to spreading the tapenade on to flounder fillets and rolling them up.

8 flounder fillets, about 1¼ pounds, skinned
4 tablespoons tapenade
⅔ cup fish stock (see page 231)
4 tablespoons extra-virgin olive oil
1 lemon, grated rind and juice
freshly ground black pepper
2 medium tomatoes, peeled, deseeded and diced
basil leaves, for garnish

Protein 32%
Carbohydrate 9%
Fat 59%
GI: low
GL: very low

Preheat the oven to 350°F.

Spread the flounder fillets with tapenade and roll up. Place the rolled fillets in an ovenproof dish, small enough that they fit snugly, and pour the fish stock over them.

Bake in the preheated oven for 15–20 minutes, until just cooked. Remove from the oven and pour off the cooking juices into a small pan. Keep the fish warm.

Reduce the cooking juices over high heat until there are only about 4 tablespoons left. Whisk this with the olive oil, lemon juice, and grated rind and pepper. The dressing should not need salt because of the saltiness of the tapenade. Add the diced tomatoes.

Serve the fish with the tomato dressing spooned over, and garnish with basil leaves.

PER SERVING

Calories 326 ▶ Protein 27g ▶ Carbohydrates 7g ▶ Fiber 3g ▶ Sugar—Total 2g ▶ Fat—Total 22g ▶ Saturated Fat 3g ▶ Vitamin C 34mg ▶ Magnesium 75mg

▶ Flounder, being a white fish, doesn't have the same benefits as the oily fish such as salmon and trout. However, it is still an excellent low-fat source of protein and still relatively abundant and not too expensive.

trout fillets with lettuce and fennel

■ ■ ■

SERVES 4 ▶ TIME TAKEN: 40 minutes

*Y*ou can use wild salmon, organic salmon, or sea bass instead of the trout, if you prefer. This is a delicately flavored dish so assertive fish such as mackerel would not do.

4 small firm organic lettuces, such as Bibb
2 fennel bulbs, finely sliced
1 tablespoon organic unsalted butter
½ cup fish stock (see page 231)
⅓ cup dry white wine
4 rainbow trout, filleted (8 fillets)
sea salt and freshly ground black pepper
4 tablespoons soy cream
squeeze of lemon juice

Protein 44%
Carbohydrate 20%
Fat 36%
GI: low
GL: low

Wash the lettuces well and cut in half vertically. Blanch in boiling water for 2–3 minutes, then drain. Melt the butter in a wide pan over gentle heat, and cook the fennel for 2 minutes. Place the lettuce on top of the fennel, add the wine, cover and simmer for 10 minutes.

Now put the trout fillets on top of the lettuce, season, cover, with the lid, and continue cooking until the trout is done—about 10 more minutes.

Take the trout out of the pan. Remove the lettuce and fennel with a slotted spoon, place on individual plates and put the trout on top. Turn up the heat under the pan to reduce the cooking liquid. Add the soy cream and lemon juice, adjust seasoning, then pour over the fish.

── PER SERVING ──
Calories 322 ▶ Protein 34g ▶ Carbohydrates 14g ▶ Fiber 5g ▶ Sugar—Total 2g ▶ Fat—Total 13g ▶ Saturated Fat 4g ▶ Vitamin C 30mg ▶ Magnesium 86mg

▶ I specify organic lettuce because lettuces have a large surface area, and therefore nonorganic lettuces are likely to harbor more pesticide residue than most other conventionally grown vegetables.

roasted mackerel with horseradish cream

■ ■ ■

SERVES 4 ▶ TIME TAKEN: 25 minutes

Mackerel's pink, firm flesh is tasty, nutritious, and inexpensive. The skin should shine— if it doesn't, don't buy it. It has a strong flavor that works well with robust accompaniments such as horseradish, and is one of the best sources of omega-3 fatty acids.

1½ pounds fresh mackerel, cut into 4 ¾-inch thick pieces
1 organic lemon, grated zest and juice
2 garlic cloves, peeled and finely chopped
cherry tomatoes on the vine
1 tablespoon extra-virgin olive oil

Protein 33%
Carbohydrate 7%
Fat 60%
GI: low
GL: low

horseradish cream:
2–3 tablespoons grated fresh horseradish
2 teaspoons wine vinegar
1 teaspoon lemon juice
3 teaspoons prepared English mustard
1 teaspoon sea salt
freshly ground black pepper
1 teaspoon concentrated apple juice
½ cup plain yogurt

Preheat the oven to 450°F.

First make the Horseradish Cream: scrub the horseradish root well, peel, and grate. Put the grated horseradish into a bowl with the vinegar, lemon juice, mustard, salt, freshly ground pepper, and sugar. Fold in the yogurt but do not overmix or the sauce will curdle. There will be more than enough for this recipe, but save the rest for another dish. It keeps for 2–3 days in the fridge.

To make the fish, rub the flesh with the lemon zest and garlic. Place on a baking tray and drizzle with the lemon juice. Arrange the tomatoes on the baking tray and drizzle with the olive oil. Bake in the preheated oven for 10 minutes, until the fish is cooked through and flakes easily with a fork.

Serve the mackerel and tomatoes with the horseradish cream on the side. Steamed green beans make a good accompaniment.

PER SERVING

Calories 459 ▸ Protein 38g ▸ Carbohydrates 7g ▸ Fiber 1g ▸ Sugar—Total 2g ▸ Fat—Total 30g ▸ Saturated Fat 7g ▸ Vitamin C 18mg ▸ Magnesium 147mg

▸ To prepare fresh horseradish, scrub the root well, remove the skin with a vegetable peeler, then grate the white flesh. Avoid touching your eyes while preparing horseradish, as it is very pungent and can sting them. This property is what makes it so good for clearing stuffy noses and blocked sinuses. If you can't get fresh horseradish, substitute prepared horseradish and reduce the amount of yogurt.

sea bass with soba noodles

■ ■ ■

SERVES 4 ▶ **TIME TAKEN:** 30 minutes

This recipe contains some Japanese ingredients, which should be available from oriental shops and large supermarkets. If you can't find wasabi, substitute ordinary horseradish; pickled ginger can be replaced by grated fresh ginger root; and white-wine vinegar could substitute for rice-wine vinegar.

6 ounces buckwheat noodles (soba)
8 scallions, sliced diagonally
1½ cups snow peas, trimmed and cut in half
4 fillets of sea bass, about 7 ounces each, skin on
olive oil spray
coriander sprigs

> Protein 46%
> Carbohydrate 38%
> Fat 17%
> GI: medium
> GL: medium

dressing:
1 tablespoon oriental sesame oil
½ teaspoon wasabi paste (Japanese horseradish paste)
½ fresh red chili, deseeded and finely chopped
2 teaspoons japanese pickled ginger
2 tablespoons tamari sauce
3 tablespoons rice vinegar

Cook the soba noodles according to the directions on the package—they usually only require about 6 minutes in boiling water. Be careful not to overcook them or they can become gummy in texture. Drain and put in a large bowl.

Blanch the scallions and snow peas in boiling water for two minutes. Drain and refresh under cold water. Mix into the cooked noodles. Whisk all the dressing ingredients together and pour over the noodles, tossing gently to mix. Cover and set aside while you cook the fish.

Preheat the grill to high. Slash the skin of the sea bass fillets and spray with olive-oil spray. Grill the fish for 3–4 minutes on each side until cooked and the skin is starting to crisp.

Serve the sea bass fillets on a bed of noodle salad. Garnish with sprigs of coriander.

Calories 435 ▸ Protein 49g ▸ Carbohydrates 40g ▸ Fiber 3g ▸ Sugar—Total 3g ▸ Fat—Total 8g ▸ Saturated Fat 2g ▸ Vitamin C 31mg ▸ Magnesium 107mg

▷ Thanks to the sea bass, this recipe has more protein than any other in the entire book.

grilled trout with salsa verde

■ ■ ■

SERVES 4 ▶ **TIME TAKEN:** 30 minutes

*S*alsa verde is a wonderful Italian sauce, just right with grilled trout, but it could equally well be served with grilled mackerel or other strongly flavored fish. It is traditionally made with a pestle and mortar, but I'm afraid I cheat and use the food processor.

1 large bunch flat leaf parsley
8 anchovy fillets, drained and chopped
2 tablespoons capers, rinsed and drained
2 teaspoons dry mustard powder
3 garlic cloves, peeled and chopped
1 lemon, juice only
2 tablespoons fresh basil, chopped
freshly ground black pepper
8 tablespoons extra-virgin olive oil
8 trout fillets, about 1½ pounds
1 lemon, sliced

Protein 31%
Carbohydrate 4%
Fat 65%
GI: low
GL: low

Remove the stems from the parsley, reserving a few for stuffing the trout. Wash and chop the parsley leaves.

Place the anchovies, capers, mustard, garlic, lemon juice, parsley, basil, and pepper in the food processor, and process to a paste. With the machine running, gradually pour in the olive oil, as for mayonnaise. Taste and adjust seasoning. The salsa will separate on standing, so leave in the food processor while you grill the trout, then give it a final whizz just before serving to recombine.

Preheat the grill to high. Grill the trout for about 3–5 minutes per side, or until the fish flakes easily with a fork. Serve with the salsa verde.

PER SERVING

Calories 553 ▶ Protein 42g ▶ Carbohydrates 6g ▶ Fiber 2g ▶ Sugar—Total 1g ▶ Fat—Total 40g ▶ Saturated Fat 7g ▶ Vitamin C 50mg ▶ Magnesium 74mg

▶ Trout have less fat than other oily fish, so therefore less of the beneficial omega-3 fatty acids. However, they do contain some, and are also a very good source of potassium.

vegetables
AND salads

VEGETABLES SHOULD BE the mainstay of any diet, accounting for at least half of every meal, but too often they are treated as an afterthought. Eating them raw in salads, or as juices, is the way to get maximum benefit from all the nutrition they provide. The next best thing is to steam them, as few of their nutrients are lost this way— even the water over which they have been steamed can be used as a vegetable stock, or even drunk as a light soup.

Microwaving vegetables, on the other hand, can cause them to lose 97 percent of the antioxidants that help us fight cancer and heart disease, according to the *Journal of the Science of Food and Agriculture*. Deep-frying is just as harmful, as it produces free radicals that destroy essential fats in food and can damage cells. Ironically it is the polyunsaturated oils that oxidize most rapidly, becoming dangerous "trans" fats. So it is safer to use butter or coconut oil, which are saturated fats, or olive oil, which is monounsaturated. When stir frying, keep the frying part to a minimum, adding liquid as soon in the process as possible to cut down the frying time.

Here is a handful of tasty vegetable dishes, intended to be accompaniments to protein foods such as fish, chicken, or beans, although some of them would work as light meals in their own right.

vegetables

braised kale

■ ■ ■

SERVES 4 ▶ TIME TAKEN: 20 minutes

This is a quick and tasty way to cook kale, which some people find a dull vegetable. It's anything but dull like this, though. Alternative ways to cook kale are to boil it just in the water clinging to the leaves, for 6 minutes, or stir-fry it with ginger, garlic, and sesame seeds.

1 pound kale
2 tablespoons extra-virgin olive oil
2 garlic cloves, chopped
½ cup vegetable stock (see page 229)
2 tablespoons shoyu sauce
2 tablespoons rice vinegar
1 lemon, juice and finely grated rind
sea salt and freshly ground black pepper to taste
1 tablespoon flaked almonds, lightly toasted

Protein 11%
Carbohydrate 26%
Fat 63%
GI: low
GL: low

Wash the kale, separate the stems from the leaves, and chop both coarsely, discarding the very woody parts of the stems. Heat the oil in a wok or large sauté pan over medium heat. Sauté the garlic and kale stems for 3 minutes, then add the kale leaves, vegetable stock, and shoyu. Cover and cook until the kale is tender, about 5–7 minutes. Remove from the heat and add the vinegar, lemon juice and rind, and seasoning to taste. Toss well. Serve topped with toasted flaked almonds.

PER SERVING
Calories 150 ▶ Protein 4g ▶ Carbohydrates 11g ▶ Fiber 3g ▶ Sugar—Total 3g ▶ Fat—Total 11g ▶ Saturated Fat 1g ▶ Vitamin C 53mg ▶ Magnesium 28mg

▶ Kale is rich in potassium and folate, calcium, thiamine, and vitamin B_6. In addition, it is positively bristling with cancer-fighting phytochemicals and glucosinolates. Kale consumption has been linked with lower incidences of colon and bladder cancer.

broccoli with garlic

■ ■ ■

SERVES 4 ▸ **TIME TAKEN:** 10 minutes

This is an oriental way of cooking broccoli that can also be used with cauliflower. The broccoli is steamed for a few minutes first, which ensures it is tender before the final stir-frying. Don't throw away the broccoli stems—either peel, cut into discs, and steam together with the florets, or use raw in salads.

2 pounds broccoli
2 tablespoons extra-virgin olive oil
1 teaspoon fresh ginger root, peeled and finely chopped
2 garlic cloves, peeled and finely chopped
½ fresh red chili, deseeded and finely chopped (optional)
freshly ground black pepper
2 tablespoons pine nuts
2 teaspoons tamari

> **Protein 18%**
> **Carbohydrate 30%**
> **Fat 52%**
> **GI: low**
> **GL: low**

Wash the broccoli and divide into florets. Steam over boiling water for 2 minutes only, then set aside.

Heat the olive oil in a wok over medium heat. Add the ginger, garlic, and chili (if using), stir once, then add the broccoli florets. Stir fry for about 4 minutes, and season with pepper. Toss in the pine nuts and serve sprinkled with tamari.

Variations: Try this with sesame seeds instead of pine nuts.

PER SERVING
Calories 143 ▸ Protein 7g ▸ Carbohydrates 12g ▸ Fiber 6g ▸ Sugar—Total 4g ▸ Fat—Total 9g ▸ Saturated Fat 1g ▸ Vitamin C 172mg ▸ Magnesium 62mg

---

▸ Broccoli is an amazingly nutritious vegetable. It contains twice as much vitamin C as an orange; it has almost as much calcium as whole milk—and the calcium is better absorbed; and it contains selenium, a mineral that has been found to have anticancer and antiviral properties. It is also a modest source of vitamin A and alpha-tocopherol vitamin E.

green vegetable stir-fry

■ ■ ■

SERVES 4 ▶ TIME TAKEN: 15 minutes

*T*his recipe is an adaptation of one by Dr. Mercola, a doctor with quite radical views who runs one of the best independent health sites on the Internet, www.mercola.com.

2 tablespoons coconut oil
2 garlic cloves, peeled and crushed
2 medium leeks, washed and sliced
1 pound brussels sprouts, washed and quartered
1 teaspoon fresh chopped rosemary
1 pound bunch of kale, stems removed and coarsely chopped
4 tablespoons water
2 tablespoons Dijon mustard
freshly ground black pepper

Protein 12%
Carbohydrate 48%
Fat 40%
GI: very low
GL: low

Heat a wok or heavy saucepan with a cover over high heat. Add oil and garlic and stir for a few seconds. Then add the sliced leeks. Stir-fry, stirring constantly, for about 2–3 minutes or until the leeks start to wilt. Add the Brussels sprouts and rosemary and stir-fry for 2–3 minutes. Reduce the heat to medium, add the chopped kale and water, stirring to combine. Cover and steam for 3–5 minutes, until the vegetables are tender. Remove the cover and stir in the Dijon mustard. Season with freshly ground black pepper. Remove to a serving dish and serve immediately.

─── PER SERVING ───
Calories 171 ▶ Protein 6g ▶ Carbohydrates 23g ▶ Fiber 6g ▶ Sugar—Total 8g ▶ Fat—Total 9g ▶ Saturated Fat 6g ▶ Vitamin C 119mg ▶ Magnesium 54mg

▶ Kale contains lutein and zeaxanthin, phytonutrients that protect the eyes from macular degeneration. Leeks, being a member of the onion family, contain quercetin, which protects against heart disease. So this mixture of vegetables is particularly good for people with diabetes whose heart and eye health are especially at risk.

arame with baked vegetables

■ ■ ■

SERVES 4 ▶ TIME TAKEN: 50 MINUTES

---

*A*rame is a mildly flavored seaweed that has been precooked and sliced finely. It is therefore an ideal food with which to start your exploration of sea vegetables. It expands hugely when soaked and cooked, so though a handful might seem like a small amount, it will swell dramatically.

½ ounce arame (a large handful)
2 medium onions, peeled and quartered
2 medium carrots, peeled unless organic,
    and cut into chunks
2 zucchini, thickly sliced
2 red peppers, deseeded and cut into pieces
4 ounces mushrooms, cut in half if large
2 garlic cloves, peeled and finely chopped
4 tablespoons extra-virgin olive oil
2 tablespoons concentrated apple juice

Protein 5%
Carbohydrate 37%
Fat 57%
GI: medium
GL: medium

to serve:
1 tablespoon tamari sauce
2 tablespoons coriander leaves, roughly chopped

Preheat the oven to 375°F.

Rinse the arame under cold water. Place it in a bowl and cover with cold water. Soak for 10 minutes, then rinse again and drain well.

Place the drained arame and all the other ingredients (except the tamari and coriander) in a large ovenproof casserole, and mix well. Add about 6 tablespoons of boiling water, just enough to moisten. Cover with a lid and bake until the vegetables are tender (approximately 35–40 minutes). Sprinkle with the tamari sauce, garnish with the chopped coriander, and serve hot.

PER SERVING

Calories 221 ▶ Protein 3g ▶ Carbohydrates 21g ▶ Fiber 3g ▶ Sugar—Total 13g ▶ Fat—Total 15g ▶
Saturated Fat 2g ▶ Vitamin C 122mg ▶ Magnesium 29mg

▶ Like other seaweeds, arame contains all of the minerals required by human beings, including calcium, sodium, magnesium, potassium, iodine, iron, and zinc.

In addition, there are many trace elements in seaweeds. The alginic acid in sea vegetables actually helps bind and draw out toxins such as lead, cadmium, mercury, and radioactive strontium that are stored in the body. Oriental medicine has long recognized that sea vegetables contribute to the health of the endocrine and nervous systems. In recent decades, medical researchers have discovered that a diet that includes sea vegetables reduces the risk of some diseases, including diabetes.

spiced red cabbage with prunes

▪ ▪ ▪

SERVES 4 ▸ **TIME TAKEN:** 3¼ hours

*T*his recipe is brilliant because it contains not only cinnamon, the virtues of which I have
mentioned elsewhere, but also juniper berries. Juniper berries have the reputation of being
able to regulate blood sugar. I have not found any clinical trials to support this theory, but it's
always worth paying attention to folk medicine.

1½ pounds red cabbage
2 small onions, peeled and sliced
3 tablespoons butter
½ teaspoon ground cinnamon
4 whole cloves
½ teaspoon freshly grated nutmeg
½ teaspoon crushed juniper berries
½ cup dried, ready-to-eat prunes
3 tablespoons concentrated apple juice
3 tablespoons red wine vinegar
sea salt and freshly ground black pepper to taste

> **Protein 6%**
> **Carbohydrate 56%**
> **Fat 38%**
> **GI: low**
> **GL: low**

Preheat the oven to 300°F.

Shred the cabbage finely, discarding the core. Place half the cabbage in the bottom
of a casserole. Place half the onions on top and then all the spices and the prunes.

Add half the butter in knobs and season with salt and pepper. Top with the rest of the
cabbage and the onions. Mix the vinegar and apple-juice concentrate together and pour
over the cabbage. Top with the rest of the butter.

Cover with a lid and bake for 3 hours, stirring occasionally, until tender. Taste and
adjust the seasoning. Serve hot.

PER SERVING

Calories 217 ▸ Protein 3g ▸ Carbohydrates 32g ▸ Fiber 6g ▸ Sugar—Total 22g ▸ Fat—Total 10g ▸
Saturated Fat 6g ▸ Vitamin C 62mg ▸ Magnesium 31mg

▸ Red cabbage has all the virtues of green cabbage, with the added advantage of
lycopene, which is responsible for the red coloring, also found in tomatoes.
Research has found that higher intakes of this antioxidant in the diet are associated with lower levels of heart disease, especially in men.

stir-fried bean sprouts

■ ■ ■

SERVES 4 ▶ **TIME TAKEN:** 10 minutes

M*ung bean sprouts are specified here, but feel free to use any sprouted beans or seeds in this stir-fry.*

1 pound mung bean sprouts
1 tablespoon extra-virgin olive oil
3 scallions, split lengthwise and cut into
   1-inch lengths
1 tablespoon fresh ginger root, peeled and finely chopped
½ teaspoon freshly ground black pepper
tamari

Protein 18%
Carbohydrate 42%
Fat 40%
GI: very low
GL: very low

Wash, drain, and dry the bean sprouts on kitchen paper.

Heat the olive oil in a wok over medium-high heat. Add the scallions and ginger, and stir-fry for a few seconds. Then add the bean sprouts and stir-fry for 1 minute. Do not overcook—sprouts should remain crunchy but lose their raw bean taste.

Season to taste with pepper, and sprinkle with tamari.

Mix well and serve.

PER SERVING

Calories 75 ▶ Protein 4g ▶ Carbohydrates 9g ▶ Fiber 2g ▶ Sugar—Total 4g ▶ Fat—Total 4g ▶ Saturated Fat 1g ▶ Vitamin C 17mg ▶ Magnesium 27mg

---

▶ Mung beans are small dried green beans with yellow flesh. Like all beans, they are rich in protein, calcium, phosphorus, and iron, but they are mainly grown for sprouting. Mung bean sprouts have long been a familiar ingredient in many Asian dishes. Traditional Chinese medicine maintains that mung beans have a "heat-clearing, toxin-resolving" effect that eases conditions such as diarrhea. They should be of particular interest to people with diabetes because they contain chiro-inositol, an ingredient also present in buckwheat, which may prompt cells to become more insulin-sensitive.

warm east-west salad

■ ■ ■

SERVES 4 ▶ **TIME TAKEN:** 20 minutes

---

*T*he style of this warm salad is oriental, but the vegetables come straight from an English garden.

3 small carrots
½ pound French beans, trimmed
1 cauliflower weighing about 1 pound
½ fresh red chili, deseeded and finely chopped
1 teaspoon apple juice concentrate
2 tablespoons shoyu sauce
1 tablespoon oriental sesame oil
1 tablespoon sesame seeds, toasted

Protein 14%
Carbohydrate 50%
Fat 36%
GI: medium
GL: low

for the broth:
2 cups vegetable stock (see page 229)
1 medium onion, peeled and finely chopped
1 teaspoon ginger root, grated
3 sprigs of thyme
1 lime, juice only

Put all the ingredients for the broth into a pan, bring to a boil, cover, and simmer for 5 minutes. Leave to infuse while you prepare the vegetables.

Cut the carrots into sticks about 2 inches long, and cut the beans the same length. Separate the cauliflower into small florets.

Strain the broth and return it to the pan. Bring to a boil and cook the vegetables in it for 3–4 minutes—not more, as they should retain some "bite." When cooked, drain the vegetables, reserving 3 tablespoons of the cooking broth. Place the vegetables in a serving bowl. Reserve 3 tablespoons of the cooking broth.

For the dressing, whisk together the reserved cooking broth, chopped chili, apple-juice concentrate, shoyu sauce, and sesame oil. Pour this over the vegetables and sprinkle with sesame seeds. Serve warm or at room temperature.

PER SERVING

Calories 123 ▶ Protein 5g ▶ Carbohydrates 17g ▶ Fiber 7g ▶ Sugar—Total 6g ▶ Fat—Total 5g ▶ Saturated Fat 1g ▶ Vitamin C 69mg ▶ Magnesium 34mg

---

beet, dandelion, and radish salad

■ ■ ■

SERVES 4 ▶ **TIME TAKEN:** 15 minutes

Beets can be eaten raw rather than cooked. For people with diabetes, raw beet is prefer-able because the GI of root vegetables is invariably higher when the vegetables are cooked. Dandelion makes a piquant addition to this salad, but only use the young spring leaves before the flowers appear, as older leaves are very bitter. If you don't have a source of clean dandelion leaves, or if it is the wrong time of year, use watercress instead.

3–4 small beets, weighing about 12 ounces
12 radishes
a good handful of fresh dandelion leaves,
    picked away from busy roads or
    where pesticides are used

for the dressing:
3 tablespoons sunflower seeds, ground
3 tablespoons extra-virgin olive oil
1 tablespoon apple-cider vinegar
sea salt and freshly ground black pepper

Protein 7%
Carbohydrate 24%
Fat 69%
GI: very low
GL: very low

Peel the beets and grate finely into a bowl. Slice the radishes and mix in with the grated beets. Wash the dandelion leaves well, dry, and tear into bite-sized pieces. Arrange the dandelion leaves in the bottom of a salad bowl.

For the dressing, whisk all the ingredients together. Toss with the beets and radishes, then pile this mixture onto the dandelion leaves.

PER SERVING
Calories 215 ▶ Protein 4g ▶ Carbohydrates 13g ▶ Fiber 4g ▶ Sugar—Total 7g ▶ Fat—Total 17g ▶ Saturated Fat 2g ▶ Vitamin C 22mg ▶ Magnesium 29mg

▶ This salad is particularly good for the liver, as beets, radishes, and dandelions are known to be beneficial.

vegetables in curried coconut cream

■ ■ ■

SERVES 4 ▶ TIME TAKEN: 20 minutes

serve this delicious vegetable mixture with plain brown rice, but you could serve it as an accompaniment to a Thai meal. Root vegetables increase their glycemic index as they cook, so serve this when the carrots and celeriac still have some "bite."

1 tablespoon coconut oil
1 large onion, thinly sliced
2 garlic cloves, crushed
1 inch piece of ginger root, peeled and finely chopped
1 tablespoon curry paste
1 teaspoon ground turmeric
½ teaspoon chopped fresh chili
sea salt and freshly ground black pepper to taste
1 cup vegetable stock (see page 229)
1¼ pounds celeriac, peeled and cut into 1-inch cubes
2 carrots, sliced
¼ pound French beans, cut into 2-inch lengths
7 fluid ounces coconut cream
fresh coriander, chopped, for garnish

Protein 10%
Carbohydrate 34%
Fat 56%
GI: medium
GL: very low

Heat the coconut oil in a large saucepan over low heat and add the onion, garlic, and ginger. Cook for about 5 minutes, until softened but not brown. Stir in the curry paste, turmeric, chili, and seasoning. Add the stock, bring to a boil, and add the celeriac, carrots, and green beans. Cover and cook over gentle heat for 10 minutes. Stir in the coconut cream and continue cooking for another few minutes, until heated through and the vegetables are just tender but still resistant to the bite. Serve garnished with chopped fresh coriander.

━━━ **PER SERVING** ━━━
Calories 151 ▶ Protein 4g ▶ Carbohydrates 13g ▶ Fiber 4g ▶ Sugar—Total 5g ▶ Fat—Total 10g ▶ Saturated Fat 3g ▶ Vitamin C 18mg ▶ Magnesium 36mg

avocado, grapefruit, and alfalfa salad

■ ■ ■

SERVES 4 ▶ **TIME TAKEN:** 15 minutes

---

*T*his started out as an attempt to design a salad full of foods rich in vitamin E. However, it turned out to be too high in fat, as vitamin E is a fat-soluble vitamin. So I added grapefruit to cut the richness. It still has quite a lot of fat, although mostly monounsaturated, so I would serve it with plain grilled fish or chicken and a steamed green vegetable.

2 avocados
½ lemon, juice only
2 pink grapefruit
alfalfa sprouts, a handful
¼ cup sunflower seeds, toasted
vinaigrette made with walnut or avocado oil
    (see page 235)

Protein 5%
Carbohydrate 21%
Fat 74%
GI: very low
GL: very low

Peel and slice the avocados. Brush the cut surfaces with lemon juice to prevent discoloration. Peel the grapefruit, removing all the pith, and slice thinly into segments.

Fan out the avocado slices and grapefruit segments on individual plates, and put a mound of alfalfa sprouts on each serving. Garnish with toasted sunflower seeds and dress with walnut or avocado oil vinaigrette.

PER SERVING

Calories 372 ▶ Protein 5g ▶ Carbohydrates 21g ▶ Fiber 8g ▶ Sugar—Total 9g ▶ Fat—Total 33g ▶ Saturated Fat 4g ▶ Vitamin C 60mg ▶ Magnesium 70mg

▶ Avocados are nutritionally rich and should not be avoided on account of their fat content. They contain 4 times as much monounsaturated, and 4.5 times as much polyunsaturated fat (the good kinds) as saturated fat (the "bad" kind). They are also a good source of minerals, particularly potassium, and most of the B vitamins that we need for energy. As for grapefruit, recent research has shown that grapefruit really does contribute to weight loss, by moderating both insulin and blood glucose. It appears that grapefruit contains enzymes that help control insulin spikes after a meal. This frees the digestive system to process food more efficiently, which means that fewer nutrients are stored as fat.

bean and seed sprouts with avocado dressing

SERVES 4 ▶ TIME TAKEN: 15 minutes

*U*se whatever sprouts you have available for this salad—below are only suggestions. If you want to try growing your own sprouts, look for sprouting kits in the produce section of your local health-food store. If you don't have a juicer with which to make the carrot juice, cook and purée a couple of carrots and thin the purée with a little water.

½ cup mung bean sprouts
½ cup sprouted chickpeas
1 cup alfalfa sprouts
1 tablespoon sprouted fenugreek seeds
1 red pepper, deseeded and thinly sliced
2 tomatoes, peeled, deseeded and diced
½ cucumber, peeled and sliced

Protein 12%
Carbohydrate 41%
Fat 47%
GI: very low
GL: very low

for the dressing:
1 ripe avocado
1 tablespoon lime juice
4 tablespoons carrot juice, preferably freshly made
1 garlic clove, finely chopped
sea salt and freshly ground black pepper

For the dressing, peel and roughly chop the avocado. Put all the ingredients in the blender and blend to mix. The avocado should not discolor due to the lime juice.

For the salad, mix all the ingredients. Toss with the avocado dressing and serve.

PER SERVING

Calories 147 ▶ Protein 5g ▶ Carbohydrates 17g ▶ Fiber 6g ▶ Sugar—Total 4g ▶ Fat—Total 8g ▶ Saturated Fat 1g ▶ Vitamin C 75mg ▶ Magnesium 41mg

---

▶ Mung beans are thought to be beneficial as an antidiabetic, low-GI food, rich in antioxidants. I have included sprouted fenugreek seeds as they have similar properties.

egyptian broad bean salad

■ ■ ■

SERVES 4 ▶ **TIME TAKEN:** 40 minutes

There is a wonderful Egyptian dish made with dried brown broad beans called ful medames. *This is a variation made with fresh broad beans, best made with the first beans of the season before they have grown their thick skins, as it is a bit tedious to remove them, though well worth it. If you can find dried* ful, *available from Middle Eastern groceries, do try this dish with them.*

2 pounds fresh broad beans in the pod
low-sodium salt and freshly ground
    black pepper to taste
fresh sage leaves
1 dried red chili pepper or pepper flakes
1 tablespoon whole cumin seeds, dry roasted
fresh coriander leaves
basic vinaigrette (see page 235)
4 organic free-range eggs, hard boiled

> Protein 15%
> Carbohydrate 17%
> Fat 67%
> GI: very low
> GL: very low

Pod the broad beans and cook in boiling water for 10 minutes with the sage leaves. Drain and slip off the outer skins, unless very young and tender. Mix together the chilies, cumin seeds, and dressing. Pour over the beans. Shell the eggs, cut them into quarters, and serve with the beans, garnished with coriander leaves.

PER SERVING

Calories 316 ▶ Protein 12g ▶ Carbohydrates 14g ▶ Fiber 5g ▶ Sugar—Total 3g ▶ Fat—Total 24g ▶ Saturated Fat 4g ▶ Vitamin C 23mg ▶ Magnesium 50mg

---

▶ One of the really good things about broad beans is that they have very long tap-roots, going down five feet or more into the soil, where they are able to tap into minerals that other plants will not reach. This means that they have a better chance than other vegetables of delivering trace minerals to you when you eat them, for example selenium and zinc, which are both needed for thyroid function.

chinese-style broccoli salad

■ ■ ■

SERVES 4 ▶ TIME TAKEN: 35 minutes

T*he origins of this recipe lie in Elaine Bruce's* Living Foods for Radiant Health. *Elaine runs the Living Foods Clinic in Ludlow, the theory behind which is that only by eating raw foods can we obtain all the nutrients we need for maximum health. This dictum is quite hard for most people to follow, but it is certainly wise to incorporate a generous proportion of raw vegetables into our diet. Elaine's broccoli salad incorporates raw peppers and no dressing. This is my not-quite-authentic version.*

1 red pepper
1 yellow pepper
1 pound raw broccoli florets, finely chopped
4 zucchini, grated

dressing:
1 tablespoon toasted sesame oil
2 tablespoons extra-virgin olive oil
2 tablespoons fresh lemon juice
2 garlic cloves, peeled and crushed
1 tablespoon fresh ginger root, peeled and grated
sea salt and freshly ground black pepper
To serve: green salad leaves

Protein 11%
Carbohydrate 29%
Fat 60%
GI: very low
GL: very low

Grill the peppers under a hot grill, turning from time to time, until just charred. Leave to cool, then skin, deseed, and cut into strips.

Save a few tiny leaves and florets of broccoli for decoration. Mix the chopped broccoli with the grated zucchini. Whisk together all the ingredients for the dressing, then stir into the broccoli and zucchini, mixing thoroughly to balance the flavors. Turn the salad onto a dish of green leaves and decorate with strips of red and yellow pepper.

PER SERVING
Calories 154 ▶ Protein 5g ▶ Carbohydrates 12g ▶ Fiber 5g ▶ Sugar—Total 4g ▶ Fat—Total 11g ▶ Saturated Fat 2g ▶ Vitamin C 230mg ▶ Magnesium 46mg

▶ This salad is a rich source of beta-carotene, vitamin B$_6$, folic acid, and particularly vitamin C, of which it has a staggering 230 mg per serving, which is nearly four times the recommended daily allowance (RDA) for this vitamin.

fennel and red cabbage salad
with pumpkin seeds

◼ ◼ ◼

SERVES 4 ▶ TIME TAKEN: 20 minutes

---

*R*aw fennel is my absolutely favorite vegetable. If you can get hold of organic fennel, you will notice that its aniseed taste is much more pronounced than that of the convention-ally grown vegetable.

2 fennel bulbs
½ small red cabbage (about 8 ounces)
3 scallions, finely chopped
2 tablespoons pumpkin seeds
2 tablespoons plain yogurt
1 tablespoon extra-virgin olive oil
squeeze of lemon juice
sea salt and freshly ground black pepper

Protein 15%
Carbohydrate 40%
Fat 45%
GI: very low
GL: very low

Trim the fennel, reserving the frondy tops. Cut vertically into quarters, then slice as finely as possible. Shred the cabbage as finely as possible. Put the vegetables into a salad bowl and add the chopped scallions.

Toast the pumpkin seeds in a small dry pan until they begin to give off their aroma, but be careful not to let them get too dark.

For the dressing, mix together the yogurt and olive oil, sharpen with a little lemon juice, and season to taste. Stir the dressing into the fennel mixture until well combined.

Chop the fennel fronds and use them to garnish the salad, together with the toasted pumpkin seeds.

PER SERVING

Calories 129 ▶ Protein 5g ▶ Carbohydrates 14g ▶ Fiber 5g ▶ Sugar—Total 3g ▶ Fat—Total 7g ▶ Saturated Fat 1g ▶ Vitamin C 48mg ▶ Magnesium 68mg

---

▶ Besides its other virtues, fennel contains a good range of microminerals—those minerals of which we only need a small amount, such as selenium, iron, manganese, and molybdenum. Molybdenum is needed by some of the enzyme systems in the body that are involved in detoxification.

greek mushroom salad

■ ■ ■

*O*therwise known as *"champignons à la grècque,"* this is a French rather than a Greek salad.

12 ounces small button mushrooms
½ cup dry white wine
½ cup water
½ cup extra-virgin olive oil
1 lemon, juice only
1 bay leaf
2 tablespoons chopped onion
2 teaspoons fresh thyme leaves
pinch of ground coriander
1 teaspoon fennel seeds
sea salt and freshly ground black pepper

Protein 7%
Carbohydrate 18%
Fat 75%
GI: very low
GL: very low

Wipe the mushrooms, but do not peel them. If the mushrooms are very small, leave them whole. Otherwise, cut them in half or into quarters, depending on their size. Put all the remaining ingredients into a saucepan, bring to a boil and simmer them for 5 minutes. Add the mushrooms and simmer for another 5 minutes. Let the mushrooms cool in the liquid before placing in a bowl to serve.

PER SERVING

Calories 142 ▶ Protein 3g ▶ Carbohydrates 5g ▶ Fiber 2g ▶ Sugar—Total 2g ▶ Fat—Total 12g ▶ Saturated Fat 2g ▶ Vitamin C 8mg ▶ Magnesium 14mg

▶ Because mushrooms contain chromium, it is important for people with diabetes to include them in their diet, as it is one of the major components of glucose-tolerance factor, a molecule that improves insulin's ability to lower blood-sugar levels. Chromium also helps to reduce sugar cravings.

lime-scented carrot and cumin salad

■ ■ ■

SERVES 4 ▶ **TIME TAKEN:** 20 minutes

---

*T*his is a good way to use the larger, older carrots. Given this treatment they appear to regain their youth.

2 teaspoons cumin seeds
3 tablespoons extra-virgin olive oil
1 organic lime, grated zest and juice
sea salt and freshly ground black pepper
3–4 large organic carrots, peeled and finely grated
    (about 1½ pounds)
1 red onion, peeled and thinly sliced into rings
1 tablespoon coriander leaves, chopped

Protein 4%
Carbohydrate 39%
Fat 57%
GI: very low
GL: very low

First, dry-fry the cumin seeds in a small pan until they begin to release their aroma. Be careful as they can jump out of the pan when they get hot. Set aside.

Whisk together the olive oil, lime juice and zest, and seasoning. Put the carrots and onions into a salad bowl, toss with the dressing, then stir in the toasted cumin seeds. Garnish with chopped coriander.

PER SERVING

Calories 165 ▶ Protein 2g ▶ Carbohydrates 17g ▶ Fiber 5g ▶ Sugar—Total 10g ▶ Fat—Total 11g ▶ Saturated Fat 2g ▶ Vitamin C 20mg ▶ Magnesium 24mg

---

▶ Raw carrots have a GI of 16 or thereabouts, but as much as 49 after cooking. Since they are our richest source of the antioxidant beta-carotene and other carotenoids, which help to provide protection against free-radical damage, it is a good idea for people with diabetes to eat them regularly.

pink and purple salad

■ ■ ■

SERVES 4 ▶ **TIME TAKEN:** 1½ hours, including 1 hour standing

---

I designed this salad to take advantage of the beautiful purple curly kale when it comes into season in the winter. If you can't find it, use ordinary green kale, which has the same nutritive properties.

2 small raw beets
1 pink or red grapefruit
2 cups purple curly kale, washed and torn into
   bite-sized pieces, woody stems discarded
12 radishes, sliced

for the dressing:
4 tablespoons orange juice
1 teaspoon finely grated orange zest from an organic orange
4 tablespoons extra-virgin olive oil
1 tablespoon finely grated fresh ginger root
2 tablespoons chopped parsley
sea salt and freshly ground black pepper

> Protein 5%
> Carbohydrate 31%
> Fat 64%
> GI: very low
> GL: very low

Peel and grate the beets. Whisk together all the dressing ingredients and stir half the dressing into the beets. Leave for an hour to allow the flavors to meld.

Peel and segment the grapefruit. Toss the kale with the rest of the dressing and arrange on four plates. Scatter with the sliced radishes. Pile the dressed beets on top, and decorate with the grapefruit segments.

PER SERVING
Calories 194 ▶ Protein 2g ▶ Carbohydrates 16g ▶ Fiber 3g ▶ Sugar—Total 11g ▶ Fat—Total 14g ▶
Saturated Fat 2g ▶ Vitamin C 74mg ▶ Magnesium 27mg

▶ Kale is a fantastic source of minerals, beta-carotene, and folic acid, and this puts it firmly on my list of superfoods.

spinach salad with garlic yogurt dressing

SERVES 4 ▶ **TIME TAKEN:** 15 minutes

This is a good way to use the larger spinach leaves. Baby spinach leaves don't need much jazzing up, but the larger leaves, with their strong flavor and more robust texture, take kindly to a creamy dressing.

1 pound fresh spinach
2 tomatoes, peeled and sliced
6 scallions, thinly sliced on the diagonal
5 tablespoons plain yogurt
2 tablespoons extra-virgin olive oil
2 garlic cloves, peeled and finely chopped
1 tablespoon fresh oregano leaves
sea salt and freshly ground black pepper

> Protein 16%
> Carbohydrate 31%
> Fat 53%
> GI: very low
> GL: very low

Wash the spinach well in several changes of water. Dry the leaves carefully and tear into bite-sized pieces if necessary. Place in a salad bowl together with the tomatoes and scallions.

Whisk together the yogurt, olive oil, chopped garlic, and oregano, and season to taste. Toss the salad with the dressing and serve.

PER SERVING
Calories 124 ▶ Protein 5g ▶ Carbohydrates 11g ▶ Fiber 4g ▶ Sugar—Total 3g ▶ Fat—Total 8g ▶ Saturated Fat 1g ▶ Vitamin C 49mg ▶ Magnesium 101mg

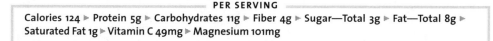 Spinach is an excellent source of magnesium, needed by people with diabetes, because magnesium can help promote healthy insulin production. It can also reduce the craving for sweet foods that can contribute to the development of Type 2 diabetes.

desserts

apple and passion fruit pudding
with almond wafers

■ ■ ■

SERVES 4 ▶ TIME TAKEN: 1 hour

Apple pudding was one of my favorite desserts from childhood, and here I have updated it with the addition of passion fruit, which weren't available back then. Make sure the passion fruit are ripe—the skin should be wrinkled and hard.

for the almond wafers:
1 tablespoon unsalted butter, softened
2 tablespoons organic raw cane sugar
1 organic, free-range egg white
scant ¼ cup plain or gluten-free flour
1 tablespoon flaked almonds

for the apple and passion fruit snow:
1 pound cooking apples
3 tablespoons concentrated apple juice
3 passion fruit
3 organic, free-range egg whites

Protein 9%
Carbohydrate 73%
Fat 18%
GI: medium
GL: medium

Preheat the oven to 350°F. Cover a large flat baking tray with a sheet of nonstick baking parchment. Cream the butter and sugar until well mixed then beat in the egg whites followed by the flour.

Spoon a level tablepoonful on to the baking tray and spread with the back of the spoon round and round into a flat circle. Sprinkle with the flaked nuts.

Repeat three more times so you have four thin wafers on the sheet. Bake for 8–10 minutes until the edges turn light brown and the centers are pale golden. Remove from the oven, wait a few seconds then slide off with a palette knife on to a rack to cool. Repeat with the rest of the mixture. You should have 8 thin wafers.

For the apple and passion fruit snow, peel, core, and roughly chop the apples and put them in a pan with the concentrated apple juice and 3 tablespoons water. Bring to a boil, lower the heat, and simmer gently, covered, until the apple has cooked down to a mush. This will take about 20 minutes. Remove from the heat and stir vigorously with a wooden spoon to break down any remaining pieces of apple.

Cut the passion fruit in half and spoon out the pulp. Add to the apple purée and mix thoroughly.

Put the egg whites in a bowl and whisk until they form soft peaks. Fold the egg whites into the apple-passion fruit mixture. Spoon the apple foam into individual glass dishes and serve cold, accompanied by the almond wafers.

PER SERVING

Calories 212 ▸ Protein 5g ▸ Carbohydrates 41g ▸ Fiber 4g ▸ Sugar—Total 31g ▸ Fat—Total 4g ▸ Saturated Fat 2g ▸ Vitamin C 10mg ▸ Magnesium 19mg

Note: Because this recipe contains uncooked egg whites, it should not be served to pregnant women.

▸ Apples are an excellent choice for people with diabetes as their glycemic index is low and they provide soluble fiber, which slows down glycemic response.

apricot and tofu cheesecake

■ ■ ■

SERVES 6 ▶ TIME TAKEN: 30 minutes plus setting time

---

*F*resh apricots are tricky customers. They can be utterly delicious if you catch them at the right moment, but so often they are picked before they are ripe and never reach ripe perfection. You can use well-drained apricots canned in their own juice for this recipe if you cannot find good fresh ones.

Protein 18%
Carbohydrate 45%
Fat 37%
GI: medium
GL: low

for the base:
2 tablespoons butter
2 tablespoons apple juice
4 ounces oat and almond muesli (see page 46)

for the filling:
10 ounces silken tofu
1 cup plain or soy yogurt, drained in a sieve overnight
4 tablespoons apple juice
2 teaspoons agar-agar powder
   (or 1½ tablespoons agar-agar flakes)

for the topping:
6 fresh apricots, halved and stoned
2 tablespoons all-fruit apricot jam

Preheat the oven to 350°F.

For the base, process the muesli in a food processor until it forms fine crumbs. Melt the butter and apple juice over gentle heat and mix it with the ground muesli. Spread it in an oiled 9-inch flan pan with a removable base, and bake for 5 minutes. Cool and chill while you make the filling.

Place the tofu and drained yogurt in a food processor and process until smooth. Put the apple juice and agar agar powder into a small pan and cook until the agar-agar has dissolved—about 5 minutes. If you are using the agar-agar flakes, you will need to cook a bit longer. Stir into the yogurt and tofu mixture.

Spread this mixture on to the chilled base and refrigerate until set.

Remove the flan ring and place on a serving plate. Arrange the apricot halves on the cake. Mix the apricot jam with a tablespoonful of warm water, and brush onto the apricots. Serve chilled.

PER SERVING

Calories 210 ▸ Protein 10g ▸ Carbohydrates 25g ▸ Fiber 2g ▸ Sugar—Total 10g ▸ Fat—Total 9g ▸
Saturated Fat 4g ▸ Vitamin C 4mg ▸ Magnesium 34mg

▶ Apricots are a useful source of beta-carotene, a good antioxidant protective against free-radical damage. They taste sweet but provide relatively few calories. They also supply fiber and have a low glycemic index, so they make an excellent choice for people with diabetes and for those who need to lose weight.

baked blackberry cheesecake

■ ■ ■

SERVES 4 ▶ **TIME TAKEN:** 1¼ hours

I love blackberries, especially the fact that they are free. My husband and I pick as many as possible during the season. I like them raw on my cereal at breakfast, or just simply mixed with yogurt, and they're good, too, stewed lightly with apple for all sorts of pies and puddings. This cheesecake is best made with fresh raw blackberries, but frozen, thawed blackberries will do almost as well. Drained blackberries canned in natural juice are a third choice.

⅔ cup cottage cheese
scant ⅔ cup plain or soy yogurt
1 tablespoon wholegrain or gluten-free flour
2 tablespoons organic raw cane sugar
1 organic, free-range egg
1 organic, free-range egg white
½ lemon, finely grated rind and juice
1½ cups fresh or thawed frozen blackberries

Protein 32%
Carbohydrate 49%
Fat 19%
GI: low
GL: low

Preheat the oven to 350°F. Oil a 7-inch loose-bottomed round cake pan, and line with greaseproof paper.

Place the cottage cheese in the food processor and process until smooth, or rub through a wire sieve into a bowl. Add the yogurt, flour, sugar, whole egg, and egg white, mixing well. Then stir in the lemon rind and juice and the blackberries, reserving a few for garnish.

Spoon the mixture into the prepared cake pan and bake for 30–35 minutes, or until set. Turn off the oven and leave the cheesecake in the oven for another 30 minutes.

Take the cheesecake out of the oven, run a knife around the perimeter, then turn it out of the pan. Remove the greaseproof paper and leave to cool.

Serve the cheesecake at room temperature, sliced into sections and decorated with the reserved blackberries.

PER SERVING

Calories 137 ▶ Protein 11g ▶ Carbohydrates 18g ▶ Fiber 3g ▶ Sugar—Total 6g ▶ Fat—Total 3g ▶ Saturated Fat 1g ▶ Vitamin C 21mg ▶ Magnesium 17mg

---

▶ I have used cottage cheese very little in this book, as dairy products (with the exception of yogurt) may be contraindicated for people with diabetes, particularly those with Type 1 diabetes. However, cottage cheese is a useful low-fat source of protein and can be included in the diet from time to time. If you are avoiding dairy products, you could substitute drained and mashed tofu for the cottage cheese.

apple quinoa pudding

■ ■ ■

SERVES 4 ▶ **TIME TAKEN:** 1 hour

Quinoa is a good choice for a filling winter pudding, as it's high in protein and provides less starch than a wheat-based alternative. The yogurt is important as the protein and fat it contains balance the carbohydrate and help to reduce the glycemic load.

½ cup apple juice
½ cup water
½ cup quinoa
3 tablespoons raisins
½ teaspoon mixed spice
3 dessert apples
2 tablespoons organic molasses sugar
to serve: vanilla yogurt

Protein 10%
Carbohydrate 82%
Fat 8%
GI: medium
GL: medium

Place the apple juice, water, quinoa, raisins, and mixed spice in a pan, and bring to a boil over medium heat, stirring. Lower the heat, cover, and simmer for 15–20 minutes, or until the quinoa is tender and most of the liquid evaporated. Drain off and discard any liquid that is left.

Preheat the oven to 400°F.

Spoon half the quinoa mixture into a 4-cup ovenproof dish. Peel, core, and slice the apples and arrange half the slices over the quinoa. Top with the remaining quinoa, and arrange the remaining apple slices on top. Sprinkle with the molasses sugar.

Bake for 25–30 minutes in the preheated oven, or until golden brown.

Serve with yogurt.

PER SERVING

Calories 233 ▶ Protein 6g ▶ Carbohydrates 51g ▶ Fiber 4g ▶ Sugar—Total 25g ▶ Fat—Total 2g ▶ Saturated Fat 0g ▶ Vitamin C 6mg ▶ Magnesium 88mg

▶ Quinoa is a rich source of magnesium, a very important mineral for people with diabetes as it is needed for the synthesis of insulin. Molasses sugar is made from the part of the sugarcane left behind after the refining process. So although it is sugar, it is rich in minerals, especially iron.

blueberry and lemon yogurt

■ ■ ■

SERVES 4 ▶ **TIME TAKEN:** 10 minutes

This is a beguilingly simple recipe but delicious. You need to use a thick yogurt—I usually use a sheep's milk yogurt, or you could substitute with a goat's milk yogurt instead. If your yogurt is a bit on the thin side, strain it in some clean muslin for a couple of hours to remove some of the whey before proceeding.

1 pound yogurt
5 ounces crème fraîche
1 tablespoon very finely grated lemon rind
3 tablespoons organic raw cane sugar
1½ cups blueberries

> **Protein 22%**
> **Carbohydrate 62%**
> **Fat 16%**
> **GI: low**
> **GL: low**

Simply mix together the yogurt, crème fraîche, and lemon rind and sweeten to taste. Place most of the blueberries into four individual glass dishes, reserving a few for decoration, then spoon over the yogurt mixture. Decorate with the remaining blueberries and serve chilled.

PER SERVING

Calories 120 ▶ Protein 7g ▶ Carbohydrates 20g ▶ Fiber 2g ▶ Sugar—Total 9g ▶ Fat—Total 2g ▶ Saturated Fat 1g ▶ Vitamin C 9mg ▶ Magnesium 3mg

▶ Variations on this theme are endless and limited only to the fruit you have on hand. This dish is delicious with strawberries and exquisite with raspberries. Kiwi fruit, pears, fresh apricots, or any other soft, sweet fruit would do very well too.

chocolate cherry soufflés

SERVES 6 ▶ **TIME TAKEN:** 40 minutes

*S*oufflés seem a bit daunting to make, but are much easier than you might suppose. The secret is to make sure that your guests are waiting to eat them, as a soufflé will collapse if kept waiting. So make the first part of the recipe in advance, then after the main course, whisk the egg whites, assemble the soufflés, bake, and serve straight from the oven.

butter for greasing
plain flour for dusting
6 ounces dark organic chocolate, at least 70% cocoa solids
2 fluid ounces cherry liqueur
5 whole organic free-range eggs, separated
2 ounces organic raw cane sugar
2 organic free-range egg whites
icing sugar, for dusting

Protein 6%
Carbohydrate 57%
Fat 37%
GI: medium
GL: medium

Preheat oven to 400°F. Grease 6 ramekins or individual soufflé moulds with butter and dust lightly with flour. Wrap a double layer of greaseproof paper around the ramekins so that it comes about 1¼ inches above the rim. Secure the paper with string and place the ramekins on a baking sheet.

Break up the chocolate and place in a heatproof bowl. Half fill a medium saucepan with water and bring to a boil. Reduce the heat to a simmer and place the bowl of chocolate over the saucepan, making sure that it is not touching the water. Stir until the chocolate melts. Whisk in the cherry liqueur until well combined. Stir in the egg yolks and sugar, and transfer to a large bowl. Up to here the recipe can be made in advance.

In another large clean bowl, beat the egg whites until firm peaks form. Fold a third of egg whites into the chocolate mixture. Fold in the rest of the egg-white mixture until just combined. Spoon the mixture into the soufflé cups and run your thumb around the inside edge to make sure the soufflés rise evenly. Bake for 12–15 minutes or until the soufflés are well risen and have just set. Do not open the oven before 12 minutes or the soufflés will collapse. Cut the string, remove the paper collars, dust the soufflés lightly with sieved icing sugar and serve immediately.

PER SERVING
Calories 232 ▶ Protein 3g ▶ Carbohydrates 30g ▶ Fiber 2g ▶ Sugar—Total 26g ▶ Fat—Total 10g ▶ Saturated Fat 6g ▶ Vitamin C omg ▶ Magnesium 1mg

▶ I included this because there just had to be a chocolate recipe for chocolate addicts. But this recipe is only to be indulged in when you have your blood sugar under control and have preceded it with a low-carbohydrate main course. The large proportion of protein-rich eggs does mitigate the effect of the sugar to a certain extent.

cherry buckwheat crêpes

■ ■ ■

SERVES 6 ▶ TIME TAKEN: 1 hour

*Y*ou could make these crêpes using only buckwheat flour, but without the addition of a
lighter flour they can be a bit heavy and strong-tasting.

for the crêpes:
¾ cup buckwheat flour
¼ cup unbleached white flour or gluten-free flour
1 large, organic free-range egg
1 cup soy or rice milk mixed with water

for the filling:
1 pound black cherries, stoned
3 tablespoons concentrated apple juice
1½ teaspoons arrowroot

Protein 11%
Carbohydrate 76%
Fat 13%
GI: medium
GL: low

For the crêpes, put the flour, egg, and milk and water mixture in the blender, and
blend until well mixed. Leave the batter to rest while you make the filling.

For the filling, put the cherries and concentrated apple juice into a pan, bring to a boil
over gentle heat, and simmer for 10–15 minutes or until the cherries are tender. Cool
a little, then drain, reserving the syrup.

Now, make the crêpes. Heat a nonstick medium-sized frying pan and spray lightly
with olive oil spray. Ladle in enough batter just to cover the base of the pan. Cook over
medium-high heat until the surface bubbles and starts to dry. Turn and cook the other
side until lightly browned, then slide the finished crêpe out onto kitchen paper and keep
warm. Repeat with the remaining mixture. This should make 12 crêpes.

To finish the filling, mix about 2 tablespoons of the syrup with the arrowroot in a
small saucepan, then stir in the rest of the syrup. Heat gently, stirring, until the mixture
boils, thickens, and clears. Add the cherries and stir until heated through.

Spoon the cherries into the crêpes and fold into quarters. Serve hot with a spoonful
of plain yogurt.

PER SERVING
Calories 173 ▶ Protein 5g ▶ Carbohydrates 35g ▶ Fiber 4g ▶ Sugar—Total 18g ▶ Fat—Total 3g ▶
Saturated Fat 1g ▶ Vitamin C 5mg ▶ Magnesium 53mg

These crêpes incorporate two ingredients that are thought to be beneficial for people with diabetes—cherries and buckwheat. The contribution of cherries is their low GI, and buckwheat has been shown in several studies to help lower blood glucose.

cherry and almond clafoutis

■ ■ ■

SERVES 6 ▶ TIME TAKEN: 1 hour

A *clafoutis is a French pudding consisting of fruit baked in a rich pancake batter. It's very easy, and delicious with apples, pears, apricots, or blackberries. But it's best of all with cherries.*

2 pounds cherries, washed and stoned
2 tablespoons brown-rice flour or gluten-free flour
4 tablespoons maple syrup
4 organic free-range eggs
⅓ cup ground almonds
1 cup soy or rice milk
1 tablespoon extra-virgin olive oil
2 teaspoons icing sugar (optional)
soy cream or yogurt to serve

Protein 12%
Carbohydrate 50%
Fat 38%
GI: medium
GL: low

Preheat the oven to 375°F.

Oil a shallow baking dish. Put the cherries in the dish. Beat together the flour, maple syrup, eggs, ground almonds, soy, or rice milk and olive oil (this is easiest done in a blender). Pour the batter over the cherries, and bake in the oven for 45 minutes, or until the clafoutis is puffed up and golden. To test whether it is cooked, insert a sharp knife or wooden skewer into the middle—it should come out clean. If it doesn't, lower the heat to 300°F and continue cooking for another 10 minutes or so.

Serve dusted with icing sugar if desired, and with soy cream or yogurt on the side.

PER SERVING
Calories 299 ▶ Protein 10g ▶ Carbohydrates 39g ▶ Fiber 5g ▶ Sugar—Total 30g ▶ Fat—Total 13g ▶ Saturated Fat 2g ▶ Vitamin C 10mg ▶ Magnesium 64mg

---

▶ Cherries are a rich source of copper, a deficiency of which may be a cause of osteoporosis. Certainly, it is known that a severe copper deficiency produces abnormalities in bone growth, which would imply that it is wise to make sure we get enough copper from our diet.

peach and cinnamon soufflés

SERVES 4 ▶ **TIME TAKEN:** 35 minutes

½ cup sugar-free peach jam or spread
butter, for greasing
plain or gluten-free flour, for dusting
3 organic, free-range eggs
½ lemon, finely grated rind
1 teaspoon cinnamon, plus extra for garnish

Protein 28%
Carbohydrate 23%
Fat 49%
GI: medium
GL: medium

Preheat the oven to 375°F. Butter four individual soufflé dishes or ramekins and dust lightly with flour.

Separate the eggs and put into a bowl together with the peach spread, lemon rind, and cinnamon. Whisk until the mixture is thick. Whisk the egg whites in another bowl until they form soft peaks. Using a metal spoon, fold the whisked egg whites quickly into the peach mixture until amalgamated.

Divide the mixture between the four prepared dishes and bake for 10–15 minutes until golden and risen. Serve immediately, dusted with extra cinnamon.

PER SERVING

Calories 128 ▶ Protein 5g ▶ Carbohydrates 4g ▶ Fiber 1g ▶ Sugar—Total 3g ▶ Fat—Total 4g ▶ Saturated Fat 1g ▶ Vitamin C 2mg ▶ Magnesium 6mg

---

▶ I used the St. Dalfour fruit spread for this recipe. It is also delicious with their other sugar-free fruit spreads, such as apricot or blueberry.

cinnamon apple yogurt cake

SERVES 8 ▶ **TIME TAKEN:** 1¼ hours

This cake is based on a recipe by Donna Hay, the gifted and innovative Australian cookery writer. Her version, using sour cream, is richer and more indulgent than my pared-down version. Don't be put off by the amount of butter and sugar—the cake serves 8 people, so each serving contains only a small amount.

1 stick butter
4 tablespoons pear and apple spread
2 teaspoons cinnamon
2 organic, free-range eggs
5 ounces plain yogurt, drained of whey
1 tablespoon lemon juice
8 ounces gluten-free flour
1 teaspoon baking powder

Protein 5%
Carbohydrate 36%
Fat 59%
GI: medium
GL: low

for the topping:
3 tablespoons gluten-free flour
3 tablespoons organic raw cane sugar
3 tablespoons ground pumpkin seeds
1 teaspoon cinnamon
3 green dessert apples, peeled, cored,
    and thinly sliced

Preheat the oven to 350°F. Grease a 9-inch round springform cake pan.

Beat together the butter, concentrated apple juice, and cinnamon, either by hand or with an electric mixer. Add the eggs and beat well. Fold in the drained yogurt and lemon juice. Sift together the flour and baking powder and fold gently into the mixture. Spoon into the prepared cake pan.

For the topping, mix together the flour, sugar, ground pumpkin seeds, and cinnamon, then toss the apple slices in this mixture. Arrange the apple slices over the top of the cake and sprinkle with any remaining topping. Bake for 1 hour or until a wooden skewer inserted in the cake comes out clean. Serve warm or at room temperature with extra yogurt if desired.

Variations: Try substituting pears, plums, or apricots for the apples. Ground almonds or walnuts would work well instead of ground pumpkin seeds for the topping.

PER SERVING

Calories 307 ▸ Protein 5g ▸ Carbohydrates 43g ▸ Fiber 2g ▸ Sugar—Total 9g ▸ Fat—Total 15g ▸ Saturated Fat 8g ▸ Vitamin C 3mg ▸ Magnesium 29mg

cinnamon clementines

■ ■ ■

SERVES 4 ▶ TIME TAKEN: 35 minutes

This is a dessert I make at Christmas as an alternative to the ubiquitous Christmas pudding, which is too heavy to eat after the turkey and all the trimmings, disliked by many people and anyway pretty much out-of-bounds for people with diabetes. This is a light but festive alternative with the added benefit of blood-sugar-lowering cinnamon.

8 clementines

1 cup apple juice

2 cinnamon sticks

2 tablespoons Cointreau or Grand Marnier (optional)

2 tablespoons shelled, unsalted pistachio nuts

Protein 6%
Carbohydrate 80%
Fat 14%
GI: medium
GL: medium-high

Using a vegetable peeler, pare the rind from two of the clementines, being careful not to include any pith, and cut into fine strips. Set aside.

Peel the clementines, removing every scrap of pith but keeping each fruit whole. Place in a heatproof bowl.

Place the apple juice, reserved peel, and cinnamon sticks into a pan, bring to a boil and cook until reduced by half. Stir in the liqueur if using. Leave the syrup to cool for about 10 minutes, then pour over the clementines in the bowl. Cool, cover, and chill overnight.

Before serving, skin the pistachios: cover them with boiling water for a few minutes. Drain and slip off the skins while still warm. Chop roughly and scatter over the clementines before serving. Serve with natural yogurt.

PER SERVING

Calories 123 ▶ Protein 2g ▶ Carbohydrates 27g ▶ Fiber 4g ▶ Sugar—Total 22g ▶ Fat—Total 2g ▶ Saturated Fat 0g ▶ Vitamin C 44mg ▶ Magnesium 24mg

▶ I make no apology for including so many recipes featuring cinnamon. There has been a lot of research into the benefits of cinnamon in the management of diabetes (see page 29) that consuming half a teaspoon per day seems like an excellent strategy. Although this doesn't sound like a large quantity, it may be quite difficult to use this much and you will be looking for innovative ways to include cinnamon in your diet. These clementines are just one idea.

floating islands with plum sauce

SERVES 4 ▶ **TIME TAKEN:** 45 minutes

1 pound plums
1 cup apple juice
2 organic, free-range egg whites
2 tablespoons organic raw cane sugar
fresh nutmeg, grated

Protein 8%
Carbohydrate 87%
Fat 5%
GI: medium
GL: medium

Halve and pit the plums. Place in a pan with the apple juice. Bring to a boil, lower the heat, cover, and simmer for 15–20 minutes or until the plums are tender. Cool and purée in a blender or food processor. Pour the resulting purée into a wide sauté pan or frying pan and leave to simmer over a very gentle heat.

For the "islands," whisk the egg whites until they hold soft peaks. Gradually whisk in the sugar, and continue whisking until the meringue is stiff.

Using two tablespoons, form the meringue mixture into 8 oval shapes and place into the simmering plum sauce. Cover and simmer gently for 2–3 minutes, until the meringues are just set. Serve hot with a sprinkling of fresh nutmeg.

PER SERVING

Calories 135 ▶ Protein 3g ▶ Carbohydrates 31g ▶ Fiber 2g ▶ Sugar—Total 27g ▶ Fat—Total 1g ▶ Saturated Fat 0g ▶ Vitamin C 11mg ▶ Magnesium 12mg

▶ The protein in the egg whites helps to mitigate the blood-sugar raising effect of the sweet plums.

poached pears in ginger yogurt sauce

SERVES 4 ▶ **TIME TAKEN:** 1 hour

Pears and ginger make a delicious combination.

4 large dessert pears, such as Comice or Bartlett
1 tablespoon lemon juice
1 cup apple juice
thinly pared rind of one lemon
2 pieces of stem ginger, chopped
2 tablespoons syrup from the jar of ginger
½ teaspoon arrowroot
½ cup vanilla yogurt

Protein 5%
Carbohydrate 88%
Fat 7%
GI: medium
GL: medium

Preheat the oven to 350°F.

Peel the pears thinly, leaving them whole with their stalks on. Brush with lemon juice to prevent discoloration. Using an apple corer or potato peeler, scoop out as much of the core as you can from the base of each pear.

Place the pears in an ovenproof dish together with apple juice and lemon rind. Cook in the preheated oven until tender—about half an hour—turning the pears from time to time so that they cook evenly.

Remove the pears to a plate to cool and pour the syrup into a pan. Bring to a boil and cook, uncovered, until reduced by half. Add the ginger and ginger syrup. Take out a spoonful or two of liquid and blend in a cup with the arrowroot, then return to the pan and mix well. Cook gently, stirring, until the mixture thickens and clears. This will only take a minute or two, then remove from the heat. Up to now the recipe can be made in advance.

Just before serving, mix the ginger syrup with the yogurt and use to cover the base of four individual plates. Then slice the pears almost all the way through from base to stem, leaving the slices attached at the stem end. Finally, fan out the pears on the yogurt and ginger sauce.

PER SERVING

Calories 180 ▶ Protein 2g ▶ Carbohydrates 43g ▶ Fiber 4g ▶ Sugar—Total 37g ▶ Fat—Total 1g ▶ Saturated Fat 0g ▶ Vitamin C 12mg ▶ Magnesium 14mg

Arrowroot is a white powder extracted from the root of a West Indian plant. The native people, the Arawaks, used the substance to draw out toxins from people wounded by poison arrows—hence the name Arrowroot. It is used today as a thickener, usually for sweet sauces. It thickens at a lower temperature than cornstarch, but cooking for more than a minute or two will cause the liquid to go thin again, so it should only be added at the end of cooking. Cornstarch can be substituted but use a bit less.

dried fruit pashka

■ ■ ■

SERVES 4 ▶ **TIME TAKEN:** 15 minutes, plus overnight draining

---

*P*ashka is a traditional Russian dessert, usually made with double cream and raw egg whites and served at Easter. My version uses strained cottage cheese and yogurt, thus cutting down on the saturated fat without sacrificing taste. You will need a clean clay flower pot and some clean muslin for this recipe.

12 ounces cottage cheese
¾ cup plain or soy yogurt
2 tablespoons maple syrup
½ teaspoon pure vanilla extract
2 tablespoons candied peel, chopped
grated rind of one orange
grated rind of one lemon
2 tablespoons unblanched almonds, chopped
1 tablespoon raisins
1 orange, for decoration

Protein 30%
Carbohydrate 48%
Fat 22%
GI: medium
GL: low

Drain any liquid from the cottage cheese. Place it in a sieve and, using a wooden spoon, rub it through the sieve into a bowl. Stir in the yogurt, maple syrup, and vanilla extract. Then add the candied peel and the grated citrus rind, reserving a little of the latter for decoration.

Line the flowerpot with the muslin, add the cheese mixture and press down firmly. Fold the muslin over the pudding and place a saucer with some weights on it on top. Put the pot on a saucer and refrigerate overnight. Any excess liquid will drip out at the hole in the bottom of the pot.

The next day, turn the pot upside down, turn out the pashka onto a serving plate and discard the muslin. Slice the whole orange and cut the slices in half. Surround the pashka with these and sprinkle it with the reserved grated orange and lemon peel.

PER SERVING

Calories 200 ▶ Protein 15g ▶ Carbohydrates 25g ▶ Fiber 2g ▶ Sugar—Total 15g ▶ Fat—Total 5g ▶ Saturated Fat 2g ▶ Vitamin C 14mg ▶ Magnesium 10mg

---

prune and orange creams

■ ■ ■

SERVES 4 ▶ **TIME TAKEN:** 20 minutes

This is very quick to make and uses ingredients you will probably already have to hand.

2 cups ready to eat prunes or soaked dried prunes,
    roughly chopped
½ cup orange juice
1 cup plain or soy yogurt
2 tablespoons Cointreau, Grand Marnier or brandy (optional)
The rind of half an orange, thinly pared and sliced
    into tiny matchsticks, to garnish

Protein 9%
GI: medium
Carbohydrate 85%
GL: low
Fat 6%

Place the chopped prunes in a pan with the orange juice and bring to a boil over a gentle heat. Cover and simmer for about 5 minutes, until the prunes are tender and the liquid is reduced by half. Remove from the heat and allow to cool, then blend to a purée in the blender or food processor.

Stir the yogurt, prune purée, and liqueur (if using) lightly together to achieve a marbled effect. Spoon into individual glass dishes and garnish with the shreds of orange peel. Serve chilled.

PER SERVING

Calories 211 ▶ Protein 5g ▶ Carbohydrates 49g ▶ Fiber 5g ▶ Sugar—Total 7g ▶ Fat—Total 1g ▶
Saturated Fat 1g ▶ Vitamin C 24mg ▶ Magnesium 27mg

▶ Prunes have many virtues, not least their laxative effect. They do this by providing fiber for the good bacteria. These bacteria then ferment the fiber and in the process increase the bulk of the stools, which helps to relieve constipation. Prunes are also an excellent source of potassium, which helps to maintain fluid balance and therefore good blood-pressure levels.

raspberries and passion fruit
with coconut custard

███

SERVES 4 ▶ TIME TAKEN: 1 hour

*P*assion fruit gives this pudding an exotic taste. As a variation, try it with pears, strawberries, or blueberries instead of the raspberries.

2¼ cups fresh raspberries
2 passion fruit
2 tablespoons organic raw cane sugar

coconut custard:
1 cup soy or rice milk, or goat's milk
1 cup coconut milk
1 cinnamon stick
¼ teaspoon freshly grated nutmeg
4 cardamom pods, crushed
1½ tablespoons arrowroot
4 raspberries and 4 sprigs of mint, to serve

Protein 7%
Carbohydrate 31%
Fat 62%
GI: low
GL: low

Using a fork, mash the raspberries in a small bowl until the juice runs.

Halve the passion fruit, scoop out the seeds and put these in a separate bowl.

For the custard, put all but 3 tablespoons of the milk into a pan, add the cinnamon, nutmeg and crushed cardamom and bring to just below boiling point over a gentle heat. Remove from the heat, cover and leave to infuse for 30 minutes. Strain through a sieve and discard the cinnamon and crushed cardamom.

Blend the arrowroot with the reserved 3 tablespoons milk and stir in the warm milk. Heat gently, stirring until boiling, then simmer, stirring constantly, for 1–2 minutes or until thickened. Leave to cool to room temperature.

Add the passion fruit pulp to the coconut custard and stir in sugar to taste, using as little as possible.

Place alternate spoonfuls of raspberry pulp and the coconut-custard mixture into individual glass dishes. Stir lightly to create a swirled effect, and decorate each serving with a whole raspberry and a sprig of fresh mint. Serve chilled.

PER SERVING
Calories 233 ▶ Protein 5g ▶ Carbohydrates 19g ▶ Fiber 8g ▶ Sugar—Total 8g ▶ Fat—Total 17g ▶ Saturated Fat 14g ▶ Vitamin C 22mg ▶ Magnesium 64mg
---

▶ Coconut milk has the same virtues as coconut oil, but in lesser proportion as it is only 24 percent fat.

basics

THE ESSENCE OF a good soup is the stock you use to make it. There are one or two good organic stocks on the market, such as Imagine Foods or Amy's, but nothing beats making your own. It should be a habit always to have some stock on hand in the fridge, but if there's simply no room, or you've got more stock than you know what to do with, you can make stock cubes to freeze. When you have made your stock, boil it hard until it is reduced to a fraction of its original volume, then freeze the resultant concentrated stock in ice-cube trays. These "stock cubes" can then be diluted with water to make instant homemade stock.

stock

vegetable stock

1 large onion
2 large carrots
3 sticks of celery
4 outside leaves of lettuce
potato peelings
parsley stalks
1 bay leaf
6 peppercorns
5 cups water

Simmer all the ingredients together for about half an hour. Drain and use as directed in soups and sauces. Since it is so quick to make I don't usually bother to keep vegetable stock on hand, but it should keep for up to a week in the fridge or four months in the freezer.

PER CUP

Calories 30 ▸ Protein 1g ▸ Carbohydrates 5g ▸ Sugar—Total 3g ▸ Fiber 0g ▸ Fat—Total 0g ▸ Saturated Fat 0g ▸ Vitamin C 0mg ▸ Magnesium 0mg

chicken stock

■ ■ ■

The longer and slower you can cook your stock the better. A slow Crock-Pot is ideal—if you have one of these, put it on low all night.

1 whole chicken, cooked
1 large onion, peeled and roughly chopped
2 large carrots, roughly chopped
3 sticks of celery, roughly chopped
parsley stalks
1 bay leaf
6 peppercorns
½ teaspoon sea salt
5 cups water

Put all the ingredients in a large pan and bring to a boil. Cover and simmer over very low heat for 1–2 hours. The slower you cook it, the more goodness will be extracted, and the clearer your stock will be. If you boil it too hard it will go cloudy.

Drain in a sieve or colander. If you are using the stock right away, skim off and discard any fat. If not, cool the stock completely before skimming the fat (it will be easier to remove when cool). It will keep for up to three days in the fridge or for three months in the freezer.

PER CUP

Calories 20 ▸ Protein 1g ▸ Carbohydrates 4g ▸ Fiber 1g ▸ Sugar—Total 2g ▸ Fat—Total 1g ▸ Saturated Fat 0g ▸ Vitamin C 0mg ▸ Magnesium 0mg

fish stock

2 tablespoons extra-virgin olive oil

1 onion, roughly chopped

2 carrots, chopped

2 sticks celery, chopped

1½ pounds bones and trimmings of any white fish such as cod,
haddock, whiting, or flounder

5 cups water

1 tablespoon white wine vinegar

3 whole black peppercorns

½ teaspoon sea salt

Heat the oil in a heavy pot over moderately high heat until hot but not smoking, then sauté the onion, carrots, and celery, stirring occasionally, until golden. Add the fish bones and trimmings, water, vinegar, peppercorns, and salt. Bring to a boil, skim the froth, then reduce heat and simmer, uncovered, for 30 minutes.

Pour the stock through a fine-mesh sieve into a large bowl. If you are using the stock right away, skim off and discard any fat. If not, cool the stock completely before skimming the fat (it will be easier to remove when cool). It will keep for a week in the fridge.

PER CUP
Calories 40 ▸ Protein 5g ▸ Carbohydrates 0g ▸ Fiber 0g ▸ Sugar—Total 0g ▸ Fat—Total 2g ▸ Saturated Fat 0g ▸ Vitamin C 0mg ▸ Magnesium 16mg

japanese stock

4 cups water
6-inch piece of dried kombu
8 large dried shiitake mushrooms

Bring all the ingredients to a boil in a large saucepan. Turn heat down to simmer, cover and cook for 15–20 minutes. Strain and use as required.

sauces
AND salad
dressings

basic tomato sauce

■ ■ ■

1 tablespoon extra-virgin olive oil
1 medium onion, peeled and finely chopped
1 carrot, finely chopped
1 stick celery, finely chopped
2 garlic cloves, peeled and finely chopped
4 tablespoons red or white wine
2 pounds fresh tomatoes, peeled and chopped, or
    2 14-ounce cans of chopped Italian tomatoes
bouquet garni of 1 bay leaf, 1 sprig each of parsley, thyme, and rosemary
sea salt and freshly ground black pepper

Heat the oil over medium heat, and sauté the onion, carrot, celery, and garlic until soft but not browned. Add the wine, tomatoes, bouquet garni, and seasoning. Bring to a boil, reduce the heat to low, cover, and simmer for one hour, stirring from time to time. Remove the bouquet garni, cool, and purée in the food processor. Keep refrigerated and use within four days or freeze for future use.

PER SERVING

Calories 81 ▸ Protein 2g ▸ Carbohydrates 12g ▸ Fiber 2g ▸ Sugar—Total 6g ▸ Fat—Total 3g ▸ Saturated Fat 1g ▸ Vitamin C 15mg ▸ Magnesium 14mg

basic vinaigrette

Whisk together 4 tablespoons cold-pressed extra-virgin olive oil, 1 tablespoon flaxseed oil, and 1 tablespoon cider vinegar, wine vinegar, or lemon juice. Season with sea salt, freshly ground black pepper, and a little dry mustard powder to taste.

Variations: Substitute walnut oil, hazelnut oil, or avocado oil for the olive oil.

soy mayonnaise

Using a blender, combine 3 ounces silken tofu, 1 tablespoon cider vinegar, 1 tablespoon concentrated apple juice, and seasoning to taste. With the machine running, add 6 tablespoons extra-virgin olive oil, drop by drop at first, and then in a steady stream, as for mayonnaise. Add a crushed clove or two of garlic for garlic mayonnaise.

miso dressing

Simply blend together 4 parts basic vinaigrette, 2 parts soy mayonnaise, and 1 part miso. This dressing is delicious on grated root vegetables.

gazpacho dressing

■ ■ ■

This is a deliciously appetizing dressing that enhances the look and flavor of different lettuces. The proportions are variable according to what you have available.

1 garlic clove
½ fresh green chili
½ small cucumber
½ red pepper
3 scallions
½ cup extra-virgin olive oil
1 tablespoon cider vinegar
1 tablespoon fresh lemon juice
1 tablespoon fresh basil, chopped
freshly ground black pepper

Whiz all the ingredients in the blender and keep in the fridge. Shake well and drizzle over salad, vegetables, or rice.

sunflower or pumpkin spread

■ ■ ■

MAKES 8 servings

Butter has its uses in cooking—being a saturated fat it is stable at high temperatures, and it adds a rich flavor to foods. However, there are many healthier and more nutritious spreads on the market. Try nut butters such as almond or cashew nut butter, or my latest favorite, brazil nut butter. For those who cannot tolerate nuts but would like a spread full of essential fatty acids and minerals, try using seeds instead.

1 cup sunflower or pumpkin seeds
1–2 tablespoons organic, cold-pressed sunflower or
   pumpkin-seed oil
sea salt and freshly ground black pepper
1 tablespoon water or lemon juice

Grind the seeds in an electric grinder until a fine powder is formed. Transfer to the food processor and, with the machine running, add half the oil. Gradually add the rest of the oil, if necessary, until the desired consistency is reached. Season to taste and stir in the water or lemon juice—this helps to emulsify the mixture. Homemade nut or seed butter is chunkier than the commercial variety because a domestic blender cannot grind as finely. Keep refrigerated and use within 3–4 days.

PER SERVING

Calories 72 ▸ Protein 3g ▸ Carbohydrates 2g ▸ Fiber 0g ▸ Sugar—Total 0g ▸ Fat—Total 6g ▸ Saturated Fat 1g ▸ Vitamin C 0mg ▸ Magnesium 59mg

---

▸ A word of caution about nuts, seeds, and nut butters. Because of their highly unsaturated fat content, they are all prone to rancidity if not stored carefully. Always make or purchase in small quantities and keep them away from heat and light, preferably in the fridge. If you don't wish to make your own, they can be purchased at health-food stores or your local supermarket.

menu
planner

IN DEVISING THESE menus I have aimed for a low ratio of carbohydrate to protein and a low glycemic load over each day.

	BREAKFAST	LUNCH	EVENING MEAL	MACRO-NUTRIENT RATIO (PROTEIN:CARB:FAT)
Monday	Apple, pear, and tofu smoothie	White bean and mint hummus with raw vegetables	Grilled chicken with quinoa and lemons Broccoli with garlic	20:35:45
Tuesday	Chickpea and tomato frittata	Two-lentil soup with coriander Fresh fruit	Tofu fajitas Mixed vegetables	20:40:40
Wednesday	Baked eggs with mushrooms	Two-lentil soup with coriander Rye toast	Grilled chicken with quinoa and lemons Steamed vegetables	25:29:46
Thursday	Poached egg with grilled tomatoes Whole grain and seed muffins	Cold chicken Avocado, grapefruit, and alfalfa salad	Lentils with olives and anchovies Blueberry and lemon yogurt	19:38:43
Friday	Apricot, soy and plum smoothie	White bean and mint hummus with crudités and rye crispbread	Trout fillets with lettuce and fennel Quinoa pilaf with green leaves	18:46:36
Saturday	Rainbow fruit salad with yogurt and 1 tbsp ground seeds	Broccoli soup with horseradish Barley bread with quick sardine pâté	Avocado, grapefruit, and alfalfa salad Grilled mackerel Butter beans with fennel	15:40:45
Sunday	Boiled egg and barley bread toast	Butter bean with parsley pesto Bean and seed sprouts with avocado dressing	Cinnamon smoked duck Stir-fried vegetables Apple and passion fruit pudding with Almond wafers	21:51:28

	BREAKFAST	LUNCH	EVENING MEAL	MACRO-NUTRIENT RATIO (PROTEIN:CARB:FAT)
Monday	Oat porridge with grated apple and ground seeds	Cream of avocado soup with coconut milk	Turkey with fennel and cashew cream Steamed vegetables	15:42:43
Tuesday	Baked beans on rye toast	Cold chicken with large mixed salad	Buckwheat pancakes with ratatouille	30:47:23
Wednesday	Buckwheat pancakes with fresh fruit	Baked eggs with mushrooms Mixed salad	Grilled trout with salsa verde Broccoli with garlic	18:42:40
Thursday	Chickpea and tomato frittata	Gazpacho with eggplant croûtons	Amaranth lentil cakes Spiced red cabbage with prunes	15:36:49
Friday	Oat and almond muesli with yogurt	Tofu fajitas Chinese-style broccoli salad	Thai-style salmon fishcakes with cucumber salad Stir-fried bean sprouts	24:32:44
Saturday	Rainbow fruit salad with yogurt and 1 tbsp ground seeds	Omelette with salad	Buckwheat noodles with tofu, tahini sauce, and vegetables	23:40:37
Sunday	Raspberry muesli sundae	Roast chicken with walnut sauce Baked blackberry cheesecake	Butter beans with fennel	23:51:26

week 2

	BREAKFAST	LUNCH	EVENING MEAL	MACRO-NUTRIENT RATIO (PROTEIN:CARB:FAT)
Monday	Yogurt cheese with apricots and walnuts	June's spicy chana dal soup	Roasted mackerel with horseradish cream Warm East-West salad	18:45:37
Tuesday	Apricot, soy and plum smoothie	Cold roasted mackerel with mixed salad	Amaranth and lentil cakes Moghlai spinach	18:37:45
Wednesday	Marion's breakfast	Fennel and red cabbage salad with pumpkin seeds	Turkey with fennel and cashew cream Steamed vegetables	25:47:28
Thursday	Oat and almond muesli with yogurt and seeds	Two-lentil soup with coriander	Baked eggs with mushrooms Fennel and red cabbage salad with pumpkin seeds	18:48:34
Friday	Chickpea and tomato frittata	Baked eggs with mushrooms Green salad	Two-lentil soup with coriander Thai-style salmon fish cakes with cucumber salad	20:42:38
Saturday	Tropical tofu smoothie	Cold poached salmon Greek whole mushroom salad, green salad	Chana dal with coconut and spices Brown rice and barley Cinnamon jelly with roasted plums	21:47:32
Sunday	Oat and almond muesli with yogurt and fruit	Grilled chicken with quinoa and lemons	Cinnamon smoked duck Raspberries and passion fruit with coconut custard	20:24:56

week 3

	BREAKFAST	LUNCH	EVENING MEAL	MACRO-NUTRIENT RATIO (PROTEIN:CARB:FAT)
Monday	Buckwheat pancakes with apple and almond filling	Cold smoked duck with mixed salad	Amaranth and lentil cakes Spiced red cabbage with prunes	25:33:42
Tuesday	Oat and citrus smoothie	Spinach salad with garlic yogurt dressing and soy beans	Salmon with minted pea purée and asparagus	29:35:36
Wednesday	Baked beans on rye toast	Cold salmon with lime-scented carrot and cucumber salad	Chili tofu and coconut stew	28:30:42
Thursday	Tropical tofu smoothie	Quick sardine pâté on rye toast Fresh fruit	Black bean cakes with tomato and orange salsa	27:36:37
Friday	Chickpea and tomato frittata	Chana dal with spinach	Coconut fish curry Brown rice Green vegetable stir-fry	22:44:34
Saturday	Apple, pear and tofu smoothie	Barley and spring vegetable risotto	Chili mussels with garlic rye toast Warm East-West salad Prune and orange creams	20:48:32
Sunday	More than tomato juice Baked eggs with mushrooms	Crispy polenta with wild mushrooms and coriander pesto	Chicken in coconut milk Stir-fried green vegetables Cinnamon clementines	22:32:46

week 4

shopping list

vegetables, emphasize:
Bean sprouts
Beets and beet greens (raw)
Broccoli
Cabbage
Celery
Chicory
Chinese cabbage
Garlic
Jerusalem artichokes\
Kale
Mushrooms
Olives
Onions
Peppers
Radishes
Sea vegetables
Spinach
Sweet potatoes
Sweetcorn
Tomatoes
Zucchini

fruits, emphasize:
Apples
Apricots, unsulphured dried or fresh
Avocados
Berry fruits
Cherries
Grapefruit
Grapes
Nectarines
Peaches
Pears
Plums

Note: treat cooked starchy root vegetables with caution owing to their high GI values (e.g., cooked parsnips, mashed potatoes)

whole grains

Amaranth
Brown rice
Buckwheat
Arrowhead Mills cereals such as
    Amaranth Flakes, Millet Flakes, etc.
Organic oat flakes and oat groats
Pearl barley
Polenta
Quinoa
Wholewheat pastas (any kind)

flour

Barley flour
Brown-rice flour
Buckwheat flour
Chickpea flour
Gluten-free flour
Stone-ground organic wholegrain
    flour such as Arrowhead Mills

legumes, any kind such as

Black beans
Butter beans
Chana dal
Chickpeas
Haricot beans
Kidney beans
Lentils, red, green, and brown
Soy beans and soy products such
    as tofu

protein foods

Oily fish such as wild or organic
    salmon, mackerel, sea bass,
    herrings, trout, anchovies
White fish such as cod, haddock,
    flounder, etc.
Chicken, duck, and guinea fowl
    (without skin)
Eggs, free-range and organic
Lean meat, all visible fat removed
Combinations of beans, whole grains,
    and nuts/seeds

nuts and seeds, raw

Flaxseed (linseed)
Pumpkin seed
Sesame seeds
Sunflower seeds
Almonds
Brazil nuts
Walnuts
Nut and seed butters (e.g., almond,
    hazelnut, tahini)

dairy products (if using)

Organic yogurt, soy yogurt
Cottage cheese
Occasional use of Parmesan and goat/
    sheep cheese

optional milk alternatives

Soy milk
Rice Dream
Oat milk
Coconut milk

fats and oils
Cold pressed extra-virgin olive oil
Organic coconut oil
Butter in moderation
Flaxseed oil, walnut oil, avocado oil,
    pumpkin seed oil for salads

spices—include
Cinnamon
Fenugreek seed
Ginger
Juniper berries

beverage options
Herbal teas
Ginseng tea
Dandelion coffee
Green tea
Carob with soy, rice, or almond milk

sweeteners—minimal use only
Apple juice
Concentrated apple juice
Molasses
A little honey or maple syrup

bread alternatives
Rye bread (100% is best)
Rye crackers
Barley bread
wholegrain breads (low GI)

seasonings
Miso
Tamari/shoyu (naturally brewed
    soy sauce)
Sea salt or low-sodium salt
Fresh herbs of all kinds

convenience foods
Canned beans—any kind
Sardines in olive oil
Tomatoes—canned/paste/dried/salsa
Hummus
Falafel
Amy's organic soups
Marinated tofu, etc.
Sugar-free jams

food equipment
Grinder—for nuts and seeds
Food processor
Juicer for vegetable juices
Pump-action spray for olive oil

THE
glycemic index
AND
glycemic load

THIS IS AN extract of the latest tables available, which were published in 2002. Not all foods have been tested, and for reasons of space I have limited the extract here to more commonly used foods. The GI in these tables is based on an assumption that pure glucose has a GI of 100. Please note the following:

- A GI of 70 or more is high, a GI of 56 to 69 inclusive is medium, and a GI of 55 or less is low
- A GL of 20 or more is high, a GL of 11 to 19 inclusive is medium, and a GL of 10 or less is low
- Look for carbohydrate foods that are both low GI *and* low GL.

FOOD	GI GLUCOSE	GL
BAKERY PRODUCTS		
Sponge cake, plain	46	16.6
Croissant	67	17.5
Crumpet	69	13.1
Doughnut	76	17.4
Pastry	59	15.4
BEVERAGES		
Cola soft drink	53	13.9
Orange soft drink	68	22.8
Sparkling glucose drink	95	39.7
Lemon soft drink	58	17.0
Apple juice, mean of three studies	40	11.7
Carrot juice, freshly made	43	10.0
Cranberry juice drink	56	16.4
Grapefruit juice, unsweetened	48	10.7
Orange juice, mean of two studies	50	12.8
Pineapple juice, unsweetened	46	15.6
Tomato juice, canned	38	3.5
BREADS		
Baguette, white, plain	95	14.7
Barley kernel bread, mean of two studies	46	9.4
Hamburger bun	61	9.2
Gluten-free white bread, sliced (gluten-free wheat starch)	80	11.9
Whole grain pumpernickel	46	5.2
Whole grain rye bread, mean of four studies	58	8.4
White bread, mean of six studies	70	9.7
White bread with butter	59	28.5
Whole grain bread, mean of thirteen studies	71	9.5
Soy and linseed bread	36	3.2
Pita bread, white	57	9.5
BREAKFAST CEREALS		
All-Bran™ (Kellogg's)	38	8.7
Bran Flakes™ (Kellogg's)	74	13.2
Cornflakes, mean of five studies	81	20.8
Natural muesli, mean of two studies	49	9.6
Muesli, toasted	43	7.1
Nutrigrain™ (Kellogg's)	66	9.9
Porridge made from rolled oats, mean of eight studies	58	12.8
Puffed Wheat (Quaker Oats Co)	67	13.5
Raisin Bran™ (Kellogg's)	61	11.7
Rice Krispies™ (Kellogg's)	82	21.0
Shredded Wheat™ (Nabisco Brands Ltd)	83	16.6
Special K™ (Kellogg's)	54	11.3
Weetabix, mean of seven studies	70	13.0
CEREAL GRAINS		
Amaranth eaten with milk and nonnutritive sweetener	97	21.0
Pearl barley, mean of five studies	25	10.6
Buckwheat, mean of three studies	54	16.1
Corn tortilla	52	12.4
Cornmeal (polenta), mean of two studies	69	9.0
Couscous, mean of two studies	65	22.7
Millet, boiled	71	25.2

FOOD	GI GLUCOSE	GL
Arborio, risotto rice, boiled	69	36.2
Boiled white rice, mean of 12 studies	64	23.3
Boiled long grain rice, mean of 10 studies	56	22.9
Glutinous rice, white, cooked in rice cooker	98	31.0
Jasmine rice, white long grain, cooked in rice cooker	109	46.1
Basmati rice, white, boiled	58	21.8
Brown rice, mean of three studies	55	17.9
Rye, whole kernels, mean of three studies	34	12.9
Wheat, whole kernels, mean of four studies	41	14.0
Wheat tortilla (Mexican)	30	7.8
Bulgur wheat, mean of four studies	48	12.4
BISCUITS AND CRACKERS		
Digestive biscuits, mean of three studies	59	9.7
Rich Tea biscuits	55	10.4
Shortbread	64	9.9
Rice cakes, mean of three studies	78	17.0
Ryvita, mean of four studies	64	10.5
DAIRY PRODUCTS AND ALTERNATIVES		
Custard, homemade from milk, wheat starch, and sugar	43	7.1
Ice cream, mean of five studies	61	7.9
Milk, full-fat, mean of five studies	27	3.1
Milk, skim	32	4.0
Milk, condensed, sweetened	61	17.0
Yogurt	36	3.4
Low-fat, fruit yogurt with aspartame	14	1.8
Soy milk, full-fat, 120 mg calcium	36	6.4
Soy yogurt, peach and mango, 2% fat, sugar	50	13.0
FRUIT		
Apples, raw, mean of six studies	38	5.5
Apricots, raw	57	5.2
Apricots, canned in light syrup	64	12.0
Apricots, dried	30	8.0
Banana, mean of 10 studies	52	12.4
Cherries, raw	22	2.7
Dates, dried	103	41.6
Figs, dried	61	15.7
Grapefruit, raw	25	2.7
Grapes, mean of two studies	46	8.2
Kiwi fruit, mean of two studies	53	6.2
Mango, mean of three studies	51	8.5
Oranges, mean of six studies	42	4.6
Papaya, mean of three studies	59	10.2
Peaches, mean of two studies	42	4.6
Peaches, canned, mean of two studies	38	4.2
Pears, raw, mean of four studies	38	4.2
Pineapple, mean of two studies	59	7.4
Plums, mean of two studies	39	4.8
Prunes	29	9.7
Raisins	64	28.5
Strawberries, fresh	40	1.3
Watermelon, raw	72	4.3

FOOD	GI GLUCOSE	GL
LEGUMES AND NUTS		
Baked beans, canned, mean of two studies	48	7.4
Black Beans	30	6.8
Blackeyed beans, boiled, mean of two studies	42	12.8
Butter beans, mean of three studies	31	6.1
Chickpeas, dried, boiled, mean of four studies	28	8.3
Haricot beans, mean of five studies	38	11.8
Kidney beans, mean of eight studies	28	6.9
Black beans, soaked overnight, cooked 45 min	20	4.9
Green lentils, mean of three studies	30	5.1
Red lentils, mean of four studies	26	4.8
Mung beans, germinated	25	4.3
Peas, dried, boiled	22	1.9
Pinto beans, dried, boiled	39	10.0
Soy beans, dried, boiled, mean of two studies	18	1.1
Soy beans, canned	14	0.8
Split peas, yellow, boiled 20 min	32	6.1
CONVENIENCE FOODS AND MIXED MEALS		
Fish sticks	38	7.3
Pizza, plain baked dough, served with parmesan cheese and tomato sauce	80	21.6
Sirloin chop with mixed vegetables and mashed potato, homemade	66	34.9
Spaghetti bolognaise, homemade	52	25.0
Stir-fried vegetables with chicken and boiled white rice, homemade	73	54.7
PASTA AND NOODLES		
Corn pasta, gluten-free	78	32.4
Gluten-free pasta, maize starch, boiled 8 min	54	22.5
Rice noodles, dried, boiled	61	23.5
Rice noodles, freshly made, boiled	40	15.4
Rice pasta, brown, boiled 16 min	92	34.8
Rice and maize pasta, gluten-free	76	36.9
Soba noodles, instant, reheated in hot water, served with soup	46	22.3
White spaghetti, boiled, mean of three cooking times	57	27.3
Whole wheat spaghetti, boiled, mean of two studies	37	15.5
Split pea and soy pasta shells, gluten-free	29	8.9
Udon noodles, plain, reheated 5 min	62	30.0
Vermicelli, white, boiled	35	15.5
SNACK FOODS AND CONFECTIONERY		
Chocolate, milk, mean of four studies	43	12.0
Mars Bar®	68	27.1
Cashew nuts, salted	22	2.8
Peanuts, mean of three studies	14	0.8
Popcorn, mean of two studies	72	7.7
Potato crisps, mean of two studies	54	11.4
Snickers Bar®	68	23.1
Twix® Cookie Bar, caramel	44	17.0
SOUPS		
Green pea soup, canned	66	27.3
Lentil soup, canned	44	9.0

FOOD	GI GLUCOSE	GL
Minestrone soup	39	7.1
Tomato soup	38	6.4

SUGARS

Honey, mean of 11 types	55	9.8

VEGETABLES

Peas, mean of three studies	48	3.4
Pumpkin	75	3.3
Sweet corn, mean of six studies	54	9.3
Beets	64	4.6
Carrots, raw	16	1.2
Cooked carrots, mean of four studies	47	2.7
Parsnips	97	12.1
Baked potato, mean of four studies	85	25.6
Boiled potatoes, mean of five studies	50	13.9
Mashed potato, mean of three studies	74	14.5
New potato, mean of three studies	57	12.0
Sweet potato, mean of five studies	61	17.0

Source: Foster-Powell, et al., International table of glycemic index and glycemic load values: 2002, *Am J Clin Nutr* 2002 ▶ 76:5-56

useful addresses

Diabetes-related Organizations and Public Health Agencies

AMERICAN DIABETES ASSOCIATION
Attn: National call center
1701 North Beauregard Street, Alexandria, VA 22311
Tel: 1 800 342 2383
AskADA@diabetes.org
www.diabetes.org
The leading organizaton working with people with diabetes.

NATIONAL DIABETES INFORMATION CLEARINGHOUSE
1 Information Way
Bethseda, MD 20892-3560
Phone: 1 800 860 8747
Fax: 703 738 4929
www.diabetes.niddk.nih.gov
A public health agency, desseminates information on diabetes including general information, treatment, complications, statistics and research. Information is also available in Spanish. The Clearinghouse is part of the National Institutes of Health (HIH), which is under the U.S. Department of Health and Human Services.

JUVENILE DIABETES RESEARCH FOUNDATION INTERNATIONAL
120 Wall Street
New York, NY 10005-4001
Tel: 1 800 533 cure
Fax: 212 785 9595
E-mail: info@jdrf.org
Web site: *www.jdf.org*
Founded in 1986 by families living with diabetes, with the aim of finding a cure and improving the lives of their children.

Diabetes-related Web sites

www.mendosa.com
David Mendosa is a freelance medical writer and consultant specializing in diabetes. Free monthly e-mail newsletter, Diabetes Update, and links to the latest diabetes research.

www.childrenwithdiabetes.com
American Web site for children, families and adults with diabetes.

www.diabetesmonitor.com
A resource for patients to educate themselves about their role as active participants in the care of diabetes.

www.diabetesportal.com
A central one-stop resource for people with diabetes and their families.

Suppliers (food)

GOLD MINE NATURAL FOOD CO.
7805 Arjons Drive
San Diego, CA 92126
Tel: 1 858 537 9830
Web site: goldminenaturalfood.com
Organic wholefoods from Japan, including shoyu, tamari and sea vegetables. Online shopping available through the Web site or call for a catalog.

RUDI'S ORGANIC BAKERY, INC.
3640 Walnut Street, Unit B
Boulder, CO 80301
Tel: 303 447 0495
Fax: 303 447 0516
Web site: www.rudisbakery.com
Suppliers of organic breads. National distribution.

SHOP NATURAL
350 S. Toole Avenue
Tuscon, Arizona 85701
Tel: 520 884 0745
E-mail customerservice@shopnatural.com
Web site: www.shopnatural.com
Comprehensive mail-order service including organics, groceries, personal and homecare products.

THE BAKERS CATALOGUE
P.O. Box 876
Norwich, VT 05055
Tel: 1 800 827 6836
Fax: 800 343 3002
E-mail: bakers@kingarthursflour.com
Web site: shop.bakerscatalogue.com
Suppliers of baking ingredients including flour.

UNITED NATURAL FOODS, INC.
P.O. Box 999 260 Lake Road
Dayville, CT 06241
Tel: 1 800 877 2240 Eastern Region
1 800 679 6733 Western Region
Web site: www.unfi.com
America's premier certified organic distributor

WHOLE FOODS MARKET
Website: www.wholefoods.com
The largest retailer of natural and organic foods, including vitamins, supplements, personal and homecare products. Find a store near you through the Web site.

references

1 Dyson, P. "Nutrition and diabetes control: advice for non-dietitians." *Br J Community Nurs*, 2002; 7:414–9.

2 White F, Rafique G. "Diabetes prevalence and projections in South Asia." *Lancet* 2002; 360: 07 September 2002.

3 Eschwege, E. "Epidemiology of type II diabetes, diagnosis, prevalence, risk factors, complications." *E.Arch Mal Coeur Vaiss*. 2000 Dec; 93 Spec No 4:13–7.

4 Wild, S, Roglic G, Green A, Sicree R, King H. "Global Prevalence of Diabetes: Estimates for the year 2000 and projections for 2030." *Diabetes Care*. 2004 May; 27(5):1047–1053.

5 Schernthaner G et al. "Progress in the characterization of slowly progressive autoimmune diabetes in adult patients (LADA or Type 1.5 diabetes)." *Exp Clin Endocrinol Diabetes*. 2001; 109 Suppl 2:S94–108.

6 Vaarala O, Paronen J, Otonkoski T, Akerblom HK. "Cow milk feeding induces antibodies to insulin in children—a link between cow milk and insulin-dependent diabetes mellitus?" *Scand J Immunol*. 1998 Feb; 47(2):131–5.

7 Murray M, Pizzorno J, *Textbook of Natural Medicine*, Seattle: John Bastyr College Publications 1988.

8 Given HDC. *A New Angle on Health*. John Bale, Sons & Danielsson Ltd. 1935.

9 Montignac, M. *Dine Out and Lose Weight*. Montignac Publishing (UK) 1996.

10 Willett, W et al. "Glycemic index, glycemic load and risk of Type 2 diabetes." *Am J Clin Nutr* 2002; 76(suppl):274S–80S.

11 Watts, DL, "Trace Elements and Other Essential Nutrients," *Writer's B-L-O-C-K*, 1999.

12 Talior I, Yarkoni M, Bashan N, Eldar-Finkelman H. "Increased glucose uptake promotes oxidative stress and PKC-delta activation in adipocytes of obese, insulin-resistant mice." *Am J Physiol Endocrinol Metab*. 2003 Aug; 285(2):E295–302.

13 Bunyard P. "Blowin' in the wind: industrial waste and the government." *The Ecologist* 22/6/2001.

14 Reitman et al., *Isr. Med Assoc J*, 2002, 4; 590–593.

15 Foster-Powell, et al., "International table of glycemic index and glycemic load values: 2002," *Am J Clin Nutr* 2002; 76:5–56.

16 Gannon et al., "An increase in dietary protein improves the blood glucose response in persons with Type 2 diabetes," *Am J Clin Nutr*. 2003; 78:734–741.

17 Sheela CG, Augusti KT. "Antidiabetic effects of S-allyl cysteine sulphoxide isolated from garlic Allium sativum Linn." *Indian J Exp Biol*, 1992; 30: 523–6.

18 Platel K, Srinivasan K. "Plant foods in the management of diabetes mellitus: vegetables as potential hypoglycemic agents." *Nahrung*, 1997; 41:68–74.

19 Madar Z, Stark AH, "New Legume Sources as Therapeutic Agents," *Br J Nutr*, 2002; 88:S287–92.

20 Montonen J, Knekt P, Jarvinen R, Reunanen A. "Dietary antioxidant intake and risk of Type 2 diabetes." *Diabetes Care*. 2004 Feb; 27(2):362–6.

21 Jiang R et al. "Body iron stores in relation to risk of Type 2 diabetes in apparently healthy women." *JAMA*. February 11, 2004;291(6):711–7.

22 Clandinin MT, Wilke MS. "Do trans fatty acids increase the incidence of Type 2 diabetes?" *Am J Clin Nutr*. June 2001; 73:1001–1002, 1019–1026.

23 Fife, Bruce. *The Healing Miracles of Coconut Oil*. Piccadilly Books, 2003.

24 Baba, N. "Enhanced thermogenesis and diminished deposition of fat in response to overfeeding with diet containing medium-chain triglyceride." *Am. J. Clin. Nutr.* 1982 35:678

25 Sircar, S. and Kansra, U. 1998. "Choice of cooking oils—myths and realities." *J. Indian Med. Assoc.* 96(10):304.

26 Liljeberg H, Bjorck I. "Delayed gastric emptying rate may explain improved glycemia in healthy subjects to a starchy meal with added vinegar." *Eur J Clin Nutr*. 1998 May; 52(5):368–71.

27 Brighenti F et al. G. "Effect of neutralized and native vinegar on blood glucose and acetate responses to a mixed meal in healthy subjects." *Eur J Clin Nutr*. 1995 Apr; 49(4):242–7.

28 Wien MA et al. "Almonds vs complex carbohydrates in a weight reduction program." *Int J Obes Metab Disord*. 2003 Nov; 27(11): 1365–72.

29 Lopez-Ridaura R et al. "Magnesium intake and risk of Type 2 diabetes in men and women." *Diabetes Care*. 2004 Jan; 27(1):134–40.

30 Grylls WK, McKenzie JE, Horwath CC, Mann JI. "Lifestyle factors associated with glycemic control and body mass index in older adults with diabetes." *Eur J Clin Nutr*, 2003:57. 1386–1393.

31 Blaylock, R. *Excito Toxins—The Taste that Kills*: pp. 39–43, 1997: Health Press, Santa Fe, USA

32 Gregersen S, et al. "Antihyperglycemic effects of stevioside in Type 2 diabetic subjects." *Metabolism* 2004; 53(1): 73–76.

33 Keijzers GB, De Galan BE, Tack CJ, Smits P. "Caffeine can decrease insulin sensitivity in humans." *Diabetes Care* February 2002; 25:364–369.

34 Salazar-Martinez E et al. "Coffee Consumption and Risk for Type 2 Diabetes Mellitus." *Annals of Internal Medicine,* 2004; 140:1–8.

35 Rosengren A, Dotevall A, Wilhelmsen L, Thelle D, Johansson S. "Coffee and incidence of diabetes in Swedish women: a prospective 18-year follow-up study." *Intern Med.* 2004 Jan; 255(1):89–95.

36 van Dam RM, Feskens EJ. "Coffee consumption and risk of Type 2 diabetes mellitus." *Lancet.* 2002 Nov 9; 360(9344):1477–8.

37 Howard AA, Arnsten JH, Gourevitch MN. "Effect of alcohol consumption on diabetes mellitus: a systematic review." *Ann Intern Med.* 2004 Feb 3; 140(3):211–9.

38 Magis DC, Jandrain BJ, Scheen AJ. "Alcohol, insulin sensitivity and diabetes." Rev Med Liège. 2003 Jul–Aug; 58(7–8):501–7.

39 Bell DS. "Alcohol and the NIDDM patient." *Diabetes Care.* 1996 May; 19(5):509–13.

40 Wannamethee SG et al. "Alcohol drinking patterns and risk of Type 2 diabetes mellitus among younger women." *Arch Intern Med.* 2003 Jun 9; 163(11):1329–36.

41 Ames RP. "The effect of sodium supplementation on glucose tolerance and insulin concentrations in patients with hypertension and diabetes mellitus." *American Journal of Hypertension,* 2001, Vol 14, Iss 7, Part 1, pp. 653–659.

42 Khan A, Safdar M, Ali Khan MM, Khattak KN, Anderson RA. "Cinnamon improves glucose and lipids of people with Type 2 diabetes." *Diabetes Care* 26:3215–3218, 2003.

43 Barringer TA, Kirk JK, Santaniello AC, Foley KL, Michielutte R. "Effect of a multivitamin and mineral supplement on infection and quality of life. A randomized, double-blind, placebo-controlled trial." *Ann Intern Med* 2003; 138(5):365–71.

44 Block G et al. "Plasma C-reactive protein concentrations in active and passive smokers: influence of antioxidant supplementation." *J Am Coll Nutr* 2004 Apr; 23(2):141–7.

45 Timms PM et al. "Circulating MMP9, vitamin D and variation in the TIMP-1 response with VDR genotype: mechanisms for inflammatory damage in chronic disorders?" *QJM.* 2002 Dec; 95(12):787–96.

46 Hypponen E, Laara E, Reunanen A. "Intake of vitamin D and risk of Type 1 diabetes: a birth-cohort study." *Lancet.* 2001 Nov 3; 358(9292):1500–3.

47 Ortlepp JR, Lauscher J, Hoffmann R. "The vitamin D receptor gene variant is associated with the prevalence of Type 2 diabetes mellitus and coronary artery disease." *Diabet Med.* 2001 Oct; 18(10):842–5.

48 Quillot D et al. "Fatty acid abnormalities in chronic pancreatitis: effect of concomitant diabetes mellitus." *Eur J Clin Nutr* 57(3): 496–503, Mar 2003.

49 Annual Experimental Biology 2002 Conference New Orleans, LA April 21, 2002.

50 Petersen M et al. "Effect of fish oil versus corn oil supplementation on LDL and HDL subclasses in Type 2 diabetic patients." *Diabetes Care* October 2002; 25:1704–1708.

51 Ma J et al. "Associations of serum and dietary magnesium with cardiovascular disease, hypertension, diabetes, insulin, and carotid arterial wall thickness: the ARIC study. Atherosclerosis Risk in Communities Study." *J Clin Epidemiol.* 1995 Jul; 48(7):927–40.

52 Arvanitakis Z, Wilson RS, Bienias JL, Evans DA, Bennett DA. "Diabetes mellitus and risk of Alzheimer disease and decline in cognitive function." *Arch Neurol.* 2004 May; 61(5):661–6.

53 www.tahoma-clinic.com.

54 Mooradian AD et al. "Selected vitamins and minerals in diabetes." *Diabetes Care* 1994 May; 17(5):464–79.

55 Ghosh D et al. "Role of chromium supplementation in Indians with Type 2 diabetes mellitus." *J Nutr Biochem.* 2002 Nov; 13(11):690–697.

56 Ambrosch A et al. "Relation between homocysteinaemia and diabetic neuropathy in patients with Type 2 diabetes mellitus." *Diabet Med.* 2001 Mar; 18(3):185–92.

57 Liu X, Zhou HJ, Rohdewald P. "French maritime pine bark extract Pycnogenol dose-dependently lowers glucose in Type 2 diabetic patients." *Diabetes Care.* 2004 Mar; 27(3):839.

58 Sotaniemi EA, Haapakoski E, Rautio A. "Ginseng therapy in noninsulin-dependent diabetic patients." *Diabetes Care* 1995 Oct; 18(10):1373–5.

59 Leatherdale BA et al. "Improvement in glucose tolerance due to Momordica charantia (karela)." *Br Med J (Clin Res Ed).* 1981 Jun 6; 282(6279):1823–4.

60 Baskaran K et al. "Antidiabetic effect of a leaf extract from Gymnema sylvestre in non-insulin-dependent diabetes mellitus patients." *J Ethnopharmacol.* 1990 Oct; 30(3):295–300.

61 Jia W, Gao W, Tang L. "Antidiabetic herbal drugs officially approved in China." *Phytother Res.* 2003 Dec; 17(10):1127–34.

62 Wannamethee SG, Shaper AG, Alberti KG. "Physical activity, metabolic factors, and the incidence of coronary heart disease and Type 2 diabetes." *Arch Intern Med.* 2000 Jul 24; 160(14):2108–16.

63 Surwit RS et al. "Stress management improves long-term glycemic control in Type 2 diabetes." *Diabetes Care.* 2002 Jan; 25(1):30–4.

64 Wang Q. "The present situation of TCM treatment for diabetes and its researches." *J Tradit Chin Med.* 2003 Mar; 23(1):67–73.

65 Galper DI, Taylor AG, Cox DJ. "Current status of mind-body interventions for vascular complications of diabetes." *Family and Community Health* 26(1): 34–40, Jan–Mar 2003.

66 Ayas NT et al. "A prospective study of self-reported sleep duration and incident diabetes in women." *Diabetes Care.* 2003 Feb; 26(2):380–4.

67 Hooper PL. "Hot-tub therapy for Type 2 diabetes mellitus." *N Engl J Med,* 1999; 341: 924–5.

68 Hayashi K et al. "Laughter lowered the increase in postprandial blood glucose." *Diabetes Care* May 2003; 26:1651–1652.

69 *Arch Intern Med,* 2000; 160:1009–13.

70 Madar Z, Stark AH. "New Legume Sources as Therapeutic Agents," *Br J Nutr,* 2002; 88:S287–92.

71 Swanston-Flatt SK, Day C, Bailey CJ, Flatt PR. "Traditional plant treatments for diabetes. Studies in normal and streptozotocin diabetic mice." *Diabetologia.* 1990 Aug; 33(8):462–4.

index